Moral Voices, Moral Selves

Moral Voices, Moral Selves

Carol Gilligan and Feminist Moral Theory

Susan J. Hekman

The Pennsylvania State University Press
University Park, Pennsylvania

First published in 1995 by Polity Press
in association with Blackwell Publishers Ltd.

First published 1995 in the United States
and Canada by The Pennsylvania State
University Press, 820 North University
Drive, University Park, PA 16802

ISBN 0–271–01483–0 (cloth)
ISBN 0–271–01484–9 (paper)

Library of Congress Cataloging in Publication Data
A CIP catalog record for this book is available from the Library of Congress.

Typeset in Palatino on 10/12 pt
by Best-set Typesetter Ltd., Hong Kong
Printed and bound in Great Britain by Hartnolls Limited, Bodmin, Cornwall

This book is printed on acid-free paper.

In memory of Douglas Anders

Contents

Acknowledgments

In their acknowledgments authors usually declare that writing the book was a cooperative task, that it would not have been possible without the help of many colleagues and friends. This is true of this book as well. But it is also true that writing this, or any book, is a lonely endeavor. It requires what seem like endless hours of solitude, sitting at a desk accompanied only by a recalcitrant, sometimes hostile manuscript. In this situation the written comments of friends and colleagues become like conversations. Reading these comments in the solitude of my study, I feel as if I am engaging the authors in extended conversations and replying by revising my manuscript. These conversations relieve the necessary solitude of writing, and for this I am very grateful.

I have been very fortunate in my conversational partners in the writing of this book. Keith Burgess-Jackson read the whole manuscript with care and gave me a meticulous catalog of my numerous errors. My "conversations" with Keith were not always harmonious, and I have not always corrected the errors he identified, but I am grateful nonetheless. C. Jan Swearingen and Harry Reeder read portions of the manuscript and helped me avoid even more errors. Dick Flathman also gave me comments on portions of the manuscript and, most important, encouraged me at a crucial point in my writing to believe that what I was saying about Wittgenstein was not crazy. I am grateful for his assistance on this project. But my debt to him goes much beyond this. He has given me unstinting support throughout my scholarly career. He is, simply, the best mentor anyone could hope for.

The University of Texas at Arlington provided a Faculty Development Leave for the completion of this book. My sister, Judy Thompson, provided a stunningly beautiful and tranquil environment in which to write. Both were essential to the completion of the project. I would also like to thank Tony Giddens for his support through what is now three book projects. Tony has set new standards of excellence as a scholar and as an editor. I and the academic world owe him a great debt.

Finally, this book could not have been written without the scholarly and emotional support of my husband, Evan Anders. His agreements and disagreements with my ideas have shaped the direction of my arguments and helped me to clarify my positions at crucial points throughout the project. My dear friends Kathleen Underwood and Laurin Porter made the years spent writing this book richer and fuller, both intellectually and personally. And Mike Moore helped me conquer the labyrinthine complexities of WordPerfect. My thanks to them all.

1

The Different Voice

In 1982 Carol Gilligan published an empirical and interpretive analysis of the decision-making process of a sample of girls and young women confronted with both hypothetical and real-life moral dilemmas. Gilligan, a Harvard psychologist who specializes in moral development, challenged the influential approach of the moral development theorist Lawrence Kohlberg, who was also her teacher at Harvard. Against Kohlberg, Gilligan argued that the women and girls she interviewed articulated their moral dilemmas in a "different voice." Kohlberg's studies had concluded that women clustered at an inferior stage of moral development; few women attained what he defined as the highest stage of moral reasoning. In order to avoid the "distortion" that female subjects created, Kohlberg conducted his studies using primarily male subjects. Gilligan's study opposed Kohlberg's findings, as well as his interpretation of them. She attempted to define a separate but equal moral sphere for the different voice and thus to reform Kohlberg's theory by describing women as equals rather than inferiors.

It does not overstate the case to say that Gilligan's work has revolutionized discussions in moral theory, feminism, theories of the subject, and many related fields. *In a Different Voice* is unquestionably one of the most influential books of the 1980s. It has been both criticized and praised by feminists, moral philosophers, and moral psychologists. Gilligan's work has been hailed both as the harbinger of a new moral theory and as the final blow to the exhausted masculinist tradition of moral philosophy. It has also been condemned as methodologically unsound, theoretically confused, and even antifeminist. Gilligan's critics and defenders have cast her, respectively, as either villain or savior in the ongoing intellectual debate of the 1980s and 1990s. Probably the only point on which they agree is that, more than a decade later, the moral, epistemological, and methodological ramifications of her work are still being explored. A pertinent question at this point in the debate is why Gilligan's study of women's and girls' moral reasoning has stirred up such a hornet's nest of controversy and evoked such vehement reactions from both critics and defenders.

One of the aims of this study is to answer this question. It is my contention that Gilligan's work is both an indication of, and a major contributor to, a sea change that is under way in late twentieth-century intellectual thought. In almost every branch of intellectual life, the twentieth century has witnessed a move away from the universalism and absolutism of modernist epistemology toward conceptions that emphasize particularity and concreteness. The linchpin of this move is the attack on the centerpiece of modernist, Enlightenment epistemology: "man," the rational, abstract, autonomous constitutor of knowledge. In opposition to this conception of the subject, many twentieth-century thinkers posit a subject who is embedded and situated, constituted by language, culture, discourse, and history.

Literary theory, deconstruction, cultural anthropology, and relational psychology have been on the cutting edge of the articulation of this new paradigm, developing a theory of the subject that deconstructs the Enlightenment edifice and proclaims the "death of man." One of the discourses that has resisted this transition and thus represents one of the last bastions of the modernist subject is moral philosophy. The reason for this is clear to anyone familiar with the still dominant tradition of modernist moral theory. It is the rationality and autonomy of the modernist subject, which provides the necessary basis for contemporary moral philosophy. The paradigm of this tradition is Kant's self-legislating moral subject. For this subject, rationality and morality are mutually dependent; this explains why Kant excludes those incapable of full rationality, such as women and idiots, from the moral sphere. Essential to this moral tradition is the ability of the subject to abstract from the particularity of his (as the writers in this tradition invariably designate the subject) circumstances and to formulate the universal principles that define the moral sphere. The situated, embedded, discursively constituted subject that is being defined in other disciplines obviates this conception of the moral agent.

Gilligan does not explicitly attack the subject of modernist thought in her work. She is not a moral philosopher; she does not define her project in terms of a deconstruction of the Enlightenment moral subject. Yet her work contributes significantly to that deconstruction. Gilligan articulates a relational subject that is the product of discursive experiences, a subject that undermines the very possibility of the autonomous, self-legislating agent. Her work has had a profound effect on the discipline of moral theory. Yet she comes from outside that discipline – indeed, from an empirical rather than a philosophical discipline. This in itself should not be surprising. In his work on the "death of man," Foucault argues that epistemological shifts necessarily originate on the fringes of intellectual life; they come from the periphery, not the center. The revolutionary impact of Gilligan's work is a function of her status outside the tradition of moral theory; it is outsiders, not insiders, who articulate new paradigms.

Although Gilligan is not offering a new, fully developed moral philosophy, theory of the subject, methodology, or epistemology, the implications of her work have radical consequences in all these areas. She is not concerned with moral philosophy per se; yet her findings have led her to an understanding of the development of moral voices that undercuts the very foundation of modernist moral theory. Gilligan is not the only contemporary theorist to advance the concept of the relational subject; yet her description of the evolution of this subject's moral voice in gendered terms reveals the radical implications of the concept in unique ways. Her work is not explicitly methodological; yet her counter to Kohlberg's method suggests a definition of the relationship between truth and method that has implications for contemporary disputes in the philosophy of social science and feminist methodology. Finally, the epistemological issues raised by Gilligan's account of woman's voice parallel those raised in many recent critiques of the modernist concept of truth. My aim in this book is to draw out the strands of meaning embedded in Gilligan's work and to relate them to the issues now being discussed in these fields. My goal is both descriptive and prescriptive: I want to describe the new paradigm of moral knowledge that I see emerging and, at the same time, to argue for its utility for feminist theory.

In a Different Voice

In the introduction to *In a Different Voice* (1982) Gilligan articulates the issues that will concern her both in that book and in her subsequent work. At the center of all these issues is what might be labeled the "woman problem": the fact that women fail to fit the existing models of human moral development (1982: 2). Beginning with Freud, theorists of moral development have cited the "failure" of woman's development (1982: 6). Piaget and other development theorists "solved" this problem by ignoring women and articulating a developmental theory based solely on the experience of men (1982: 10). Erikson and Bettelheim skirted the issue by asserting that women's development is "different" from that of men but showed little interest in defining the difference (1982: 12–13). It is precisely this "difference," however, that Gilligan wants to address. But the way in which she does so, even at this early stage in her thinking, indicates that she will be departing from the epistemological and methodological assumptions of her male predecessors.

The goal of the theories that Gilligan critiques is to find the "truth" of human moral development. Each of these theories employs the standard procedures of scientific method in order to attain this truth: hypotheses, factual evidence, empirical studies of representative subjects, and so forth. The most straightforward way to counter these theories from a feminist perspective is to assert that they are "biased" – that is, that they are incomplete, because they ignore the reality of women's experience. Following this line of argument, the solution to the problem appears to be quite simple: the theories should be completed by including women in the empirical studies, thereby supplying the missing element – women's development – and thus bringing them up to the standard of completeness and objectivity to which they aspire. Many passages of *In a Different Voice* suggest that this is precisely Gilligan's goal. She states that her intention is to yield a "more encompassing view of the lives of both of the sexes" (1982: 4), to find "the truth of women's experience" (1982: 62) and thus of human experience (1982: 63). She wants to force development theorists to "admit the truth of women's perspective" (1982: 98), because women's experience provides clues to the "central truth of adult life" (1982: 172). In what appears to be a direct appeal to the legitimizing force of standard scientific method, she argues that "by looking directly at women's lives over time, it becomes possible to test, in a preliminary way, whether the changes predicted by the theory fit the reality of what in fact takes place" (1982: 21). She concludes her study by asserting: "Yet in the different voice of women lies the truth of an ethic of care" (1982: 173).

Yet, other elements in Gilligan's work suggest that her approach departs significantly from the methodological assumptions that inform the work of the theorists she examines and that her concepts of "truth" and "method" differ significantly from theirs. At the outset, she notes that recent trends in social science have called into question the "presumed neutrality of science," recognizing instead that "the categories of knowledge are human constructions" (1982: 6). This almost offhand reference to an epistemology of science starkly opposed to that employed by standard developmental theorists continues to be a theme throughout the book. Gilligan defines women's voice as "an alternative concept of maturity" (1982: 22) and a "new line of interpretation" (1982: 26). Women's experience, she asserts, is a "vision" that "illuminates" a hitherto unseen realm (1982: 62–3). At the end of the book she brings these reflections together with the assertion that women's "underdevelopment" according to previous, male-biased theories was a result of the *construction* of those theories and not of "truth" (1982: 171). She claims that her work on the different voice results in a "new perspective" on relationships, which changes the basic constructs of interpretation and consequently expands the moral domain (1982: 173).

These passages require a good deal of unpacking. Gilligan is here appealing to an alternative conception of scientific analysis, which radically shifts the terms of the debate in which she is engaged. Advocates of this alternative conception assert that the categories of analysis create the parameters of the data analyzed. Gilligan applies this perspective to moral development theory with startling results. She asserts that defining moral development in terms of the evolution of autonomous, separate selves who are eventually capable of applying abstract universal principles to moral problems produces a particular definition of the moral realm. This definition entails that only such autonomous subjects applying such abstract principles can be considered fully moral. It defines the "truth" of moral development as the evolution of moral subjects who meet these criteria. It also relegates the different voice of women to, at the very least, moral inferiority. A strict application of this theory yields an even harsher conclusion: that women, who fail to meet the criteria of fully moral subjects, do not inhabit the moral realm at all. What Gilligan proposes in her work is a radically different perspective on moral development, which results in a different definition of the moral realm. By developing this new concept of the moral subject, she redefines the "truth" of moral development and the constitution of morality itself. She proposes a dual vision of the moral realm, one in which two interacting and intertwining voices replace the unitary view.

This way of reading Gilligan contrasts sharply with the first reading, I have suggested. On the first reading, Gilligan seems to be arguing that she is replacing one truth with another, attempting to correct the biased and incomplete masculinist theories of moral development by introducing a truer, more objective theory. On the second reading, however, she is doing something quite different. On this reading she is introducing a new interpretation of the moral realm, which wholly reconstitutes it. She is opposing the "truth" of the masculinist theories with other "truths." But if we interpret this statement in the context of the alternative scientific methodology, the conclusions that follow differ from those entailed by the first reading. Most important, it follows that Gilligan cannot claim that her interpretation is truer or more objective, because she has defined truth as a function of theoretical perspective. The "truth" that Gilligan claims for her perspective is thus a truth that is internal to the theoretical perspective itself, just as the "truth" of the dominant conception is internal to that perspective.

It is possible to interpret *In a Different Voice* from the perspective of either of these two readings. I employ the second reading in my analysis of Gilligan, for a number of reasons. First, in the studies she has published since *In a Different Voice*, Gilligan quite explicitly adopts what I am calling the second reading, embracing an alternative scientific methodology that departs from standard empiricism. In these works she employs what, in the jargon of the philosophy of science, amounts to a coherentist scientific method. Second, employing the second reading of Gilligan accomplishes a redefinition of the moral realm and the reconstitution of moral theory that are the goal of my study. Defining the moral realm as constituted by conceptions of the moral subject and of morality itself fosters an approach that is pluralistic and nonhierarchical, an approach that highlights the constitution of moral voices. Third, the second reading emphasizes the necessary connection between method and truth – that is, that the method employed in the analysis of morality cannot be divorced from the moral truths that the method produces.

In chapter 3 of *In a Different Voice*, entitled "Concepts of Self and Morality," Gilligan ties her redefinition of the moral realm to a concept of self that challenges the autonomous self of the masculinist tradition. One of the major themes of Gilligan's work – and also one of her most significant contributions – is the claim that selfhood and morality are intimately linked. Gilligan argues that subjects develop moral voices as a function of the emergence of selfhood and that the definition of the moral realm is necessarily structured by the concept of self that informs it. Moral development theory as defined by Piaget and Kohlberg is grounded in the separate, autonomous self of the modernist tradition. This separate self is both the precondition and the goal of the moral stages that Kohlberg posits. Against this, Gilligan proposes what is now called "the relational self." She defines a self that is formed through relational patterns with others, particularly in the early years of childhood. Following the psychological approach of object-relations theory, she describes the way in which girls, because they are not encouraged to separate from their mothers, develop a sense of self in which relationships are primary. Boys, by contrast, because they succeed in separating from their mothers, develop a sense of self as separate and autonomous. Thus, as a result of their different relationships with their mothers, girls develop relational skills and find autonomy problematic, while boys fear relationships but develop autonomy skills.

It is tempting to read Gilligan's argument about the constitution of the self in an empiricist vein. She seems to be proposing a corrective to the incomplete, erroneous, and biased view of the self propounded by masculinist theorists. These theorists listened to the accounts of male subjects only; Gilligan, by listening to women as well, can be interpreted as completing the faulty accounts of masculinist theorists. As is evident from the passages quoted above, there is evidence in the text for this interpretation: Gilligan several times refers to her goal as uncovering the "truth" of human development. But here, too, there are grounds for a second reading. At the very beginning of her account, Gilligan states that she is interested in listening to the "stories" that women tell about their lives (1982: 2). Her emphasis on narrative, listening, and voices introduces a different approach to the study of moral development, an approach that is incompatible with the empiricist studies she challenges.

Two points are crucial here. First, Gilligan is well aware that theorists such as Kohlberg *have* listened to women's stories, but, because they employed the interpretive framework of separate selves, they were forced to classify these stories as deficient and those who told them as lacking the qualities necessary for moral agency. What Gilligan is proposing is an alternative framework in which these women's stories are interpreted as genuine moral statements. If, as Gilligan proposes, we interpret relationship, care, and connection as integral to human life and development, then we will interpret women's stories as genuinely moral narratives, distinct from, but every bit as moral as, those based on abstract principles. Implicit in Gilligan's articulation of the different voice is the assumption that what we, as listeners, hear is a function of the interpretive framework we impose. What Gilligan is proposing is a different interpretation of the same moral experiences. These moral experiences, the voices of women that Kohlberg dismissed as deficient, Gilligan hears as genuine moral statements.

Second, Gilligan's use of the term "stories" here is significant. Kohlberg does not claim to be telling a "story" about moral development. The word *story* connotes fiction, whereas Kohlberg claims to be discovering an antecedently given truth. "Stories" suggests multiplicity, invention, interpretation; Kohlberg is searching for facts and evidence. By claiming that she is listening to women's "stories," Gilligan is advancing two key theses: first, that we need to alter our interpretive framework in order to hear these stories as *moral* stories, and, second, that women (and men) make sense of their lives by telling stories about themselves. The link between narrative and selfhood has been explored by a number of contemporary theorists.[1] Narrative theorists argue that subjects make sense of their lives and constitute themselves *as* subjects by the very activity of constructing stories about themselves. At this point in her work Gilligan does not elaborate on the role of narrative in her theory. It is clear, however, that viewing subjectivity as a function of narrative is incompatible with the empiricist accounts she is challenging. Two themes emerge from her account: that women's moral stories were not heard by her male colleagues as *moral* and that it is her intention to replace their interpretive framework with one that does not ignore or silence the moral voice of women.[2]

What, then, is the story that Gilligan wants to tell about human experiences, a story that includes the moral voice of women? And, most important, how does this story relate to the story of separate selves that has dominated accounts of moral development? In the course of her work, Gilligan proposes several different understandings of this narrative. In *In a Different Voice* her account can best be described as additive or dialogic: she proposes that women's relational, caring voice be added to the voice of the separate self. Thus she asserts that "Adding a new line of interpretation, based on the imagery of the girls' thought, makes it possible not only to see development where previously development was not discerned, but also to consider differences in the understanding of relationships without scaling these differences from better to worse" (1982: 26). She suggests that both voices are integral to the human life cycle, that "we know ourselves as separate only insofar as we live in connection with others, and that we experience relationships only insofar as we differentiate other from self" (1982: 63). The result, she claims, is a "dialogue between fairness and care" (1982: 174), a kind of complementarity of the two voices.

There are many problems with this formulation, problems that occupy Gilligan's attention in subsequent work. One is that of the relationship between gender and voice. Throughout her work, Gilligan claims that the different voice is identified by theme, not gender (1982: 2). Yet, in her descriptions it is exclusively women who speak in the different voice. Another problem concerns the issue of hierarchy. Gilligan is consistent in her claim of equality for the two voices. Here she describes their interaction as complementary and dialogic; later it becomes the interplay of themes. Yet, as she herself admits, it is difficult to claim difference without implying better or worse (1982: 14). Although, in a logical sense, positing differences or distinctions may be innocent, in a social and political context it is not. Identifying a group or social practice as "different" from an established social norm implies an inferior status for that difference, despite protestations to the contrary. As will become evident in the following discussions, this issue has continued to be problematic for Gilligan's thesis. Several feminist moral theorists have used Gilligan's work to proclaim the superiority of women's moral voice. Yet there is virtually no textual evidence for this claim in Gilligan's book.[3] The equality thesis, however, is far from satisfactory. It is naive to assume that the inferiority of women's moral voice can be overcome simply by asserting its equality. Several millennia of subordination are unlikely to be overcome by little more than a proclamation.

Subsequent work

The themes introduced in *In a Different Voice* also inform Gilligan's subsequent work, but in the later work these themes have been expanded and, in some cases, even transformed. My interpretation of this later work is guided by two theses. The first is that it is impossible to separate questions of substance from questions of method in Gilligan's discussions. In working through this literature it becomes evident that her substantive claims about justice and care are a function of the method with which she approaches the issue of moral development. Second, although Gilligan continues to claim that she is merely adding another "voice" to existing moral theory, I argue that in an epistemological sense this is not an adequate description of the theoretical import of her work. Her concepts of the moral domain and the moral subject are incompatible with the definition of morality found in modernist moral theory; thus she cannot *add* the different voice to that theory. Gilligan frequently backs away from an outright rejection of contemporary moral theory; she claims that she wants to reform rather than reconstitute it. But the elements of a radically different approach to moral theory are nevertheless present in her work.

The issue that has received most attention from critics is the relationship between the two moral voices that she analyzes: justice and care. *In a Different Voice* characterized this relationship as one of complementarity, of a dialectical interplay of two voices. As early as 1985, however, Gilligan developed a different characterization of the relationship, what she calls the "focus phenomenon." Her ongoing studies revealed that a significant majority of people interviewed – 70 percent in one study (Marcus and Spiegelman 1985: 48) and 75 percent in another (Gilligan 1988a: xviii) – described their moral conflicts in terms of either justice *or* care, but not both. Building on this evidence, Gilligan argues that the two moral perspectives are grounded in different dimensions of relationships that give rise to moral concerns. Justice and care, she argues, are not mirror images but, rather, different ways of organizing the basic elements of moral judgment. Appealing to the duck/rabbit figure to illustrate her point, Gilligan claims that individuals can see moral conflicts in terms of either justice or care but not both at once. Moral problems are thus not resolved by balancing justice and care but by taking one perspective rather than the other (1987a: 20–6; Bernstein and Gilligan 1990).

Gilligan's discussion in these articles complicates the description of moral voices which she presents in *In a Different Voice*. On the one hand, she emphasizes a theme that was present in the latter: the universality of justice and care. In a more recent discussion, for example, she asserts that, "Although these two dimensions of relationship may be differently salient in the thinking of women and men, both equality and attachment are embedded in the cycle of life, universal in human experience because inherent in the relation of parent and child" (1986a: 286). This passage is compatible with what I identified above as the first reading of *In a Different Voice*. It emphasizes Gilligan's attempt to define the universal parameters of morality, the human moral condition. But there is also another tendency that is present in this work: a movement toward the particular, away from the universal. *In a Different Voice* theorized what appeared to be a straightforward relationship between gender and moral voice. In her more recent work, however, Gilligan has come to acknowledge that this relationship is far from simple. Although she continues to find gender to be a significant factor in the expression of moral voice, Gilligan now asserts that the connection between gender and moral voice is complex, that "differences cannot be reduced to questions of gender" (Gilligan, Johnston, and Miller 1988: 54). This second tendency offers a more fruitful line of inquiry than the attempt to define the universal parameters of morality. An emphasis on the particular, on the complexity of moral voices, characterizes Gilligan's research in her most important work since *In a Different Voice*, her book with Lyn Brown, *Meeting at the Crossroads* (Brown and Gilligan 1992). What Gilligan is exploring – and what I want to explore in my examination of moral voices – is the range of factors, including but not limited to gender, that constitute these voices.

In her most recent work Gilligan has begun to articulate the relationship between justice and care by employing musical metaphors. The terms "counterpoint," "harmony," "harmonious whole," and "double fugue" have provided her with a means of redescribing the moral realm that departs radically from that of the modernist tradition (Gilligan, Rogers, and Brown 1990; Gilligan, Brown, and Rogers 1990). She rejects the language of stages and steps employed by the masculinist development theorists for a musical language of counterpoint and theme. A counterpoint is a melody accompanying another melody; it involves not opposition but the addition of a related but independent melody (Gilligan, Brown, and Rogers 1990: 115). Employing these musical metaphors allows Gilligan to define the relationship of justice and care in a way that avoids the oppositional connotations implicit in her earlier formulation. She describes the two voices as related but independent melodies, with fixed rules of harmony that constitute a harmonious whole. They play together, she concludes, like a "double fugue" (Gilligan, Rogers, and Brown 1990: 321ff.).

It is not an exaggeration to assert that both critics and defenders of Gilligan's work are obsessed with the question of the hierarchy of justice and care. Defenders of modernist moral theory have argued that justice subsumes care; feminist critics of Gilligan have argued that emphasizing women's traditional differences perpetuates their inferiority. And, most notably, feminist defenders of Gilligan have tried to enlist her as an ally in their attempts to argue for the superiority of the care voice. She neatly sidesteps this controversy, however, first, by advancing a nonoppositional understanding of justice and care through the use of musical metaphors and, second, by asserting that both justice and care are universal elements of the human condition. There is only one passage in Gilligan's work in which she succumbs to the temptation to privilege care over justice. At a conference on women and moral theory she asserted: "The promise of joining women and moral theory lies in the fact that human survival, in the late twentieth century, may depend less on formal agreement than on human connection" (1987a: 32). This passage, however, is exceptional. In all other instances Gilligan steadfastly maintains the equality of justice and care. In an interview in which she was asked whether the care voice was the "better" voice, she replied that thinking about issues of care and responsibility is better than ignoring them and that seeing detachment as morally problematic is better than not seeing it in this light. She concluded: "My argument, therefore, about better voice/ different voice, is that you really are going to have a new understanding of both attachment *and* equality. They're both vitally important. Attachment and equality will always be with us. They're built into the human experience" (Gilligan, in Marcus and Spiegelman 1985: 61).

Central to Kohlberg's articulation of the "justice voice" is his assertion that it develops in distinct steps or stages. The concept of development as a linear progression upward to better forms is constitutive of the dominant discourse of moral development. Gilligan was thoroughly trained in this discourse by none other than Kohlberg himself. It should come as no surprise, then, that at least in her early work Gilligan attempts to apply the concept of linear development in her analysis of the ethic of care. In *In a Different Voice* she asserts that studies of women's lives over time "elucidate transitions in the development of an ethic of care," indicating a shift in concern "from survival to goodness and from goodness to truth" (1982: 109). It is significant that in her subsequent research Gilligan has focused her attention on adolescent girls. She argues that adolescence is a key developmental stage for girls, analogous to early childhood for boys. This implies that she is continuing the pattern established in the discourse of moral development theory: defining stages of development that progress toward more advanced forms (1991: 23).

A careful reading of Gilligan's various formulations of the issue of development, however, suggests a quite different interpretation. Although Gilligan claims that the aim of her work on adolescent girls is to add another line of development to moral development theory, her research accomplishes a much more significant feat (1988b: 14). In her studies Gilligan challenges the fundamental assumptions of development theory and, ultimately, the assumption of linear progress itself. The development theory in which Gilligan was trained identifies the linear progression in the development of the self as a movement from attachment to autonomy. In her researches on adolescent girls Gilligan defines adolescence as a "watershed in female development," a turning point in the development of the self that parallels that of early childhood for boys (1990b: 10). But, as she continued her researches, Gilligan gradually came to define this transition as a regression rather than a progression. This led her not only to articulate a new theory of female development but to question the normative, linear concept of development that grounds traditional moral development theory.

In her first series of articles on adolescent girls, Gilligan argued that adolescence is "a time when girls are in danger of drowning or disappearing" (1990b: 10). Whereas eleven- and twelve-year-old girls tend to be outspoken and sure of themselves, adolescent girls are conforming, less resistant, and more hesitant (1990a: 514). The explanation that Gilligan offers initially for this transition in girls' lives is that it is at this point that they meet what she calls the "wall of Western culture" (1990a: 502). What she means by this is that girls begin to realize that being a "good woman" in this society means becoming selfless. It follows that the adolescent girl must renounce the clear sense of self that the eleven- or twelve-year-old has developed; for continuing to assert this self will result in her being labeled selfish (1990b: 10). The crisis that this produces in girls' sense of self is devastating. But Gilligan theorizes that this crisis also produces resistance. Adolescent girls develop a resistance, because they are being asked to renounce the knowledge they have acquired, a knowledge of the body and of relationships (1990a: 504). When Gilligan first theorizes about this resistance, her goal is to devise ways in which it can be healthy, rather than corrosive, to allow girls to stay in "the open air of relationships," rather than turn inward (1990a: 533).

In their recently published study of adolescent girls, however, Brown and Gilligan (1992) articulate a more radical approach to girls' "development," one that constitutes a fundamental challenge to development theory. Gilligan and her colleagues followed a group of girls from the age of seven or eight to their mid-teens. The seven- and eight-year-olds whom they interviewed expressed the strong belief that they knew what was going on in their relational world and were willing to act on that knowledge. They expressed a wish for honest dialogue that was not always "nice" but was full of genuine disagreements and feelings; they did not feel that these disagreements jeopardized their relationships (1992: 44–53). But as early as age eight, the girls began to come up against "the wall of conventional female behavior" and were expected to give up their strong feelings. By the time they were ten or eleven, the girls were struggling against the growing pressure not to speak what they knew and to repress their strong feelings (1992: 91). Brown and Gilligan define the nature of this crisis in a unique way. They argue that the seven- to eleven-year-olds' knowledge of relationships is one in which strong feelings are expressed and disagreements occur. As they approach "the wall," however, they are asked to accept a very different model of relationship, one in which they must remain silent and be "selfless" rather than "selfish." As Brown and Gilligan put it, girls take themselves out of relationship for the sake of relationship (1992: 106).

The result is that the girls yearn for honest, open relationships but fear such relationships as dangerous because they conflict with the image of the good – that is, "selfless" – woman (1992: 175).

A number of significant conclusions emerge from these studies. Gilligan is suggesting an understanding of "development" that constitutes a radical departure from that of Kohlberg. Kohlberg's theory of moral development defined development as a progression from dependence to independence, from reliance on relationships to autonomous selfhood. Gilligan's observations of adolescent girls, however, lead her to a different interpretation. In her first studies, Gilligan noted that many of the girls she interviewed resisted the move to detachment from relationships, a move that, they were told, constitutes mature selfhood. Instead, they attempted to remain attached, to continue their relationships, but to change the character of their attachments. Gilligan found that adolescent girls defined "dependence" as positive, not negative; they found that depending *on* someone is a good thing (1988b: 14–15). From this Gilligan concluded that adolescent girls' resistance to detachment may not signal a failure of individuation but "may lead to a different vision of progress and civilization" (1988b: 14). She reminds her readers that, since Freud, detachment has been identified as the key to civilization, that the individual's move to disengagement from relationships signaled his entry into mature selfhood. The alternative that Gilligan derives from her study of adolescent girls is one in which psychological health is defined not as disengagement but, rather, as staying in relationships: with oneself, with others, and with the world (1991: 23). In a closely related study, one of Gilligan's colleagues, Lori Stern, showed that adolescent girls resisted the opposition of separation and connection; instead, they wanted to define separation and independence in the context of relationship (1990).

The conclusions that Gilligan and her colleagues drew from these first studies were relatively optimistic: they defined a developmental pattern for girls that identified relationships in positive terms. This optimism was abandoned, however, in *Meeting at the Crossroads*. Although Brown and Gilligan have not relinquished the latter's earlier claim that girls' development constitutes "a different vision," the choice that girls make to stay in relationships is now defined more negatively. At the end of *Meeting at the Crossroads* Brown and Gilligan conclude that the movement experienced by girls from outspoken to "selfless" relationships is "movement into the sea of Western culture and a profound psychological loss" (1992: 180).

There are two aspects of Gilligan's interpretations of these studies which have important theoretical implications. First, Gilligan's "model of development," if it can even be called such, cannot be added to the masculinist model but, rather, negates it. Gilligan assumes that selves

develop in relationships. It necessarily follows from this that detachment from those relationships must be psychologically unhealthy. But
if this is the case, it also necessarily follows that the model of moral
development that demands such detachment is not just "a different
vision" but a wrong-headed one. Gilligan comes close to acknowledging this in her later work. Discussing the problem of girls and resistance, she directly attacks the definition of development that grounds
the dominant tradition of moral development (Gilligan, Brown, and
Rogers 1990). Appealing to the etymology of the word *development*, she
points out that only one definition of the word presupposes a linear
model of progression to a better form. Another definition proposes an
unfolding, the realization of a fuller potential. Applying this definition
of development, she claims that development need not be exclusively
defined in terms of linear, progressive steps or stages. Rather, she
proposes an understanding in terms of musical themes, melodies
repeated in different keys or notes heard in relation to other notes; she
suggests the metaphor of a double fugue (1990: 113–15). It is this
definition of development that Gilligan hears in the voices of adolescent girls. But it is not a vision that can simply be added to the existing
development literature. It is, rather, a radical reconceptualization that
opposes the linear developmental model.

Gilligan's position also entails that the dominant tradition of moral
development, a tradition that defines detachment and separation as the
hallmarks of mature selfhood, creates severe psychological problems
for women, who define themselves in relational terms.[4] In one of her
most pessimistic passages, Gilligan admits that women are excluded
from the male definition of selfhood, a definition that labels them
inferior because of their inability to separate themselves from others.
Women cannot be mature moral agents according to this tradition,
because they fail to achieve the autonomy it demands: "The wind of
tradition blowing through women is a chill wind, because it brings a
message of exclusion – stay out; because it brings a message of subordination – stay under; because it brings a message of objectification –
become the object of another's worship or desire, see yourself as you
have been seen for centuries through a male gaze" (1990b: 20).

The second theoretically significant aspect of Gilligan's position
emerges most clearly in *Meeting at the Crossroads*. Gilligan's initial
optimism with regard to defining a relational developmental pattern
for girls is abandoned in this work. What was earlier defined as a
progression in the development of girls toward a mature selfhood
defined in terms of relationship is now redefined as a regression. The
kind of relationships women are encouraged to form, the authors now
argue, are psychologically unhealthy. Gilligan's initial understanding
of the developmental pattern of girls offered an alternative of sorts:
mature selfhood defined in terms of relationship rather than autonomy.

This new study closes off that option. The authors' conclusion is now that women are doubly handicapped: they are excluded both from the masculine model of autonomous selfhood and from the kind of open, honest relationships that they knew as preadolescent girls.

Gilligan's challenge to the linear concept of development and its masculinist bias is a function of her more fundamental challenge to the paradigm of the autonomous self that grounds that concept. This challenge was launched in her early work and is strongly reinforced in subsequent studies. In her discussion of the autonomous and relational concepts of self in *In a Different Voice*, Gilligan argued that the two concepts, like the two moral voices, can and do coexist because they are necessary aspects of the human condition. In her subsequent work Gilligan amplifies this theme. In an article written soon after *In a Different Voice* was published, Gilligan characterizes the relationship between these two senses of self as a "tension": women define selfishness as a moral failing, yet selfishness is necessary for autonomy. Gilligan concludes that this tension between responsibilities and rights "complicates" moral judgments (1983a: 59). In a later work, however, this reference to tension is dropped in favor of the musical language that she now prefers. Gilligan now asserts that these two concepts of self are "counterpoints," that they play together in a harmonious whole. The shift to musical language, she sees as taking us out of the "deadlocked paradox of relationship that continues to plague the fields of personality and developmental psychology: that one can only experience self in the context of relationships with others and that one can only experience relationship if one differentiates other from self" (Gilligan, Rogers, and Brown 1990: 328).

In several other contexts, however, Gilligan's work suggests an alternative interpretation of the differences between her concepts of self and development and those of the dominant tradition. In an article written with Grant Wiggins (1988), Gilligan argues that their explorations of moral voice call for a reversal of Piaget's conception of self and development. While Piaget (1932) claims that the individual *remains* egocentric in the absence of contrary influences, Gilligan's and Wiggins's researches show that the individual *becomes* egocentric if left to himself. The recognition of these two moral orientations, the authors conclude, necessitates a change in our concepts of development, stages, and moral maturity (1988: 136). Finally, in another context, Gilligan defines this situation as a "challenge": female development challenges the male model of self with a self defined within the context of continuing relationships (1988b: 18).

Gilligan's discussion here parallels her discussion of the relationship between justice and care. In both cases her conception effectively deconstructs the justice/autonomous self conception. Two elements of Gilligan's argument are crucial. First, the relational self that she posits cannot exist in "harmony" or "counterpoint" with the autonomous self. As her criticism of Piaget reveals, this tradition presupposes a given, egocentric, autonomous self. This self can *become* dependent on others, but within this discourse dependence is defined as a distortion of the true self, a state to be avoided or transcended if autonomy is to be achieved. Gilligan, by contrast, rejects the notion of a given self. The self, for her, is formed through relationships, particularly those of early childhood. Thus there is no authentic self to return *to*. In other words, the two conceptions are incompatible. Their relationship is not merely a case of "tension" or "challenge" but one of negation: each negates the other.

The second radical element of Gilligan's conception also follows from her discussion of Piaget. For Piaget and the tradition he represents, the separate self is given, whereas relationships are, by definition, incidental rather than constitutive. The relational self that Gilligan articulates, by contrast, claims that relationships are constitutive of the self, that there is no given core that is definitive. One of the most significant aspects of the object-relations theory on which Gilligan depends is the claim that the existence of autonomous selves is itself a product of relationships. According to object-relations theory a boy *develops* into an autonomous self, because his mother forces him to separate from her. A girl, on the other hand, because her mother does not enforce such a separation, fails to develop the autonomy that is fostered in her brothers. There is a cruel irony in this state of affairs; for when these girls become women, they are told that autonomy is the natural and proper state of mature selfhood, a selfhood that they cannot hope to attain. The relational pattern that produces the masculine autonomous self is thus privileged over that which produces the feminine relational self. What I would like to emphasize, though, is that Gilligan's theory displaces the separate self tradition by asserting that the allegedly given autonomous self is itself a product of relationships.

If, as the coherence theorists and Gilligan herself argue, theories constitute the evidence they examine, it follows that the displacement of modernist moral theory that Gilligan effects must necessarily be a function of her reliance on a radically different methodology. The move toward a coherentist conception of truth and method that was nascent in *In a Different Voice* has developed gradually in Gilligan's subsequent work; in particular, her opposition to the empiricist methodology that informs behaviorist psychology has become more explicit. In an early article written with John Murphy, Gilligan established the pattern she followed in *In a Different Voice*: first an empirical critique of Kohlberg (the assertion that he was getting it wrong), then the assertion that a new theoretical approach is necessary (Murphy and Gilligan 1980). In this article, however, Murphy and Gilligan raise an issue that will concern Gilligan for the next decade, an issue that reveals her initial ambivalence about embracing an alternative methodology: relativism. Arguing that abandoning Kohlberg's scheme would result in a relativism that constitutes moral regression, the authors argue instead for what they call "contextual relativism." It is significant that at this stage in her thinking Gilligan remains within Kohlberg's scheme. She and Murphy attempt to place their "contextual relativism" in Kohlberg's postconventional stage and give it equal billing with postconventional formal (rights) thinking, Kohlberg's highest stage (1980: 83). This thesis is an early formulation of the separate-but-equal concept of the different voice that informs her initial studies. But it is also an attempt to deal with the methodological problems entailed by that thesis.

In an article published only a year after *In a Different Voice*, Gilligan's position has evolved considerably (1983b). She specifically identifies the positivist/behaviorist trend in the social sciences as the root of the problem she is addressing. She asserts that the development of the social sciences toward increasingly formal and analytic modes of thought, the separation of subject from object, and the claim of value neutrality and objective truth foster studies focused on an ethic of justice. By contrast, she states that the ethic of care is based on an "understanding of the narrative of social relations" (1983b: 46). In this context she also introduces a theme that she subsequently reiterates throughout her work: dialectical moral theory. At this stage of her argument, Gilligan asserts that her advocacy of two voices in dialectical tension is opposed to pluralism and value relativism (1983b: 35). In later work she defines this opposition differently: relativism on the one hand and "monotheism" on the other (1987b: 77). With this formulation of her position, Gilligan takes on the entire Western tradition. In one of her most sweeping pronouncements she asserts: "If you want to support what has been in the Western tradition since Plato – that is, the notion of a unitary truth, that virtue is one, that its name is justice, that it is part of the sense of one right answer upon which we do, in the end, agree – then you will select an all-male sample" (Gilligan, in Marcus and Spiegelman 1985: 49).

A lot is at stake here, despite a dubious interpretation of Plato. Gilligan is linking the desire for unitary truth with the Western moral tradition itself and with its founding father, Plato. She specifically identifies this tradition as masculinist and describes her inclusion of women as a direct challenge to that tradition. Yet, despite the boldness of this claim, Gilligan, like many other critics of empiricism, falls prey to the assumption that abandoning unitary truth necessarily courts the "danger" of relativism. In order to avoid this danger, she proposes replacing unitary truth with dualistic truth. She asserts that her perspective "offers the possibility of a more adequate representation of human experience by including what was formerly ruled out by definition and then sustained by a major flaw in research" (Gilligan, in Marcus and Spiegelman 1985: 49).

Although she never refers to Kuhn's theory of paradigm change, I think that the best way to interpret Gilligan's methodology is to say that she is proposing a new paradigm. What these passages imply is that her research is an attempt to account for "anomalous data" in moral development that do not fit into Kohlberg's scheme (1987b: 81). Such a Kuhnian reading of Gilligan yields some very useful results. Gilligan is asserting that the different voice of women has no place in Kohlberg's scheme, despite his attempt to categorize it as an inferior stage of moral development. Kuhn's theory can also be used to explain why Gilligan "hears" this different voice while Kohlberg does not: theories constitute their own set of facts. Kohlberg's definition of morality constitutes the moral realm in a particular way, specifically in a way that silences women's moral voice. One of the most poignant aspects of Gilligan's research is her discovery that many of the adolescent girls whom she interviewed shared the dominant tradition's definition of the moral realm. Consequently, these girls were unwilling to label their moral problems, problems concerned with relationships, as properly "moral," because they fail to meet the principled criteria of the justice perspective. One of Gilligan's colleagues maintains that "the values and concerns expressed by these girls in their dilemmas are not moral problems as morality has been defined for them by those in authority in this society" (Brown 1990: 103). Gilligan's redefinition of the moral realm constitutes a new set of facts not discernible in terms of the traditional definition of morality. In Gilligan's terms, it gives women a moral voice where previously there was only silence.

Many of those who criticized Gilligan after the publication of *In a Different Voice* focused on her methodology, arguing that her evidence was faulty and that sex differences in moral voice were not statistically significant. These criticisms, as well as Gilligan's own researches, led her to reformulate her position in terms of the "focus phenomenon" discussed above. But Gilligan also offers a more comprehensive response to this criticism, one that is compatible with a Kuhnian interpretation of her position. She claims that her position has nothing to do with the statistical evidence that does or does not support her theory but concerns, rather, an interpretive point. She concedes that if we remain within the parameters of Kohlberg's theory, men and women do not differ statistically in moral voice. Rather than seeing this as a refutation of her theory, however, Gilligan asserts that she is offering a different way of defining moral problems. She argues: "There is no data independent of theory, no observations not made from a perspective. Data alone do not tell us anything; they do not speak, but are interpreted by people" (1986b: 328). What she is asserting here is that statistical evidence is theory-relative and thus that the "disproof" of her evidence from Kohlberg's perspective does not constitute a refutation. Her theory creates its own data and generates evidence that is relative to it; no theory-independent proof or disproof is possible.

In her recent articles, and most notably in *Meeting at the Crossroads*, Gilligan has begun to define quite clearly the nature of the new paradigm she is articulating. At its center is the concept of narrative. One of the themes of Gilligan's recent work is that, by moving away from a narrative art to a science that rejects narrative, psychology has been impoverished. She defines her goal as an attempt to return to an awareness of voice and vision, the recognition that stories can be told from more than one point of view (Gilligan, Brown, and Rogers 1990: 89). Citing several contemporary theorists who attempt to account for what she calls the "messiness" of human life, she once more places her work between the "Platonic legacy" of a single form and "endless relativism" (Gilligan, Brown, and Rogers 1990: 93). She describes the method employed in the study she is discussing as "reading" – that is, interpreting – the narratives that were collected for moral voice and sense of self. The researchers in the study explicitly rejected the notion of a neutral, objective observer, claiming instead that they were "glued to [their] own shadows," that they always interpreted what they observed from a particular perspective (Gilligan, Brown, and Rogers 1990: 122–3).[5]

Gilligan refines and redefines this narrative-based methodology in the coauthored study, *Meeting at the Crossroads*. The thesis guiding this extended study of girls at the Laurel School is that early adolescence constitutes a crossroads in women's lives, yet a hitherto unchartered territory. The aim of the study, the authors claim, is to learn about women's psychological development by employing a method that joins women and girls. They assert that women can reclaim lost voices and lost strengths by listening to girls' voices. The major finding of the study is that even though connection is central to women, women silence themselves in relationships rather than risk open conflict. Brown and Gilligan found that girls' voices were strong before adolescence, but that in early adolescence disconnection and repression occur. It is at this point that girls silence their voices and move from "authentic" to "idealized" relationships (1992: 5). The authors use the findings of the study to articulate a new developmental model for girls that focuses on the changes occurring in early adolescence.

The significance of this new developmental model is overshadowed, however, by the significance of the new method that Brown and Gilligan employ. The authors recount the methodological problems they encountered and the research design they employed to overcome these problems. Early in the book they report that, as a result of employing "tried and true research methods" (i.e., the narrative-based method employed in previous studies), the girls suddenly withdrew –

held their stories in and silenced their voices (1992: 12). The problem, the authors note, is that "Many of the questions we had asked . . . did not seem right; they were no longer useful, they seemed to be cutting off girls' voices, preventing them from speaking their experiences" (1992: 18). The girls' silence forced Gilligan and Brown to develop a new method, one in which the questions came from the girls rather than from the researchers: "We needed to create a practice of psychology that was something like the practice of relationship" (1992: 15). This practice of psychology entailed a method in which the researchers were actively engaged with the girls. "We would stay in relationship with the girls and move where they seemed to be taking us, change our design and rewrite our questions so that we could explore the changes we were hearing in girls' voices. . . . We would follow the associative logic of girls' psyches, we would move where the girls led us" (1992: 18–19).

The voice-centered, relational method of doing psychological research that Gilligan and her colleagues developed is based on that employed in *In a Different Voice*: listening to women's voices and trying to sort out the narratives being told. But the method employed in *Meeting at the Crossroads* is more clearly developed, detailed, and explicit. Most important, it reveals the nature of the paradigm shift that Gilligan is effecting. Four aspects of this new paradigm are definitive. First, it assumes that the task of the psychologist is to gather and analyze narratives, to collect stories rather than objective data. Thus the presupposition of objective facts, the centerpiece of empiricism, is jettisoned.[6] Second, the presupposition of the objective researcher is likewise abandoned. Brown and Gilligan repeatedly state that they are articulating a *relational* psychological method. The key to this method is voice, the "channel of connection" between researcher and subject (1992: 20). "Voice, because it is embodied, connects rather than separates psyche and body; because voice is language it also joins psyche and culture" (1992: 20). Third, the new method is hermeneutical. One of the largely unintended results of the study was that the researchers learned as much about themselves as they did about their subjects: the knowledge they gained from the girls was inseparable from self-knowledge. For the women conducting the research, listening to the girls' voices meant hearing their own voices, voices that had been silenced in their own early adolescence (1992: 216). "No longer steeped in a dispassionate discipline of testing and assessment, we entered into relationships which changed with each new encounter, and we began to learn from the girls and the women who were now joining us in this study" (1992: 15). Finally, the new method is explicitly political and engaged. Brown and Gilligan define their method as relational *and feminist* (1992: 24); the aim of their research is to "create a more caring and just society" (1992: 6) and to "extricate themselves from the constraints of patriarchal logic" (1992: 30). The ultimate goal of such research, therefore, is social change: "When women and girls meet at the crossroads of adolescence, the intergenerational seam of a patriarchal culture opens up. If women and girls together resist giving up relationship for the sake of 'relationships,' then this meeting holds the potential for societal and cultural change" (1992: 232).

It is my contention that, in *Meeting at the Crossroads*, Brown and Gilligan articulate a clear alternative to the empiricist tradition of psychological research. Taken in conjunction with Gilligan's other work, the methodology employed here constitutes a paradigm shift: a move from an objectivist method to a relational one, from the search for factual data to the collection of stories, from a detached, "scientific" approach to a committed, political one. It is her use of this method that allows Gilligan to "hear" silenced moral voices. Her method constitutes her data just as, in Kohlberg's researches, his method constitutes the parameters of the moral domain.

In what follows I explore the significance of Gilligan's work, making explicit what is only implicit in her studies. My central argument is that Gilligan's researches entail that there are many moral voices, not just two. Gender is one, but not the only, factor in the constitution of moral voices; other factors are also constitutive. Gilligan has begun to explore the influence of race in the constitution of moral subjects. I contend that this theme should be pursued further and that the influences of class and culture should be explored as well. Another way of putting this is to say that I am picking up where Gilligan left off, exploring themes that she suggests but does not pursue. I am grounding my discussion in her work, because I think that her approach, more than that of any other contemporary theorist, has made possible a radical restructuring of the moral domain. She has allowed us to hear silenced moral voices. To this I would only add: "Let many voices be heard."

Interpreting the different voice

The critical response to *In a Different Voice* and, to a lesser extent, to Gilligan's subsequent work, has been tremendous. Over a decade after the publication of *In a Different Voice* the literature on Gilligan's theory is vast and still growing. The assessment of the significance of her work varies widely, particularly among feminists. Gilligan is, on the one hand, praised for ushering in a new era of feminist thought and, on the other hand, condemned for subverting the gains made by previous feminists. Agreement exists only on the fact that Gilligan's work has had a profound impact on discussions in both moral theory and feminism. My intent in what follows is not to review this extensive literature. Rather, I will highlight salient reactions to Gilligan's work in

order to clarify my thesis regarding its significance. Despite the extensive literature, few of her critics discuss what I see as the radical
character of the claims about moral voice implicit in it.

One of the most common interpretations of Gilligan's work is that
she is making strictly empirical claims, that her central argument is that
it is a statistically provable fact that men and women have different
moral voices. Defined as an empirical claim, however, Gilligan's thesis
can be dismissed quite easily. Debra Nails, for example, argues that
Gilligan's data are so distorted that the result is "social science at sea
without an anchor," ideology rather than science (1983: 664).[7] The
clearest statement of the presuppositions informing such empiricist
criticisms was published in the pages of the prominent feminist journal
Signs. In an issue devoted to assessments of *In a Different Voice*, several
critics express the sentiment aptly summed up in the following: "We
only urge that the claims about these differences should be subject to
the empirical tests that are the basis of social science" (Greeno and
Macoby 1986: 316). Throughout the volume, Gilligan's critics claim that
her research lacks objectivity and is not adequately supported by
evidence (Kerber et al. 1986). But the whole of this acrimonious debate
remains firmly within the empiricist tradition that Gilligan is calling
into question. It is therefore wonderfully ironic that, in their introduction to the debate, the editors pose the question of whether this
"dialogue" on *In a Different Voice* constitutes a break from the "male-
dominated tradition of confrontational debate" (Kerber et al. 1986: 304).
The answer to this question must be a resounding "No."

As noted above, Gilligan's reply to these criticisms was to state
unequivocally that her point is interpretive rather than empirical. Yet
the persistence of these empiricist criticisms calls for comment. Implicit
in the empiricist understanding of scientific method is the assumption
that, without a grounding in unbiased, objective, factual evidence,
social science is indistinguishable from ideology: the specter of relativism once more looms on the horizon. Gilligan's theory is threatening
not only because it displaces traditional moral theory but also because
it challenges the foundations of empiricist, objective social science.
Claiming that Gilligan's work is factually inaccurate is one way of
dismissing its radical implications.

Another way of doing so is to claim that there is no clear distinction
between justice and care. Following Kohlberg's lead,[8] several critics
have suggested that as women move into traditionally male pro-
fessions, they, too, will adopt the justice perspective, thereby erasing
the clear, gendered distinction between justice and care (L. Walker
1984; Stocker 1987; Baumrind 1986). Others have argued that our goal
should be to create a marriage between justice and care (Baier 1987b)
or, in the words of Marilyn Friedman, that the best way to care for
persons is to respect their rights (1987a: 106). Friedman also suggests

that Kohlberg tacitly concedes the collapsing of justice and care in his famous Heinz dilemma. Kohlberg uses the Heinz dilemma to test his subjects' ability to apply abstract moral principles. Subjects are asked to "solve" Heinz's dilemma: whether to steal in order to save his wife's life. Yet the dilemma works as a moral problem only if it is Heinz's *wife* who is sick: it necessarily presupposes this caring relationship (Friedman 1987b: 198).[9]

Yet another approach to the relationship between justice and care that dismisses the impact of Gilligan's work is what some critics have called "domain relativism." Those who advocate this position claim that we need what amounts to a division of moral labor, employing different moral approaches in different domains (Flanagan and Jackson 1987). It is significant that Kohlberg himself advances this thesis. For him, domain relativism is the most convenient answer to the challenge posed by Gilligan's researches (1984: 348). It allows him to incorporate the care voice as another, albeit implicitly inferior, moral realm without altering his original theory. The advocacy of domain relativism, however, has given rise to a sharp controversy among feminist theorists. In a biting critique of Gilligan's work, Joan Tronto (1987) argues that the care voice that Gilligan "discovers" is a function of the subordinate position of women. The domain relativism that some have derived from Gilligan's work, she notes, has disturbing similarities to the public/private split in Western culture, a division that has been used to legitimize the inferiority of women. Thus, Tronto concludes, far from raising the moral status of women, Gilligan's work perpetuates women's inferiority.[10] In the introduction to her recent book on feminist ethics, Claudia Card goes even further, arguing that Gilligan's approach is "conservative," because it promotes a revival of traditional, middle-class conceptions of femininity (1991: 17). What these theorists are arguing is that the deficiency implicit in Gilligan's different voice cannot be removed by *fiat* (Nails 1983: 643). For millennia women have been associated with the realm of care, particularity, and relationships. Gilligan's declaration that this moral realm is equal to the masculine justice realm will not, these critics claim, remove this deeply rooted inferiority.

Other feminist theorists, conversely, have taken exactly the opposite approach to the status of the different voice. These theorists reject the notion that the care voice represents women's deficiency, as well as Gilligan's insistence on the equality of the two voices. Instead, they argue for the superiority of the different voice. Sarah Ruddick's *Maternal Thinking* (1989) and Nel Noddings's *Caring* (1984) are the most noteworthy examples of this genre; both assert the superiority of women's moral voice vis-à-vis the masculine justice voice. Despite the criticisms of Card and others, this position has had a significant impact on the feminist community. The argument that the justice voice has produced continual war; class, race, and gender oppression; and the rape of the natural world is an appealing one to many feminists. The conclusion that a care orientation rooted in traditional "feminine" virtues would result in a more humane world is similarly appealing.

Neither of these two strands of criticism – that of the empiricists who fault Gilligan for her methodology or that of the feminists who question the relationship between the two moral voices – grasps what I am arguing are the radical implications of Gilligan's work. Although she can be faulted for not making her methodological stance clearer, Gilligan obviates the criticisms of the empiricists by adopting what amounts to a Kuhnian or coherentist theory of evidence. She herself admits that the statistical evidence on its own does not support a different moral voice for women. What Gilligan has succeeded in articulating, however, is women's moral self-representation. The immense influence of her work can be attributed to the fact that she has accurately described how many women represent themselves in moral terms – that is, the symbolically female moral voice (Eisenberg and Lennon 1983: 125; Friedman 1987a: 96). What Gilligan is discussing are the beliefs, self-representations, and self-interpretations that many women bring to their moral dilemmas. Statistics are only tangentially relevant to this discussion, if they are relevant at all. Her research has resonated strongly with women, because she is describing a moral self-representation that many women hold.[11]

The theorists who are concerned with the relationship between justice and care raise a different set of questions: whether justice is superior to care and whether a convergence between justice and care is implied. In most of these discussions justice and care are seen to constitute a dichotomy or, at best, a continuum on which the moral voice is located. This in itself is not surprising. The history of Western thought, particularly since the Enlightenment, has been a history of dichotomies, hierarchical and oppositional. That the discussion of justice and care should conform to this pattern is thus unexceptional. But I think there is another way to read Gilligan that moves beyond dichotomies and the hierarchies they entail. Her discussion of the relationship between justice and care as a "double fugue" and her assertion that both moral voices have a relational basis suggest that she is displacing oppositional thought rather than continuing that tradition. Her move from visual metaphors, in which opposition and hierarchy are prominent, to metaphors of hearing, listening, speech, and voices also supports this interpretation. In discussing the implications of Gilligan's moral theory, my goal is to explore this displacement rather than continue the ultimately futile dispute over the relationship between the two moral voices.

Finally, some commentators on Gilligan's different voice have suggested an interpretation that has more affinity to the radical interpretation I am advancing. These commentators argue that Gilligan represents a major alternative to the form of Western moral theory that has been dominant since the Enlightenment, an alternative that has its roots in Aristotle's practical ethics and is manifest in thinkers like Hume, Weil, Murdoch, and Anscombe (Flanagan 1991: 180; Jaggar 1991: 83; Code 1988: 196; Nunner-Winkler 1984). In the next chapter I argue that there is much to this thesis but that the implications of Gilligan's work go beyond a mere reconstitution of the tradition that these philosophers represent. What Gilligan's approach entails is not a contemporary form of Aristotelian or communitarian ethics but, rather, a new moral language altogether (Baier 1985b; Jaggar 1991).

Displacing the tradition

[Women's] super-ego is never so inexorable, so impersonal, so independent of its emotional origins as we require it to be in men. Character traits which critics of every epoch have brought up against women – that they show less sense of justice than men, that they are less ready to submit to the great exigencies of life, that they are more often influenced in their judgment by feelings of affection or hostility – all these would be amply accounted for by the modification in the formation of their super-egos which we have inferred above. (Freud 1961: 257–8)

The individual, left to himself, remains egocentric. . . . The individual begins by understanding and feeling everything through the medium of himself. . . . It is only through contact with the judgments of others that this anomie will gradually yield. (Piaget 1965 (1932): 400)

[Stage 6] is what it means to judge morally. If you want to play the moral game, if you want to make decisions which anyone could agree upon in resolving social conflicts, Stage 6 is it. (Kohlberg 1981: 172)

The thesis that guides my discussion in the following is that Gilligan's research on the different voice does far more than reform the dominant moral tradition of Western thought; it radically transforms it. By untangling the strands of meaning embedded in Gilligan's work, I will attempt to establish that it is epistemologically incompatible with that tradition. Thus Gilligan's research does not, as she herself suggests in her early work, merely add another dimension to existing moral theory. The moral dimension that she propounds does not exist in the same epistemological space as that of Western moral theory. It stands not as a supplement to that tradition but in an other, incompatible theoretical space.

I have already alluded to this incompatibility. But I must now articulate this thesis more explicitly, because it is crucial to my subsequent arguments. Gilligan's paradigm shift can be seen most clearly in opposition to the moral development theorists whose position she is challenging. Her claim is that she is articulating a "different" moral voice, a voice that has been silenced by the dominant tradition. But, strictly speaking, this is not the case. As the quotation from Freud indicates, the "moral" voice of women, a voice rooted in emotion rather than reason, in particularity rather than universality, has not been ignored by moral theorists. Plato excluded his Guardians from family life because he saw the emotional bonds involved in family attachments as detrimental to the unity he wished to foster among them. The equality of women that he proposed rested on a renunciation of such familial ties by both men and women. Enlightenment philosophers in general, and Kant and Hegel in particular, condemned women for their inferior moral sense. Significantly, they traced this inferiority to women's connectedness, to their inability to abstract from the particularity of situations. Even the nineteenth-century feminist John Stuart Mill argued that women are more biased than men and are thus handicapped in the moral realm. He qualified his claim with the assertion that this bias was not natural and would probably disappear if women were educated to perceive their duty to more than their families (1971: 519–32). Throughout the Western tradition, then, women's moral voice has been not so much silenced as marginalized. That women's moral voice is distinctive, that it is inferior to that of men because it lacks objectivity, and that it is only marginally "moral" have been very much a part of Western moral theory.

Gilligan's argument in *In a Different Voice* is framed in opposition to Lawrence Kohlberg's stage sequence of moral development. Kohlberg's theory is closely related to the work of the contemporary moral and political philosopher John Rawls. In *A Theory of Justice* (1971) Rawls articulates a theory of moral development that is similar to Kohlberg's six stages, and, indeed, his approach was influenced by Kohlberg's. But the influence goes both ways: Kohlberg's theory reveals the influence of Rawls's approach as well. There is an advantage to looking carefully at Rawls's work in this context, moreover. Because it is more sophisticated philosophically than Kohlberg's, Rawls's theory reveals the presuppositions informing Kohlberg's stage sequence.

What Rawls identifies as the first stage of moral development, the morality of authority, is defined as a temporary stage based on love. The second, the morality of association, is based on conformity to societal rules. The third and highest stage, the morality of principles, is identified as abstract and above "contingencies" (1971: 462–79). On a first reading, this sounds like standard Enlightenment moral theory: a hierarchy of moral principles beginning with an inferior set based on love and culminating in abstract, universalizable principles. But there is an important sense in which Rawls departs from that tradition. Rawls claims that he is an antifoundationalist looking not for a priori moral principles or moral truths but for the moral sentiments that people in a particular society actually espouse (1980). He states: "The social role of a conception of justice is to enable all members of society to make mutually acceptable to one another their shared intuitions and basic arrangements by citing what are publicly recognized as sufficient reasons, as identified by that conception" (1980: 517).

This sounds very open and egalitarian, even pluralistic. It can even be read as a description of what Gilligan herself is attempting to do. But several factors constrain Rawls's task and prevent him from hearing the moral voice that Gilligan describes. First, Rawls makes a number of assumptions about the individuals who articulate the moral principles he is seeking. They are defined as rational and autonomous and, most important, as disembodied. In the "original position" that he posits, these individuals are ignorant of their race, sex, and class, "contingencies" that would cloud their judgment.[12] A second constraint is one that has important ramifications in the theories of both Gilligan and Kohlberg: Rawls claims to be seeking what individuals in a given society *define* as moral principles. Significantly, Gilligan, Kohlberg, and Rawls all come to the same conclusion when they investigate what individuals in our society define as "moral": it is the realm of abstract, universal principles formulated by disembodied subjects. What they all discover is that both men and women in our society have learned their moral lessons very well. Since the Enlightenment they have been taught that morality is defined as the realm of abstract principle, that it eschews the particular, the contingent, and the emotional. Ironically, the women and girls whom Gilligan interviewed illustrate this point even more clearly than the men whom Kohlberg examined. These women and girls are reluctant to label their moral voice – a voice rooted in emotion, particularity, and connectedness – as "moral" at all.[13]

Kohlberg follows Rawls's lead very closely. Invoking both Plato's *Republic* and Rawls's theory, Kohlberg defines moral development as a stage sequence moving from inferior relational stages to the ultimate stage of abstract principles (1984: xi). His six stages are divided into three levels: the preconventional, in which behavior is punishment- and obedience-oriented; the conventional, in which maintaining good relations is paramount; and the postconventional, in which individual principles of conscience are paramount (1984: 17–19). Kohlberg makes a number of bold claims regarding these stages. First, he asserts that they are developmental, both individually and culturally. As they mature morally, individuals in all societies move from the lower to the higher stages. The same, he claims, is true of cultures. The two highest stages are absent in more "primitive," preliterate cultures, making their appearance only in more "developed" cultures. From this Kohlberg concludes that what he calls "social evolutionism" is at work (1984: 128).

Kohlberg is at times defensive about the sweeping breadth of his claims. He supports his position by arguing that "moral judgments and moral development are part of human nature" (1982: 528). Although he concedes that his theory may sound like cultural imperialism, he denies that this is the case. He claims that his argument is not that moral philosophy as the West has defined it is universal but, rather, that the basic moral principles that Western philosophy has defined are universal (1981: 98). In the same vein, he argues that his stage sequence may appear elitist but that in actuality it is not. His claim is that the higher stages are not superior but, rather, of greater adequacy (1981: 169). In another formulation of the same point, he argues that individuals who reach the higher stages are not, according to his theory, more moral but, rather, that the universal principles he defines are more likely to resolve moral problems (1984: 331). What his argument comes down to is that reference to universal principles is simply what morality *is*: "moral judgments, unlike judgments of prudence or esthetics, tend to be universal, inclusive, consistent, and grounded on objective, impersonal or ideal grounds" (1981: 170). He is thus claiming both that the definition of morality that his theory articulates is what morality really *is* and that this is what his subjects conceive morality to be.

Kohlberg's response to Gilligan's work indicates his unwillingness to seriously alter his approach to moral theory. In several passages he praises Gilligan for extending the moral domain, opening it to new approaches (1984: 335). As his position unfolds, however, it becomes apparent that his intent is to subsume her work into his developmental scheme. He changes his scheme only by espousing what amounts to a form of the domain relativism discussed above. Kohlberg agrees with Gilligan that women fall into the conventional category in his schema but rejects Gilligan's contention that this phenomenon requires a new approach to moral theory. Rather, he optimistically argues that this fact is merely a temporary phenomenon. He claims that as women move into men's occupations, they will, like men, adopt the postconventional morality that, on his view, defines the moral realm (1984: 347–8). The clearest statement of how Kohlberg's definition of morality dismisses Gilligan's work is found in his claim that what she subsumes under the care perspective are personal, not moral, dilemmas (Kohlberg et al. 1983: 141). He even indicates that relegating the care perspective to the personal realm is an instance of the public/private dichotomy that, for most of Western history, has defined women's concerns as inferior to the public realm of men (1982: 515). By embracing domain relativism, Kohlberg can accommodate Gilligan's theory without altering the central tenets of his own: the superiority of the justice voice and the inferior moral status of the conventional stage of morality that the different voice represents.

Kohlberg concedes that there are problems with his theory. Thus he admits that there is little empirical evidence for the existence of Stage 6 (Kohlberg et al. 1983: 60) and that only 5 percent of adult Americans test out at this highest stage of morality (1981: 192). Despite his claim that he welcomes Gilligan's "opening up" of the moral domain, it emerges that the moral domain he describes after his "accommodation" to Gilligan has not been significantly altered. He continues to assert that "The scientific facts are that there is a universal moral form successively emerging in development and centering on principles of justice" (1981: 178) and that his theory is a "rational reconstruction of the ontogenesis of justice reasoning." Invoking Socrates' claim, he argues that virtue is not many but one and that that one is justice (Kohlberg et al. 1983: 17–18). And, most succinctly, "I argue, however, that the objective study of the history and development of moral ideas must be guided not by cultural and ethical relativism, but by reflective rational standards and principles of morality" (1981: 98). At various points in his work he tries to argue that justice and care considerations are linked (Kohlberg et al. 1983: 138) or that justice subsumes care (Kohlberg et al. 1983: 24). But these assertions fly in the face of the epistemological assumptions on which his theory rests. His approach cannot subsume Gilligan's, because the two are epistemologically incompatible. Kohlberg, relying on a long tradition of moral philosophy, defines the moral realm as constituted by abstract principles. On this definition, the care perspective is necessarily classified as morally inferior and, in a strict sense, outside the domain of the moral altogether.

Kohlberg's single-minded application of the widely accepted definition of the moral realm provides an excellent illustration of the connection between theory and observation, a point that Gilligan makes in her critique of his work. Armed with a definition of the moral realm as constituted by abstract principles and peopled by autonomous subjects, Kohlberg proceeds to "discover" the "facts" of moral development that are consistent with these preconceptions. He even goes so far as to "discover" these "facts" of moral development in non-Western cultures. When confronted by a different moral voice, he can easily dismiss it as not within the moral realm, a dismissal facilitated by the fact that his (Western) subjects agree with him, because they have been taught the same definition of the moral realm. It is only by discarding this definition, by employing another theoretical perspective, that Gilligan can "hear" another moral voice. Like Kohlberg's, Gilligan's theory creates its own facts; she can hear the different voice as moral only because her conception of morality encompasses the realm of the particular and the personal.

Gilligan's approach to the question of method and related epistemological issues is, from the perspective of the philosophy of social science, ambiguous. In her early work she seems intent on the goal of discovering the "truth" of human moral development. She claims that the two moral voices represent two universal aspects of the human condition. Thus she defines Kohlberg's error as incompleteness: he ignores a central aspect of the truth of the human moral condition. In the foregoing, however, I have suggested that there is another way to read Gilligan's work. I have argued that, particularly in her later work, Gilligan employs a Kuhnian or coherentist methodology. She defends her approach by claiming that it is interpretive rather than empirical. She asserts that there is no neutral observation language, that all theories create their own data.

It would be pointless to fault Gilligan for her lack of clarity on methodological questions. It is not her aim to formulate a new methodology, feminist or otherwise, to guide her empirical research. At root, she is interested in getting on with her research rather than dealing with methodological questions. Particularly in her most recent work her aim is to listen to the disparate moral voices of girls and women and develop a theory that incorporates these voices. But for the purposes of my interpretation of Gilligan, the question of method is central. It is my contention that particular moral theories are inextricably linked to particular epistemologies. More specifically, I am arguing that the epistemology that informs modernist moral theory necessarily assumes a disembodied knower that constitutes abstract, universal truth. The individual who occupies Kohlberg's Stage 6 is such a knower. The moral truth that this knower constitutes is singular, universal, and absolute; it is a truth that is disembodied, removed from the relationships and connectedness of everyday life that, on this view, distort moral judgments.

Gilligan has effectively deconstructed this moral knower and his abstract moral knowledge. The epistemology implicit in her work replaces the disembodied knower with the relational self. The knowledge constituted by this relational self is a very different kind of knowledge. The relational self produces knowledge that is connected, a product of discourses that constitute forms of life; it is plural rather than singular. Gilligan hears moral voices speaking from the lives of connected, situated selves, not the single truth of disembodied moral principles. She hears these voices because she defines morality and moral knowledge as plural and heterogeneous.

These speculations raise a host of complex issues that I cannot explore fully here. They include the status of the critique of modernist epistemology, as well as whether feminist approaches to knowledge and method constitute a deconstruction of masculinist science. It is important for my purposes, however, to locate my interpretation of Gilligan in terms of two issues raised in the extensive literature on feminist critiques of science.[14] First, I am claiming that Gilligan is doing far more than what Sandra Harding calls "feminist empiricism" (1986). Feminist empiricists claim that the masculine tradition of science is biased and incomplete, because it excludes the experiences of women. Without challenging the fundamental principles of scientific investigation, feminist empiricists seek to remove the biased, incomplete perspective of masculinist science and replace it with a truly objective science that includes the experiences of women. I have argued in the foregoing that, although Gilligan appears to be following this pattern in her early work, a coherentist, Kuhnian interpretation better explains her overall approach and, particularly, her most recent work.

Second, much of the discussion in the feminist critique of science revolves around the absolutism/relativism dichotomy. Critics of the position I am espousing claim that it courts the "danger" of relativism; that is, that once we abandon the goal of objective, absolute knowledge, "anything goes." There have been many attempts to deal with this question in the feminist literature on science. Sandra Harding has proposed what she calls "strong objectivity," a position that recognizes the social situatedness of knowledge but "also require[s] a critical evaluation to determine which social situations tend to generate the most objective knowledge claims" (1991: 142). In one of the most ambitious and successful feminist critiques of science, Lynn Hankinson Nelson (1990) develops a feminist empiricism rooted in the work of W. V. O. Quine. Nelson argues that the definition of "empiricism" which feminists have condemned is outdated and that her own definition meets the criticisms that feminists have leveled at science. She defines science as a communal activity wedded to both values and metaphysical commitments; yet she also sees it as constrained by the world and resting on a theory of evidence rooted in sensory experience.

The question of absolutism or objectivity versus relativism that informs these theories impinges on both Gilligan's position and the approach to moral theory I am advancing here. Defenders of modernist moral theory argue that if we abandon the conception of the disembodied knower who constitutes universal moral principles, we are condemned to moral relativism, to the babble of countless moral voices. This is a salient criticism, but only if the issue continues to be cast in terms of the opposition between absolute and relative, between objective and subjective knowledge. Against this I am arguing that posing the issue in these terms poses an unanswerable question. The category of "relativism" is parasitic on its opposite, the possibility of absolute knowledge. Perspectival, connected, discursive knowledge does not obviate the possibility of truth, evidence, or critical judgment. The criteria of judgment within any discursive system are a function of the internally constituted rules of that system. Thus we have narratives about the world, not a single meta-narrative.[15] Gilligan's recent work offers one of the best examples of this methodology, a methodology

that is empirical but not objectivist. Another way of putting this point
is that the discursive account of knowledge I am advocating explicitly
challenges the modernist epistemology that grounds both contemporary scientific method and traditional moral theory. It does not embrace
relativism but moves to an epistemological stance that displaces the
absolute/relative dichotomy. It does not define knowledge as *either*
absolute *or* relative but, rather, as situated, connected, and discursively
constituted.

There are many different ways of conceptualizing what I am identifying as the epistemological incompatibility between traditional moral
theory and the Gilligan-inspired approach I advocate. One is that
Gilligan, along with many contemporary theorists, is proposing a
conception of the subject that violates the autonomous self of the
Enlightenment conception. The relational self that Gilligan espouses
cannot, as she sometimes seems to argue, coexist with the autonomous
subject of traditional moral theory (Benhabib 1987; Pateman 1989).
Other theorists of the relational subject have shown more clearly than
Gilligan that it rests on an entirely different understanding of the
constitution of subjectivity. Another way of characterizing this incompatibility is to assert that the equality of two moral voices that Gilligan
proposes, particularly in her early writings, will not work, because
dualities always impose hierarchies. Thus, proposing a "different
voice" along with the justice voice will not, as Gilligan hopes, avoid
"invidious comparisons" (1987b: 88); the hierarchies that permeate
Western thought reveal the difficulty of avoiding such comparisons.
Yet another characterization is that what Gilligan has shown is that
justice and care, the moral voice of autonomy and that of connection,
are not opposites at all but, rather, "inhabit"[16] each other. The double
fugue, the focus phenomenon, the insistence that separation and connection are both part of all human life – all suggest this theme. Consider
the infamous Heinz dilemma: as we saw, the issue hinges on the fact
that it is Heinz's *wife* who is dying; without that connection the dilemma loses its sense. Thus the opposition/hierarchy between contextual and abstract moral reasoning that grounds Kohlberg's theory
dissolves in Gilligan's studies.

I explore the ramifications of these characterizations in what follows.
My principal argument is that the logic of Gilligan's approach entails a
radical restructuring of moral theory. The logic of voices and discourse,
of relational selves, belies the possibility of a single theory. It suggests
multiple moral language games rooted in multiple subjects. Although
in her early work Gilligan seems to be continuing the search for one,
true moral theory, her more recent work abandons this goal. A recent
study by Gilligan and her colleagues reveals that adolescent girls
from different ethnic and class backgrounds have distinctly different
senses of self, community, and identity (Gilligan, Rogers, and Tolman

1991). This and similar studies point to the existence of more than two moral voices, rooted in different subjectivities. My thesis is that the whole tenor of Gilligan's work leads to the conclusion that we should stop trying to "get it right" in moral theory and instead explore the constitution and interaction of multiple moral voices.

2
Alternative or Displacement?

"The tradition"

> To deny that standards need, or can arise from some universal ground is to weaken the walls of civilization, letting the barbarians trash all decent forms and folks. (Nelson 1990: 258)

> The separateness of persons is the basic fact for morals. (Findlay 1978: 235)

Can we speak of such a thing as "the Western moral tradition"? Does an alternative moral tradition exist today, specifically a tradition that can be traced to the work of Aristotle? If such an alternative moral tradition does in fact exist, how does it relate to the different voice theorized by Gilligan? The only way to offer a definitive answer to these questions would be to present a comprehensive history of Western moral philosophy since Plato, with an emphasis on the gendered connotations of that tradition. My aim is much more modest. I begin by outlining the characteristics of the dominant tradition of Western moral theory that have been central to the feminist critique. I then turn to a detailed examination of the claim that an "alternative moral tradition" is gaining widespread acceptance today and that this approach offers the possibility of a restructuring of moral theory that meets the objections of feminist moral theorists. Throughout, my goal is to argue that certain aspects of the feminist critique of moral theory, specifically those suggested by Gilligan's work, entail an approach far more radical than that presented by theorists of the "alternative tradition." I argue that the Gilligan-inspired approach I am advocating does not merely present an alternative to the moral theory of the dominant tradition but, rather, calls into question the very conception of what the West has defined as moral theory.

The basic assumption of feminist critics of traditional moral theory is that Western moral and political philosophy are founded on the

gendered dichotomy between the public and the private realms
(Elshtain 1981; Okin 1979). This dichotomy relegates women to an
inferior status in a number of crucial respects. The public realm is the
realm of culture, rationality, and universality, of the universal citizen
who rises above the particularities of his situation; this realm has been
defined in exclusively masculine terms since the beginning of Western
philosophy. The private realm, by contrast, is the realm of the body and
nature, irrationality and particularity, the situated individual; this
realm has been identified as the sphere of the feminine. These gendered
distinctions have defined Western discussions of the parameters of the
moral as well as the political realms. Rationality and universality stand
out as the key attributes of the moral sphere; their opposites, irrationality and particularity, conversely, are defined as symptomatic of the
failure of moral reasoning. That this definition of the moral realm is as
old as Plato is not difficult to establish. Plato's insistence that justice is
a universal, an end in itself, echoes throughout the Western tradition
and is repeated almost verbatim by Kohlberg. Plato also establishes
another dominant theme: the identification of the family, and hence
women, with the realm of the emotional and the particular, a realm that
threatens the universality and rationality of the moral and political
sphere. In the *Republic* Plato forbids the Guardians to participate in
family life and the "sordid troubles" that it entails. The Guardians, he
claims, "will not rend the community asunder by each applying that
word 'mine' to different things and dragging off whatever he can get
for himself into a private home, where he will have his separate family,
forming a center of exclusive joys and sorrows" (5. 464). At the very
beginning of the West's attempts to define the moral, then, the private
sphere of the family, a sphere that engenders a separate realm of joys
and sorrows, is defined as a threat to the unity of the *polis*. The *polis*,
Plato argues, must be preserved from this threat at all costs.

Plato need not have worried. His successors in the Western tradition
have continued to preserve the moral sphere from the encroachments
of the feminine; emotion, irrationality, and particularity have consis-
tently been defined as enemies of the moral and political spheres. The
Romans, for example, defined morality as an exclusively masculine
preserve by identifying it with "virtue," whose root, *vir*, means "man."
This definition of morality was strongly reinforced in the Enlightenment, particularly by Kant's moral philosophy. Kant defined an entity
that has become the centerpiece of modern moral theory: the disembodied subject, a subject that knows no culture, history, class, race, or
gender. This subject qualifies as a moral subject only in the sense that he
legislates for himself. Furthermore, the laws that this autonomous subject legislates and executes (the political terms here are no accident) are
moral only in that they are universalizable; the deciding factor in moral
judgments cannot be particular circumstances, concrete empirical con-

ditions, but must always be the universalizability of the abstract principle. That women are excluded from this realm should be obvious,
but, just in case his readers have missed the point, Kant notes: "of
course, I exclude women, children and idiots."

It is significant that when women began to agitate for entry into the
public sphere, the greatest impediment was precisely this legacy of
their long association with the private realm of the family and the
moral inferiority that this association entailed. John Stuart Mill, the
nineteenth-century advocate of women's rights, expresses this point
succinctly:

> Women, we are told, are not capable of resisting their personal partialities;
> their judgement in grave affairs is warped by their sympathies and
> antipathies. . . . All the education women receive from society inculcates in
> them the feeling that the individuals connected with them are the only
> ones to whom they owe any duty . . . while, as far as education is con-
> cerned, they are left strangers even to the elementary ideas which are
> presupposed in any intelligent regard for larger interests or higher moral
> objects. (1971: 519)

> I am afraid it must be said that disinterestedness in the general
> conduct of life – the devotion of the energies to purposes which hold
> out no promise of private advantages to the family – is very seldom
> encouraged or supported by women's influence . . . the consequence is
> that women's influence is often anything but favorable to public
> virtue . . . the education given to women – an education of the sentiments
> rather than of the understanding – . . . make them both unable to see and
> unwilling to admit the ultimate evil tendency of any form of charity or
> philanthropy which commends itself to their sympathetic feelings. (1971:
> 531–2)

The solution to this problem was, for Mill, quite simple. Educating
women for "larger interests or higher moral objects" would allow them
to abstract from these prejudicial attachments to the "individuals connected to them" and attend to the demands of public virtue. Mill's
ruminations reveal a presupposition about women and morality that
would extend into the twentieth century: the public sphere, the sphere
of moral universals, must remain the same; women must adapt themselves to it by abandoning their different, inferior morality.

The history of the marginalization of the feminine moral voice has
been extensively chronicled by feminist theorists.[1] Instead of reviewing
this literature, I will turn instead to a nonphilosophical source, in order
to highlight the themes that are central to my discussion. In *The Mer-
chant of Venice* Shakespeare portrays the complex interaction between
the masculine voice of justice/law and the feminine voice of mercy. A
superficial reading of the play suggests that Shakespeare is privileging
mercy over justice, reversing the priorities implicit in his culture's

definition. Indeed, Portia's famous speech appears to argue such a position:

> The quality of mercy is not strained.
> It droppeth as the gentle rain from heaven
> Upon the place beneath. It is twice blessed:
> It blesseth him that gives and him that takes,
> 'Tis mightiest in the mightiest, it becomes
> The throned monarch better than his crown:
> His sceptre shows the force of temporal power,
> The attribute to awe and majesty,
> Wherein doth sit the dread and fear of Kings:
> But mercy is above this sceptred sway,
> It is enthroned in the heart of Kings,
> It is an attribute to God himself:
> And earthly power doth then show likest God's,
> When mercy seasons justice.

But attention to the context of this speech yields a different interpretation. The speech is delivered by a woman; yet she is speaking not as a woman but as a man. In the scene from which this passage is taken, Portia is disguised not only as a man but as a doctor of law. As a woman, her voice could not and would not have been heard; she can only plead for mercy (the feminine voice) disguised as a man. Just as significantly, her speech is addressed to another marginalized voice/ character: the Jew Shylock. Shylock's reply, "I crave the law," indicates his unwillingness to speak in a marginalized voice; unlike Portia, he cannot or will not disguise himself, hide his marginality. This suggests that it is only safe to speak in the marginalized voice of mercy if one can do so from the safety of the dominant discourse. Rejecting Portia's plea for mercy, Shylock forces her to retreat to the discourse they both share: legal justice. Applying a loophole in the law that prevents Jews from spilling Christian blood, Portia accomplishes her objective of saving Antonio's life. She does so not by granting a hearing for the feminine voice of mercy but by using the dominant legal discourse to defeat Shylock. In other words, she uses the masculine voice of the law more cleverly than the men themselves, in order to reinforce the inferior status of an already marginalized member of that society. Those already marginalized cannot speak from the margins, because they will not be heard. The final proof of this is that it is the Duke, in the end, who speaks the voice of mercy that saves Shylock's life.[2]

The "alternative tradition"

Anglo-American moral philosophy is turning from an ethics based on enlightenment ideals of universality to an ethics based on tradition and

particularity; from an ethics based on principles to an ethics based on
virtue; from an ethics dedicated to the elaboration of systematic theoretical
justifications to an ethics suspicious of theory and respectful of local wis-
dom; from an ethics based on the isolated individual to an ethics based on
affiliation and care; from an ahistorical detached ethics to an ethics rooted
in concreteness and history. (Nussbaum 1992b: 9)

Martha Nussbaum's assessment of the current state of Anglo-American
moral philosophy aptly summarizes the challenge to the hegemony of
"the tradition" in moral philosophy. A growing number of contemporary moral philosophers are articulating an alternative to the dominance of Kantianism and utilitarianism in moral philosophy. They
argue for a particularistic and, in some cases, even a relativistic approach to ethics. Many of these theorists, Nussbaum among them,
identify the roots of their alternative approach in the work of Aristotle.
This not only lends legitimacy to their alternative approach but also
suggests that it has as much claim to the Western heritage as does its
rival.

Nussbaum is widely recognized as one of the principal forces in the
attempt to both define and promote a return to a specifically Aristotelian approach to ethics. Yet, as she makes clear, particularly in her most
recent works, she rejects a simple-minded opposition between universality and particularity in ethical theory. She argues instead for a link-
age between universal normative principles and contextual factors.
In her path-breaking *The Fragility of Goodness* (1986) she posits a dichotomy between Socratic ethics and the ethical approach of Aristotle.
She claims that Socrates' definition of virtue entails a turning away
from responsive intercourse with others and hence an ethics that is
hard, abstract, removed, and disembodied (1986: 195). She defines
Aristotle's ethics, by contrast, as an ethics that recognizes external
circumstances as important to happiness; it is an ethics that recognizes
the fragility of human love, as well as the necessary role of love in our
ethical life and achievement of happiness (1986: 361–2). These themes
become more pronounced in the essays collected in *Love's Knowledge*
(1990), in which Nussbaum develops her self-consciously Aristotelian
ethical perspective. Central to this approach is the concept of "perception," the ability to discern acutely and responsively the salient features
of one's particular situation (1990: 37). The key to Nussbaum's approach is her claim that "moral philosophy requires attentive and
loving novel reading" (1990: 27). Novels, she claims, force us to attend
to the concrete; they ask us to imagine possible relations and hence help
us to understand our own (1990: 95).

Nussbaum maintains that the Aristotelian particularism she advocates provides a contrast to the dominant tradition in moral philosophy
while at the same time encompassing normative principles of broad

applicability. The alternative she proposes has some striking parallels to Gilligan's work. Nussbaum argues that while traditional moral philosophy seeks to remove the subject from the "messiness" of human life, her own approach attends to this "messiness." Similarly, Gilligan insists that abstraction from the messiness of moral dilemmas distorts moral theory. Gilligan's emphasis on narrative as a central component of moral subjectivity is echoed in Nussbaum's reliance on novels. An important aspect of Nussbaum's approach is her claim that novels are a tool of moral education, which enable us to draw moral lessons from the particularities of human lives.[3]

Nussbaum's Aristotelian approach nevertheless differs in significant ways from the approach to morality that, I am claiming, flows from Gilligan's account. Nussbaum's approach illustrates what I see as three drawbacks of the "alternative tradition" that is gaining ground in contemporary moral philosophy. First, like many other contemporary Aristotelians, Nussbaum casts her argument in terms of the absolutist/relativist dichotomy that characterizes modernist moral philosophy. She feels compelled to take a stand on this dichotomy and, specifically, to firmly reject the "threat" of relativism. She insists that an Aristotelian ethics does not lead to relativism but, rather, that Aristotle's particularism is compatible with the view that what perception aims at is "the way things are" (1990: 96). Aristotle's attention to the particular and the concrete, she asserts, does not preclude a universalizing tendency, the conviction that persons in the same situation *should* act the *same* way (1990: 165–6). She argues that the ethics of virtue is concerned with both particularity and broad normative principles and that it does not preclude human universality (1992b: 9). She defines her position as "internal realism," the claim that, although reality is not given to us independently of our conventions, within the world as perceived and interpreted by human beings, we can find truth (1990: 223–4). In a provocative article in *Political Theory* she argues for a "historically informed essentialism" that can provide a historically sensitive account of basic human needs and functions (1992a).

This concern with relativism is echoed in the work of many of the "alternative tradition" philosophers discussed below. Against them, I argue that the compulsion to take a stand on this issue is self-defeating. These theorists claim to be offering an alternative to modernist moral theory. Yet, by remaining within the epistemological parameters of that theory, specifically the absolutist/relativist dichotomy, they preclude the possibility of defining such an alternative. The approach I am advocating, by contrast, eschews the dichotomy between absolute and relative, between universal moral principles and moral relativism. I argue instead that continuing to examine human moral practices in terms of this dichotomy is futile and that we need to move to another epistemological dimension. It may be the case, as Nussbaum argues, that it is possible to identify a list of universal human needs. But I do not think that the identification of such needs is a fruitful direction for moral theory. Moral practices are cultural products, and needs are constituted in different ways in different cultural settings and in varying ways even within cultures. In order to understand those moral practices, we must seek to understand that contextualized constitution. Defining the broad, universal parameters of human moral practices will not lead to the kind of moral knowledge we require. As Stuart Hampshire notes, human nature always underdetermines human needs and thus, likewise, moral prohibitions and injunctions (1989: 150).

The second drawback to the Aristotelian approach adopted by Nussbaum and other theorists in this tradition is that, with few exceptions, they ignore the issues of power and the hegemony of dominant moral discourses. One of the principal theses of the alternative moral philosophers is that ethical systems are specific to particular cultural/ societal settings. But these theorists fail to explore the hegemonic forces that establish the dominant ethical system within a cultural setting. Feminist theorists such as Gilligan, as well as those who explore the roles of race and class, are acutely aware that there *is* a dominant ethical code within every culture and that powerful social institutions maintain the hegemony of that code. But, unlike the Aristotelians, they seek to explain how that hegemonic moral discourse marginalizes other moral discourses, silencing other moral voices.

Third, this alternative tradition, again with a few notable exceptions, ignores the role of subjectivity in the construction of morality. Gilligan describes in detail how moral notions and concepts of the subject are inextricably intertwined. Her approach entails that questions concerning the construction of morality cannot be examined apart from questions concerning the construction of subjectivity. It also entails that the construction of subjectivity that defines modernist philosophy be jettisoned in order to accommodate a truly alternative moral philosophy. In sum, what I am arguing is that the approach to moral philosophy suggested by Gilligan's work is one in which questions of absolutism versus relativism do not arise, because it rests on an understanding of subjectivity that renders these questions irrelevant. I am arguing that questions of power and hegemony *must* arise, because within any given culture there will be a plurality of moral voices and, necessarily, a hierarchy of moral discourses; and, finally, I am arguing that the best way to approach moral questions is through an examination of the constitution of moral subjects.

Simone Weil and Iris Murdoch have been identified as both alternative moral theorists and predecessors of Gilligan's feminist approach. Weil's moral theory constitutes a direct attack on the concepts of rights, democracy, and individualism that inform modernist moral theory

(1977: 338). Arguing that the notion of rights that was articulated in 1789 has not realized the hopes it fostered, she proposes replacing the contentious personalistic tone of rights with the impersonal (1977: 314–23). Human beings, Weil claims, can rise above the collective only by rising above the personal to the realm of the impersonal (1977: 300). This impersonality can be achieved through what she calls a form of "attention," something that is possible only in solitude and only by an individual who does not think of himself [sic] as part of a collectivity (1977: 318). In a move that reverses the definitions of modernist moral theory, Weil goes on to oppose rights thinking to what she calls "justice." "Justice consists in seeing that no harm is done to men" (1977: 334); it is the concept that dictated Christ's "surfeit of love" (1977: 325).

Weil's work has been enormously influential among both alternative moral theorists and feminist ethicists, particularly those who take their inspiration from Gilligan. But more than terminological differences separate the approaches of Gilligan and Weil. The justice/love ethos that Weil advocates is far removed from the connected, nurturing, relational care voice that Gilligan describes. Weil's justice/love is remote and impersonal, removed from the everydayness of human life, monklike. The connection with Gilligan's work is clearer in Iris Murdoch's extension of Weil's theory of "attention." Murdoch, like Weil, finds modernist moral philosophy seriously deficient. She rejects the concept of the detached, rational individual that informs modernist moral philosophy. She argues that this view of the individual entails a definition of moral action whereby a detached observer freely and rationally chooses a moral course of action (1970: 4–8). Against this, she asserts that people neither do nor should act in this manner and that this picture is not philosophically convincing (1970: 9). As an alternative, she proposes a morality rooted in the concept of love. Moral choice, she argues, is not detached, rational, and free but, rather, is structured by the values by which we live (1970: 37). It is in her attempt to define the precise nature of this alternative morality that Murdoch turns to Weil's concept of "attention." Morality, Murdoch asserts, is "attention" to ongoing activity, not discrete acts of will (1970: 56). We act rightly not from strength of will but out of "the quality of our usual attachments" (1970: 92).

Murdoch's conception of morality exhibits two elements that are central to the formation of an alternative moral tradition. First, she rejects the concept of the rational, disembodied individual, countering it with an embedded, situated subject. She argues:

> We are not isolated, free choosers, monarchs of all we survey, but benighted creatures sunk in a reality whose nature we are constantly and overwhelmingly tempted to deform by fantasy. Our current picture of freedom encourages a dream-like facility; whereas what we require is a

renewed sense of the difficulty and complexity of the moral life and the
opacity of persons. (1983: 49)

Second, she identifies the rationalistic concept of the subject as the root
of the problem of modernist moral philosophy. Unless we replace this
concept, she argues, we will understand neither the complexity of the
moral life nor its connection to loving relationships.

Murdoch's thought has been very influential in the attempt to articulate an alternative moral theory. A good example of this influence is
found in the work of Lawrence Blum. In *Friendship, Altruism, and Morality* (1980), Blum, like Murdoch, rejects modernist moral philosophy for
its rationalism. His stated aim is to "loosen the profound grip the
Kantian view has on our moral thought" (1980: 11). Unlike Murdoch,
however, Blum does not want to deny that the impartiality whereby
Kant defines the moral sphere is erroneous; but, rather, to insist that
there is more to morality than this Kantian definition. Specifically, he
wants to claim that emotions, altruism, and friendship must be in-
cluded in the moral sphere. There are, he claims, various types of moral
goodness and no single foundation for morality (1980: 1–8). In a more
recent article he explicitly connects his approach to that of Murdoch
(1986). He asserts that Murdoch's emphasis on the personal in the
moral domain is too often ignored in contemporary moral theory. He
praises Murdoch's attention to the personal in moral actions and her
attack on the tradition of impartiality that is dominant in moral theory.
He argues that Murdoch's analysis of moral actions transcends the
objective/subjective, personal/impersonal distinctions that characterize modernist moral theory (1986: 359).

Blum's theory both extends and reinforces Murdoch's brief sketch of
an alternative to rationalistic modernist moral theory.[4] Blum also
makes explicit the connection between Murdoch's view and Gilligan's
different voice. In an article on Murdoch he links his and Murdoch's
approaches to the Gilligan–Kohlberg controversy, arguing that
Gilligan's "care voice" is compatible with the attack on impartialism
(1988). There are, however, several questionable aspects of Blum's approach. Despite his insistence that he is formulating an alternative to
Kantian impartiality, he himself is held captive by that concept. Several
hundred pages of his book are devoted to the attempt to establish what
would seem to be an obvious point: that friendship and altruism are
legitimate moral concerns. Yet, it is only from the perspective of modernist moral theory that such an argument is necessary or even makes
much sense. What Blum is offering is not so much an alternative to the
dominant impartiality tradition as an addition to it. This intention is
revealed in his analysis of Murdoch's theory. Blum argues that
Murdoch's view is incomplete, because it fails to account for morality's
less personal and individualized aspects (1986: 360). He asserts that

Murdoch has defined not morality per se but only one of its various spheres. Most significantly, he suggests that the personal sphere that she defines may not be moral at all (1986: 361) and that there is nothing morally or philosophically distinct in a morality of care (1988: 484). These comments dictate two conclusions: first, that Blum is not challenging the hegemony of modernist moral theory but merely extending it, and second, that he defines this extension, the care voice of Murdoch and Gilligan, as inferior to the impartiality voice. What we are left with, in the end, is yet another version of domain relativism.[5]

One of the names that frequently appears in discussions of an alternative moral tradition, particularly among feminists, is that of Hume. Annette Baier has sought to resurrect Hume's approach to moral theory, even claiming that his theory has much in common with Gilligan's "different voice" (1987a). In *Postures of the Mind* (1985a) Baier identifies her aim as working out a Wittgensteinian approach to ethics based on Hume's model. She claims that she wants to define a "way to think reflectively about human lives without relying on faith in any sovereign reason . . . and without oversimplifying the history-bound complexity of human life" (1985a: xii). Following Wittgenstein, she argues that moral convictions are imparted to children by their parents. Central to this argument is her assertion that, in teaching morality, parents employ examples rather than teach their children moral laws. The Humean model that Baier articulates entails the plurality of moral traditions in our society. The key to this model is the notion that moral reflection is empirically informed; the Humean morality that Baier espouses is a descriptive moral and social psychology (1985a: 237–8). She concludes:

> To have any confidence that a proposed new [moral] guide will work better than the guides it would replace, will conduce more to the human good of those using it and those affected by its use, one would need not merely economic and sociological generalizations confirmed by past history, but also something of the novelist's imagination of the detailed human consequences of its use, its full effect on people's lives. (1985a: 242)

Baier's approach offers several advantages. She clearly rejects Kantian rationalism and, unlike most other "alternative tradition" philosophers, even argues for a plurality of moral traditions within a society. Her reference to a Wittgensteinian approach to ethics, furthermore, offers intriguing possibilities.[6] Unfortunately, this promise is not fulfilled in the course of her book. There is no discussion of how moral subjects are constituted or of the differences between various moral discourses. More significantly, in a number of passages Baier indicates that she has not entirely abandoned the modernist morality she claims to challenge. At one point, she praises Frankena's theory of "the" moral point of view because it avoids both absolutism and relativism (1985a: 157). At another, she identifies Hume's morality with "one aspect of the enlightenment project." She also claims that Hume was attempting to give morality a secure basis in human active capacities for cooperation (1985a: 230–1). Such statements indicate that although Baier has taken important steps away from modernist moral theory, she has not abandoned key elements of it: the absolutism/relativism dichotomy and the search for "the" secure basis for morality. Alasdair MacIntyre once commented that "Contemporary confidence in the single unitary character of morality is part of our inheritance" (1983: 7). Baier has not altogether succeeded in freeing herself from this inheritance, despite her claim to be offering an alternative to it.[7]

The theorists whom I have discussed so far are self-consciously on the fringes of academic Anglo-American moral philosophy. Defying Kant's rejection of psychology, they pay serious attention to psychological issues; they take their cue from nontraditional philosophers like Weil. But there is another group of moral theorists writing today who also claim to be challenging the dominant tradition in moral theory. They are more mainstream than the theorists considered above. They write from within the Anglo-American analytic tradition and employ the style of argument that characterizes that tradition. Their arguments are relevant here, however, because they specifically characterize themselves as "relativists," defining their positions in opposition to the absolutism dominant in modernist moral theory.[8] These theorists form a kind of continuum from, at one end, those who are somewhat skeptical about relativism to, at the other, those who enthusiastically espouse it. Across this continuum, however, several problems persist. First, despite their move toward relativism, these authors remain caught in the dominant tradition's desire to find *the* right moral theory, *the* explanation for moral behavior. Second, and more important, all these theorists are working within the epistemological parameters of the absolute/relative dichotomy. Most of their accounts, while conceding that morality is relative to particular historical situations, nevertheless reject what is defined as "extreme relativism." Most of these authors would agree with Jeffrey Stout's pronouncement that skepticism, nihilism, and relativism are "spectres" that "haunt the philosophy of moral diversity" (1988: 3). There is, in short, an ambivalence toward the issue of relativism: an acknowledgment that morality must be historically and socially situated, coupled with a fear that taking this position too far is dangerous.

Against this, I am arguing that theorists who define their approaches somewhere along the absolutism/relativism continuum fail to offer an alternative to modernist moral theory. Rather, they perpetuate the sterile dichotomy between absolute and relative knowledge that is the centerpiece of modernist epistemology. Any discussion of relativism is parasitic on an epistemological commitment to the absolute/relative dichotomy. None of these authors embraces the position that I am advocating, namely, that we move to an understanding of moral knowledge that eschews this dichotomy. Yet, unless we abandon this dichotomy, specifically by focusing on moral voices and moral subjects, moral theory cannot move beyond its modernist boundaries.

The best illustration of what I am claiming is the ambivalence of contemporary Anglo-American philosophers toward the issue of relativism in morality is the influential work of Thomas Nagel. Nagel is not just caught up in the absolute/relative, objective/subjective dichotomies; he is obsessed by them. His persuasive work *The View from Nowhere* (1986) begins with a statement of his central problem: all people are both particular persons *in* the world and capable of taking an objective view *of* that world (1986: 3). The tension between these two viewpoints structures his whole discussion; his aim is to combine "recognition of our contingency" with our "ambition of transcendence" (1986: 3). But although he claims to be both defending and criticizing objectivity – that is, treating the phenomena of contingency and transcendence equally – as his argument unfolds, it becomes clear that he is more interested in formulating a positive account of objectivity than in exploring the contingencies of morality. "Objectivity," he claims, "is the central problem of ethics . . . If we can make judgments about how we should live even after stepping outside of ourselves, they will provide the material for moral theory" (1986: 138). The basic question of ethics, he claims, is not "what shall I do?" but "what should this person do?" It follows that, for Nagel, the best method in ethics is to take the perspectiveless view (1986: 141).

This is not to say that Nagel ignores the contingent side of the two dichotomies. Near the end of the book, he declares that "Objectivity needs subjective material to work on, and for human morality this is found in human life" (1986: 186). Morality, he concedes, is socially inculcated, and radical disagreements about it exist over cultures (1986: 147). He also concedes that to apply the objective standard in close personal relationships is inappropriate, because to do so would destroy precisely what is valuable in those relationships (1986: 155). As his argument develops, it emerges that Nagel sees the unavoidable presence of subjective and relative elements in human life as an unfortunate fact that must be tolerated but to which we must not succumb. It is, he claims, part of human nature to have a dual vision of the world; thus a fully agent-neutral morality is impossible. His discontent with this state of affairs, nevertheless, is revealed by his conclusion that we are presently at a primitive stage of moral development (1986: 185–6).

Nagel's work has been widely read and discussed by moral philosophers. It is perhaps rash to infer from this that his position is representative of the positions held by most contemporary Anglo-American moral philosophers. But I think it is safe to conclude that Nagel is asking questions that are germane to the concerns of most contemporary Anglo-American moral philosophers and, further, that his work illustrates three key problems of the approach to relativism that most of these philosophers adopt. First, most contemporary moral theorists, like Nagel and unlike Kant, recognize and try to account for the situatedness of moral agents. Yet they attempt to do so by negotiating the absolute/relative and objective/subjective dichotomies. The results vary: some tend toward the absolute side, others toward the relative. But these negotiations are never successful. The dichotomies posit a false opposition; their supposed polarities inhabit each other. As long as moral knowledge is defined as *either* absolute *or* relative, moral philosophy will consist in chalking up points on either side of the dichotomy rather than rethinking the question of moral knowledge. Another way of putting this is to say that pursuing this dichotomy is not the most fruitful way to think about moral knowledge.

The second problem illustrated by Nagel's work is that although his account of the absolute/objective sides of the dichotomies is well developed, that of the opposite side is seriously flawed. A passage from *The View from Nowhere* is instructive: "From the objective standpoint we see a world which contains multiple individual perspectives" (1986: 168). Nagel defines these multiple individuals as situated and contrasts their perspectives with that of the perspectiveless observer. But when he gives examples of the situatedness of moral dilemmas, what emerges is a description of a bizarre world in which isolated persons are forced to resolve improbable moral problems without the aid of others. Wittgenstein once remarked, "A main cause of philosophical disease – a one-sided diet: one nourishes one's thinking with only one kind of example" (1958: §593). This is true of analytic moral philosophy in general and Nagel in particular. What is missing from Nagel's world is any sense that the situated persons he posits are connected to others or that their moral perspectives are communally grounded. Instead, his situated persons are isolated and hence able to take the objective view even in personal moral dilemmas. There are two points in Nagel's moral landscape: the isolated, situated individual and the perspectiveless observer. Communities of moral belief do not make an appearance.

Third, Nagel's work illustrates yet another form of domain relativism. In his most recent book, *Equality and Partiality* (1991), Nagel adds the impersonal/personal dichotomy to the other two dichotomies he has considered. Following the long tradition of Western moral theory, he equates the impersonal with the political, the personal with the private. In the course of his book he makes it clear that he privileges the impersonal/political over the personal/private. Although he never discusses explicitly the gendered connotations of this dichotomy, neither does he deny them. The modernist moral tradition, however, has most decidedly defined these dichotomies in terms of gender and hierarchy: the disprivileged side of each is unambiguously feminine. Thus it is difficult not to come to the conclusion that, despite Nagel's avowed interest in situatedness and the realm of the personal, he is very much in the modernist moral tradition, in that he both privileges and genders impersonal moral knowledge. Once more, women's moral concerns, the realm of the personal, are relegated to an inferior status in moral theory.

I conclude my discussion of the possibility of an alternative moral philosophy in contemporary thought by examining two of the most prominent discussions of moral relativity in the current literature: David Wong's *Moral Relativity* (1984) and Michael Walzer's *Spheres of Justice* (1983). These two works and the positions espoused in them are frequently cited as evidence that even Anglo-American moral philosophy has definitively abandoned its Enlightenment absolutism. Wong expresses several viewpoints that set him apart from the relativists discussed above. He begins with the assumption that the task of the moral philosopher is to explain moral experience. His claim is that a relativist moral theory is best able to do this. Unlike Nagel, Wong sees morality as operating within a moral community and, unlike most relativist moral theorists, even argues that there are subgroups within a moral community. He emphasizes the role of language in morality, arguing that growing up in a moral community means learning a moral language (1984: 64–5). He concludes from this that few people *choose* a moral language; most just accept the one they are taught (1984: 75). Finally, at the end of the book, he argues that different moral perspectives arise out of different ethnic, class, and race perspectives and that students should be exposed to these different viewpoints (1984: 209).

Despite these advantages, however, vestiges of modernist moral theory remain in Wong's account. His argument is organized around the objective/subjective dichotomy, a variant of the absolute/relative dichotomy that informs modernist moral theory. As a result, Wong wants to maintain the idea of an "adequate moral system," albeit suitably qualified (1984: 65). Further, although he concedes that there may be subgroups within a moral community, he does not discuss the relationship of these groups in terms of power or dominance. We are given no hint that certain moral systems may be hegemonic and that marginalized groups may be disadvantaged. More important, he does not even mention gender as a constituent factor in the construction of moral discourse. This is perhaps due to the fact that, although he refers to moral experience and the role of language, he fails to develop these themes into an account of the constitution of moral subjects and the role of morality in the development of subjectivity. Although it might be argued that these are not goals that are important to Wong's project, I do not think that this is an adequate excuse. It is my contention that gender, race, class, hegemony, and subjectivity are not optional aspects of moral theory but, rather, necessary elements of any account of morality.

Michael Walzer's *Spheres of Justice* (1983) is, like Wong's book, a sustained effort to outline a nonabsolutist approach to morality. The key to Walzer's moral theory is his definition of the character and purpose of human society; this definition informs his advocacy of an egalitarian, pluralistic community. At the beginning of the book he states: "Human society is a distributive community. . . . We come to-gether to share, divide and exchange." It follows from this that dis-tributive justice is *the* moral problem that human societies must face (1983: 3). This in turn leads to his central thesis: principles of justice are pluralistic, and thus different social goods ought to be distributed according to different principles and by different procedures (1983: 6). A pluralistic conception of justice is necessary, Walzer argues, because how we conceive of goods is necessarily a product of our historical and cultural situation. Distributions are thus just or unjust relative to the socially created meanings of the goods at stake (1983: 9).

The major concern of Walzer's book is to describe the different spheres of justice that characterize human societies. Central to his argu-ment is the assertion that these different spheres must be kept separate from one another: "Good fences make just societies" (1983: 319). In his description of these spheres Walzer is bound by a social constructionist definition of meaning:

> We are (all of us) culture-producing creatures; we make and inhabit mean-ingful worlds. Since there is no way to rank and order these worlds with respect to their understanding of social goods, we do justice to individual men and women by respecting their particular creations. . . . Justice is rooted in the distinct understandings of places, honors, jobs, things of all sorts that constitute a shared way of life. (1983: 314)

This notion of a shared, common way of life is a key element of Walzer's theory. In his introduction to the book he defines the practice of philosophy as the attempt "to interpret to one's fellow citizens the world of meanings we share." He then immediately informs his readers that the meaning we share is that of an egalitarian society. For "If such a society isn't already here – hidden, as it were, in our concepts and categories – we will never know it concretely or realize it in fact" (1983: xiv). Walzer's assumption that egalitarianism is embedded in our con-cepts leads him to consider the problem of domination. He states that "The aim of political egalitarianism is a society free from domination" (1983: xiii) and that "My purpose in this book is to describe a society where no social good serves or can serve as a means of domination"

(1983: xiv). He claims that the "complex equality" that he outlines in his book establishes a set of relationships that makes domination impossible; spheres are autonomous, with no one sphere dominant (1983: 19–20). At the end, he summarizes his argument thus:

> To argue against dominance and its accompanying inequalities, it is only necessary to attend to the goods at stake and to the shared understandings of these goods. When philosophers do this, when they write out of a respect for the understandings they share with their fellow citizens, they pursue justice justly, and they reinforce the common pursuit. (1983: 320)

The image that Walzer presents of an egalitarian, pluralistic, nondominating society is inspiring. But whether it successfully grapples with the problem of moral diversity is another question. Walzer's pluralism has an odd twist: it rests on the assumption that the diverse spheres of society are united by common meanings. But, as he himself admits, under conditions of domination, no sharing of a common life is possible: "slaves and masters do not inhabit a world of shared meanings" (1983: 250n.).[9] This raises the question of who, exactly, shares this world of common meanings. Walzer answers this question very clearly. He states: "Nevertheless, the political community is probably the closest we can come to a world of common meanings" (1983: 28).

Walzer's appeal to the political in this passage is revealing. It indicates both his basic orientation toward moral issues and why that orientation is inadequate from a feminist perspective. He appeals to the political because it is the realm of equality, the place where we come together to decide our common fate and distribute the goods of our society. The various spheres he defines all derive ultimately from the political community; they coincide with the divisions that constitute our political and economic lives. This becomes clear when Walzer discusses, albeit briefly, the private realm. He declares that "Kinship ties and sexual relations are commonly thought to constitute a domain beyond the reach of distributive justice." This, he claims, would be a mistake. He proposes instead that these ties and relations be thought of as closely connected to other distributive spheres (1983: 227). His discussion of "The Woman Question" (which comprises a total of three pages), furthermore, reveals that he does not identify women as connected in any distinctive way to the sphere of kinship and sexuality or as constituting a special or problematic sphere within society. Rather, he sees the barriers to full equality for women, both politically and economically, as merely temporary obstacles (1983: 239–42).

Walzer's approach to the "problem" of women's morality is even less successful than that proposed by the advocates of domain relativism. For Walzer, the political is the *only* baseline for morality. The spheres he describes are defined by their relationship to the political realm; the common world that is the foundation of his moral perspective is rooted in the political. The private realm does not even constitute a "sphere" in his schema; the realm of the moral just *is* the realm of the political. That the political is a discursive sphere in which women have been labeled inferior is not of serious concern to him. He implies that the barriers to full equality for women can quite easily be dismantled. That there may be moral discourses that are not defined in terms of a distribution of societal goods; that race, class, and gender might be constitutive of moral discourses; or that morality might be linked to subjectivity do not enter into Walzer's analysis. As a result, feminist concerns regarding the silencing of marginalized moral voices cannot even be raised in Walzer's schema.

Feminism and the communitarian critique of liberalism

One of the most notable influences on moral and political theory in the past few decades has been the communitarian critique of liberalism.[10] No discussion of alternative moral theories would be complete without careful attention to this critique. If any moral/political theory can lay claim to be *the* alternative moral theory today, it is the communitarians' approach. The communitarians are particularly relevant to this discussion, furthermore, because many of their positions are at least superficially similar to those of feminist moral theorists. Most important, both communitarians and feminists focus on the question of the subject. Communitarians have argued that the autonomous, or "unencumbered," subject of liberalism (and, by extension, modernist moral theory) is incoherent and unintelligible. They further assert that it is this concept of the subject that fosters the loneliness and alienation that characterize liberal society. Although the feminist critique of the liberal, modernist subject differs in emphasis, there are striking similarities. Feminists have argued that the definitive characteristics of this subject, rationality and autonomy, have been defined as exclusively masculine qualities, whereas the characteristics defined as feminine, connection and caring, have been excluded from the concept. Against this, feminists, like communitarians, have argued for a concept of the subject as connected, rather than unencumbered, and as constituted by the necessary relationships that bind us as human beings to those around us.

The following examination of the communitarian critique of liberalism from a feminist perspective has several goals. First, through a detailed analysis of the most prominent "alternative moral theory," it seeks to give further substance to my claim that the Gilligan-inspired moral theory that I am advocating cannot be described as an "alternative morality." Second, it seeks to define the parameters of that moral theory. Feminist reactions to the communitarian critique reveal that many feminist theorists are unwilling to shed the epistemological assumptions of the modernist tradition. My argument is that shedding these assumptions is precisely what is required by a feminist moral theory. There are elements of the feminist critique of moral theory that suggest a truly radical reconstruction of morality, one that involves more than a modification of modernist dichotomies. I argue that the best strategy for feminist moral theory is to pursue these radical tendencies.

The communitarian critique of liberalism

In a recent article in *Political Theory* Michael Walzer (1990) argues that communitarian critiques of liberalism are not new but, rather, are recurrent phenomena that have been around at least since Marx's attack on the alienation fostered by capitalism. Nevertheless, the present version of the communitarian critique of liberalism has a number of unique aspects. First, it is a reaction against a significant revival of liberalism in the past several decades, at the center of which is John Rawls's important and influential *A Theory of Justice* (1971). Second, the intellectual context of the critique fostered by this revival of liberalism differs significantly from that of previous critiques. Hermeneutics, semiotics, and deconstruction have influenced both the articulation and the reception of the current communitarian critique. These discourses have focused attention on issues, most notably those concerning the subject, that were less central to previous critiques. As a result, the communitarian critique of liberalism, far from being merely an internal debate, has implications for the general critique of modernity that is currently under way.

The work that offers the most insight into the relevance of the communitarian critique of liberalism for feminist moral theory is Michael Sandel's *Liberalism and the Limits of Justice* (1982). This book has had an enormous impact on current discussions of liberalism, and it is not difficult to see why. Sandel launches a frontal attack on Rawls's liberal theory and, specifically, on his concept of the subject. Sandel argues persuasively that the subject that Rawls presupposes is indefensible and that, because this subject is the cornerstone of Rawls's theory, the theory itself is incoherent.[11]

Sandel begins his critique of Rawls's subject by noting that Rawls attempts to define a concept of self that avoids the pitfalls of both Kant's radically disembodied subject on the one hand and the notion of the self as radically situated on the other (1982: 23). At the outset, Sandel warns that Rawls's project is doomed to failure (1982: 19).

Central to Rawls's concept of the subject is his assertion that we are distinct persons first and that only subsequently do we form relationships with others; as Sandel puts it, for Rawls, subjects are "antecedently individuated" (1982: 53). Because Rawls espouses this view of the subject, Sandel asserts that he cannot avoid reviving Kant's disembodied subject. Despite Rawls's disclaimers, his subject is, like Kant's, beyond experience, a subject that is incapable of commitments so fundamental as to be inconceivable without them (1982: 62). For Rawls's subject, no characteristics are essential; all are contingent. For this subject, therefore, community can be only an attribute, never a constituent element (1982: 69, 74). Sandel concludes his critique with a telling point: despite the fact that self-reflection has always been regarded as central to this transcendental subject, even the possibility of self-reflection is precluded for Rawls's subject; for this subject can never reflect on itself *as* self, but only on contingent desires. Since the subject has nothing to reflect *on*, self-knowledge becomes mere awareness of desires, not true reflection (1982: 153–60).

Although the subject that Rawls creates would not have been a problem for previous social contract theorists such as Locke or Hobbes, Sandel argues that it constitutes a major problem for Rawls. Rawls's concept of justice, he argues, requires a constituent concept of community that his concept of the subject precludes. Rawls's subject cannot be even partially constituted by its connection to the community. Yet, without that connection, Rawls's central argument, his advocacy of a principle of distributive justice, loses its foundation.

Against Rawls's disembodied subject, Sandel proposes what he calls a "wider subject," a subject marked by constitutive community, a common vocabulary of discourse, and a background of implicit practices and understandings. He argues, contra Rawls, that the relationships we form, such as family, community, or nation, are both definitive and constitutive of subjects. Sandel's subject is constituted in part by aspirations and attachments and is open to growth and transformation in light of a revised self-understanding (1982: 172).

His discussion of this wider subject is far from comprehensive, but an outline of his conception emerges from his remarks. At the beginning of the book he rejects the notion of a "sociologically conditioned subject" as epistemologically incoherent (1982: 12). He further informs us that collapsing the distinction between self and situation obviates the possibility of a coherent concept of the subject (1982: 20). These remarks provide some clues to discerning the nature of the subject that Sandel explores. Like many other contemporary theorists and, indeed, many feminists, Sandel accepts the dichotomy between the disembodied subject and the radically situated (or "socially constituted") subject. His aim is to find a happy medium between these two extremes – that is, a subject that is only partly constituted by communal relationships.

He seems to imply that this subject would possess a "core self" that, although partially socially constructed, is not radically situated. One of his key points is that any subject, to be a subject, must be distanced from possessions, including relationships, rather than constituted by them. In an interesting twist to his argument, Sandel concludes that although Rawls's subject obviates the possibility of self-reflection, his own wider subject does not; Sandel's subject has a core self on which to reflect, thus repairing one of the key deficiencies of Rawls's subject.

Sandel's sketch of the wider self reveals a number of problems. He accepts almost without argument that the "sociologically conditioned subject" is incoherent, primarily because it lacks a concept of the "true self." He does not explore the possibilities of socially constructed selves or the dichotomy that defines the gap between constituted and constituting selves. Nor does he examine the necessity of a concept of a "true self" and its relationship to the transcendental self. Sandel's wider self does not so much reject the modernist (disembodied) self as repair its defects. Central to the modernist concept of the self are self-knowledge, agency, and responsibility. Sandel finds Rawls's subject lacking in these key modernist qualities and goes on to remedy this deficiency by advancing a concept of self that is partly constituted by its social setting but still not "sociologically conditioned." Sandel might well retort that his wedding of elements of the constituting and the constituted subject changes each of these concepts of the self as they are brought into relationship with each other. But this is belied by the fact that his concept of the wider self retains the definitive aspect of the modernist self: the exclusive claim to agency and self-knowledge. Like many other contemporary theorists, Sandel is unwilling to break radically with the modernist discourse of the subject or to challenge the dichotomies on which it rests. As a result, his wider subject owes much to the modernist subject; it entails a wedding of elements of the modernist subject to elements that are socially conditioned, rather than a transformation of either of these concepts.

Sandel's wider self is not the only concept of the subject that has emerged from the communitarian critique of liberalism. A second such concept is found in the work of Alasdair MacIntyre. MacIntyre proposes an alternative to the modernist subject that he labels the "narrative self." His concept of the subject is formulated in a critique that is more broadly based than that of Sandel. In *After Virtue* (1984) and *Whose Justice? Which Rationality?* (1988) MacIntyre criticizes the ethical discourse that characterizes modern thought and the concept of the self on which it rests. He identifies the modernist subject as the "emotivist self," a subject devoid of ultimate criteria or social identity. The premodern self, by contrast, was constituted by its *telos* and its identification with tribe or kin. Sandel argues that the empty self of liberal theory is inadequate to the demands of justice in communities.

MacIntyre goes beyond this to argue that the emotivist self and the ethics that it represents are a result of the failure of Enlightenment thought to find a rational basis for morality.

As an antidote to the failure of emotivism, MacIntyre advocates a return to the concept of virtue that characterized societies in the past, most notably Homeric society. He argues that the only viable basis for a moral tradition is the practice of virtue as it was exercised in these societies. Virtues operate in a society in which each individual has a specifically defined role and status; virtues are then what sustains the individual in their proper role (1984: 122). More specifically, "A virtue is an acquired human quality the possession and exercise of which tends to enable us to achieve those goods that are internal to practices and the lack of which effectively prevents us from achieving any such goods" (1984: 191). Central to MacIntyre's concept of virtue is its dependence on what he calls the "narrative" character of human life. Within a society that practices virtues, subjects find their identity and unity in the construction of a narrative linking birth to death: "It is because we live out narratives in our lives and because we understand our own lives in terms of narratives that we live out that the form of narrative is appropriate for understanding the action of others" (1984: 212). For MacIntyre, the unity of human life lies in the unity of its "narrative quest," and personal identity is the identity presupposed by the unity of the character that the narrative requires (1984: 218–19).

MacIntyre's purpose in proposing "narrative selfhood" is to oppose it to the subject of liberal individualism – what he calls the "emotivist self." Liberal individualism conceptualizes a self that is separate from the roles it assumes; the self is defined as a core that acquires a series of roles that do not alter the constitution of that core. MacIntyre's narrative self, by contrast, is defined by the roles that are available in a given community. He claims that the roles that a society provides for individuals in it are open to a range of definitions and thus that the narrative self that emerges consists in the individual's own interpretation of the role assigned him or her. What this amounts to is that the individual defines a selfhood within a given role. MacIntyre asserts that "We enter upon a stage which we did not design and we find ourselves part of an action that was not of our making" (1984: 213). The concept of the good that individuals pursue is not, as in liberal individualism, of their own design but, rather, is defined and made possible by the community. The concept that emerges from this description of the relationship between self and community is one that, as MacIntyre readily admits, is premodern. The narrative selfhood achieved by MacIntyre's subjects is a selfhood whose general form is predetermined by the communities in which they find themselves; only the individual definition of the role varies. The quality identified by MacIntyre as crucial to the practice of the virtues is *phronēsis*, which he defines as the individual's knowledge of "what is due to him" (1984: 154). The concept of self to which this understanding of the virtues gives rise presupposes a community of fixed, ascribed roles. In such a community selfhood is achieved by knowing "one's proper role," embracing the narrative required by that role, then defining it in terms of one's own characteristics.

MacIntyre's concept of the narrative self departs more radically from the modernist subject than does the wider self of Sandel. Whereas Sandel grafts some communal aspects onto the modernist subject, MacIntyre completely rejects that subject. But although his concept avoids some of the problems of Sandel's subject, it raises others. The virtuous societies that he describes are hierarchical societies in which everyone knows his or her place. Roles are fixed; status is ascribed rather than achieved; and women, slaves, and those engaged in manual labor are ascribed permanently inferior status. These societies are also thoroughly patriarchal, and the achievement of virtue is restricted to the masculine sphere. The masculine root of "virtue" (the Latin *vir*) effectively excludes women from the sphere of morality just as surely as they are excluded from the realm of politics. MacIntyre's approach exemplifies a disturbing characteristic of much communitarian literature: the romanticization of premodern societies that ignores the oppression and hierarchy endemic to them. Even Sandel, despite his modernist leanings, sometimes falls prey to the tendency to glorify traditional communities (1984: 17). The narrative selfhood that MacIntyre lauds can be achieved only at a high price: the ascription of traditional roles.

In *Whose Justice? Which Rationality?* MacIntyre addresses the question of how to adjudicate between the different concepts of justice and rationality embodied by different societies.[12] His answer is that each society develops a particular kind of rational inquiry, one that is rooted in its own traditions, and thus that the definition of rationality will vary between traditions (1988: 8). Throughout the book he emphasizes the cohesiveness of traditions, the interrelatedness of their parts. Yet, when it comes to the highly charged issues of the sexism and racism of the traditions he praises so highly, he seems to abandon his interrelationship thesis. With regard to the Aristotelian tradition, he rejects the claim that sexism and racism are integral to this system of virtues. Several feminist political theorists have argued that Aristotle's racism and sexism are inseparable from the hierarchical concept of virtues that he advances. But instead of attempting to refute this, MacIntyre asserts only that it is "clear" that Aristotle's "errors" with regard to women and slaves can be excised from his account without significantly altering it (1988: 105). This cavalier dismissal of an important point is hardly excusable. But it is consistent with the theme that MacIntyre steadfastly maintains throughout all his work: that it is this traditional community that we must foster if we are to return to any semblance of a moral life. "What matters at this stage are the construction of local forms of community within which civility and the intellectual and moral life can be sustained through the new dark ages which are already upon us" (1984: 263).

While it is MacIntyre and Sandel who advance the most comprehensive critiques of liberalism, they are by no means the only communitarian critics of liberalism writing today. An examination of this communitarian literature reveals a pattern of argument that conforms more closely to that of Sandel than that of MacIntyre. Sandel attempts what amounts to a dialectical synthesis of modernity and communalism, specifically between the "good" aspects of the modernist subject and a socially constructed subject. Most communitarian critics also attempt a synthesis of the individualism of modernity and communitarian values. MacIntyre's concept of community in which individuals have a largely ascribed status is rarely found in this literature. Instead, most communitarian writers argue that individuality and communality are not antithetical and that the communities they oppose to liberal individualism do not preclude some of the virtues of liberalism, most notably freedom and equality. They propose a dialectical concept of community, in which individuality and communality are intertwined. The concept of the self that they define as inhabiting these communities is likewise dialectical, reconciling the individual and the social self.[13]

This dialectical concept, represented in the work of Sandel and several other communitarian thinkers, is appealing, because it appears to avoid the polarities of the debate. But it incurs several problems. Such dialectical accounts are predicated on the existence of a dichotomy between individual autonomy on the one hand and communality on the other; but none of them challenges this dichotomy outright. Each sees advantages in the communality denied by liberal society, yet each wants to retain the "good" elements of individualism in the self and the community they advocate. What is missing in these accounts is any attempt to forge a discourse which avoids the polarities of this dichotomy. As in any other dichotomy, the two elements, in this case individualism and communalism, are interdependent; one cannot exist without the other. The supposed clear-cut opposition between the two concepts is thus only apparent; the concepts are intertwined. This is most evident in the fact that the discourse of each presupposes the division of the social world into public and private spheres, the public world of men (or women who enter this sphere as men) and the private world of women and family. Attempting, as these authors do, to effect a dialectical interaction between the two discourses does nothing to alleviate the polarity of the terms or to forge a discourse that displaces that polarity. Displacing the polarity would entail employing a discourse that does not attempt to graft together elements from both sides of the dichotomy; this acknowledges the legitimacy of the polarity. What is needed is a discourse that avoids the oppositional language of the dichotomy altogether, one that defines subjects and societies not as part individual and part social but as producers of discourse and knowledge.

Another significant problem with these accounts is that both the discourses they attempt to graft together are rooted in patriarchal assumptions, thus insuring that the discourse they produce is patriarchal as well. That the discourse of liberal individualism is thoroughly patriarchal has been established by several feminist writers and needs little argument here (Okin 1979; Pateman 1988; Di Stefano 1991). That the traditional discourse of communalism is likewise patriarchal is acknowledged even by its proponents. The community as it has been conceived in Western thought is hierarchical and ascriptive. This community ascribes a particular status to each category of individuals who comprise its members, and the status it has traditionally ascribed to women is clearly an inferior one. A defender of communitarianism might argue that just because extant communitarian theories are sexist, it does not follow that communitarianism is inherently sexist. There are several replies to this defense. My claim is only that there is not *at present* an alternative moral theory that can accommodate the radical issues that Gilligan raises, and that existing communitarian theories do not even come close to achieving this goal. Further, although communitarianism may not be inherently sexist, it is inherently oppositional: it is predicated on the modernist opposition between the individual and the social. We need to displace this dichotomy if we are to restructure moral theory to accommodate different moral voices.

What I am arguing, then, is that, given the patriarchal nature of the discourses of individualism and communitarianism, efforts to synthesize them can yield little that would improve the status of women. The authors who attempt this synthesis seem to implicitly acknowledge this; discussions of the status of women are extremely rare and are sketchy when they do occur. The most revealing of these discussions occurs in the work of Benjamin Barber. Barber (1974) ponders the dilemma of women in the Swiss canton of Raetia, who were denied the franchise until 1971. Although he laments this exclusion, he nevertheless argues that it was a result of the tension between equality and justice on the one hand and community and participation on the other. Unfortunate as it may be, he concludes that "The enfranchisement of women (1971) can only accelerate the ongoing erosion of direct democracy's defining conditions" (1974: 273). The exclusion of women is thus defined as a sad but necessary consequence of the "healthy" participatory community that Barber praises.[14]

MacIntyre's work provides a contrast to this dialectical concept. MacIntyre completely rejects the individualism of liberalism and espouses an uncontaminated communalism. Thus he is caught up in the dichotomy he purports to reject. But his concept raises another problem. As many of the critics of communalism have pointed out, the concept of community invoked by these theorists is a conservative, if not reactionary, one. It is at the very least a concept that, in the discourse of the West, has entailed the inferiority and subordination of women (Gutmann 1985: 309). Furthermore, this concept of community is, as one critic puts it, meant to put our critical faculties to sleep: "In the vocabulary of antiliberals, 'community' is used as an anesthetic, an amnesiac, an aphrodisiac" (Holmes 1988: 25). It is the critical analysis of community, however, that is precisely what is necessary. If feminists are enjoined to jump on the communitarian bandwagon, to embrace this alternative to modernist moral theory, then they must know exactly what "community" entails. Embracing a romantic conception of community, without scrutiny, will not solve the problems posed by the disembodied self of the liberal tradition. But existing communitarian critiques fall far short of such a critical analysis. They also fall far short of their stated goal: rejecting the problems inherent in liberal individualist discourse. What is required is a discourse about subjects and communities that rejects not only the disembodied subject of liberalism but also the liberalism/communitarianism dichotomy on which that concept rests.

Feminism and community

One of the central claims of the communitarian critique of liberalism is that the disembodied "I" of liberalism must be replaced by the embodied "we" of community. A feminist appraisal of this critique, then, must begin by questioning the constitution of this "we" that the communitarians espouse. I argued above that two senses of "community" emerge from the communitarian critique of liberalism, the dialectical concept and a premodern concept. The dialectical concept attempts to fuse elements of liberal individualism and communalism. It claims to reject, or at the very least strictly modify, the individualism of liberalism. A close look at this dialectical concept reveals, however, that, far from rejecting liberal individualism, it has an affinity with the notion of "fraternity" that is rooted in the liberal tradition. Although "fraternity" connotes emotional and affective ties, in the liberal tradition these ties exist within the context of an association of rational individuals bound together by their mutual search for autonomy and freedom. The dialectical concept of community has much in common with this notion of "fraternity." Most important, it is predicated on some of the key concepts of liberalism: voluntary choice, rationality, and autonomy. The tenuousness and fragility of this fraternal, voluntaristic sense of community have been noted by many critics of liberalism and are graphically documented in *Habits of the Heart* (Bellah et al. 1985). It is nevertheless a sense of community that has a great deal of appeal to a society schooled in liberal ideology, because it is a community of choice that does not exclude autonomous individuals.

That this notion of community is also thoroughly masculinist is evident from the designation "fraternal." Carole Pateman has argued that civil society as conceived by liberalism is based on a fraternal pact, a brotherhood of men (1988: 78). In tracing the roots of liberal contract theory, Pateman asserts that liberal society is an association rooted in the previous subordination of women and rests on sexual access to women. There are two central claims to her argument. First, the "brothers" who sign the social contract that creates the liberal community are already heads of household – that is, they already possess women. One of the principal aims of the contract is to secure that possession. This claim has been reinforced by other feminist theorists who have examined the status of women as political actors and workers in liberal society. These theorists have documented that the continued subordination of women in liberal society is due to the fact that both "citizen" and "worker" are conceived as masculine, and specifically as male heads of household (Eisenstein 1988). Women simply do not fit into this designation. The second claim is that the fraternal pact that undergirds liberal society is, by definition, a pact among equals – among men and brothers. It is a pact that denies difference; "different" groups, particularly women and racial minorities, must be excluded, because the desire for wholeness that motivates this community can be realized only among equals. This is Iris Young's point in her discussion of "the politics of difference" (1990). The "we" defined by this community identifies women as unequal because they are "different."

The premodern concept of community, by contrast, constitutes a genuine rejection of liberalism and modernism. MacIntyre's notion of a community that ascribes status, a community that is both hierarchical and deterministic, is a notion that has ancient roots, as is evident in his reliance on Greek conceptions. Yet it is a notion that is by no means obsolete. Opponents of modernity's individualism – de Tocqueville, Hegel, and Montesquieu, as well as MacIntyre himself – espouse it. A nostalgic, romantic longing for this kind of community is a major force in contemporary discussions; it surfaces in the work of the proponents of the dialectical concept of community; it also fuels conservative antifeminism. Advocates of premodern community argue that women are accorded an honored place in such communities; their difference is acknowledged, and their essential contribution valued. They argue that family is central to such communities; but it is a family in which the father is the acknowledged head. Women are assumed to have a different nature from men, but "difference" here connotes inferiority, not equality. The status ascribed to women in such communities is centered on reproduction and the nurturing roles associated with it. Communitarians can and do argue that this discourse offers the advantage of describing both men and women as embodied subjects and situated selves. But it is also a discourse in which power writes only one script for women. They are not free to enter other discourses, to resist the role scripted for them, or to create new discourses. It thus constitutes little improvement over the discourse of liberalism.[15]

Although the sexism of the discourses of both liberalism and communitarianism would seem to require that feminists look elsewhere for a political discourse of self and community, several feminists have been drawn into the liberalism/communitarianism debate and have espoused positions similar to the dialectical concept of community discussed above. Marilyn Friedman is a good example. Friedman argues for a kind of dialectical interaction between self and community as a model for a feminist political discourse (1989a, b). Although she rejects communitarianism as a "perilous ally" of feminism, because it advocates a community that is oppressive to women, she attempts to replace this concept with the notion of a community that is chosen rather than imposed. She argues that in the context of a chosen model of community "'voluntary choice' refers to motivations arising out of one's needs, desires, interests, values and attractions in contrast to motivations arising from what is socially assigned, ascribed, expected or demanded" (1989a: 286). Friedman's concept of community is one in which the voluntary choice of the individual based on personal needs and desires plays a central role. The problem with this concept is that it is closely tied to the discourse of individual autonomy that is fundamental to liberalism and modernist moral theory. Friedman assumes, like many of the communitarians discussed above, that if the model of the autonomous individual is abandoned, then choice and agency must be abandoned as well. She also assumes that a neat division can be made between "voluntary choice" and "socially assigned" motivations. Thus, like many communitarians, she seeks to retain some elements of autonomy while ostensibly espousing a communitarian model.

Feminist reactions to the liberalism/communitarian debate suggest a number of conclusions. First, the positions taken by both sides in the debate are profoundly hostile to feminism. For the debate offers women the choice of adopting either the masculinist, disembodied subject of liberalism or the subordinated, determined subject implicit in the communitarians' vision of the ideal community. Furthermore, the dialectical concept of community advanced by some communitarians offers little solace. Synthesizing the two discourses does not overcome the polarity between them or the sexism of either. Second, the mutually unacceptable alternatives of the liberalism/communitarianism debate stem from its embeddedness in modernist discourse. The polarities of the debate are misleading; the two positions are interdependent, and both are firmly embedded in dichotomous modernist thought. Both the hostility of the debate to women and its irresolvability are a result of this interdependence. Third, feminists who have attempted to join the liberalism/communitarianism debate by espousing a dialectical concept of the subject fail to displace the polarities of that debate. The futility of the debate supports my contention that we must move to a different epistemological space if we are to accomplish that displacement. Defining this epistemological space is the goal of the discussion of subjectivity in the next chapter.

At the beginning of my discussion of alternative moral theories I argued that, with few exceptions, these theories fail to supply the basis for a radical restructuring of moral theory in three areas: epistemology, power, and subjectivity. My analysis of the "relativist" moral theories offers ample support for the first claim: most of these theories remain within the epistemological parameters of the absolutist/relativist dichotomy. The defenders of relativist moral theory are, quite literally, defensive. They agree with their critics in one crucial respect: that relativism requires a substantial defense to bolster its implicitly fragile claims. The dominance of the absolutist tradition in modernist moral theory thus provides a subtext even for advocates of relativism. It does not necessarily follow, however, that a defense of relativism is the only option for the reconstruction of contemporary moral theory. In what follows I pursue another option: displacing the dichotomy altogether. This option necessarily entails confronting the epistemological issues implicit in modernist moral theory. It entails pursuing a theory of knowledge that is not dependent on the absolutist/relativist dichotomy. I explore this option in Chapter 4 through an analysis of Wittgenstein's theory of language games and a discussion of various contemporary theories of knowledge and ethics.

The foregoing analysis also substantiates my second claim: that, again with a few notable exceptions, the alternative tradition ignores the issue of power. This failure is particularly obvious in the communitarian literature. Although communitarians argue for a particularized, contextual approach to the constitution of morality, they fail to problematize the "community" they idealize. By assuming that only one moral discourse is extant in a community, they ignore the hegemonic forces that structure any community. This is Foucault's point when he asserts that we must always question what "we" means in any theory (1984a: 385). The "we" referred to by communitarians is the dominant moral discourse within the community, a discourse that excludes women and other marginalized groups. Appealing to this "we" perpetuates the power relationships that feminists and others are attempting to expose. The other alternative moral theorists discussed above are not much of an improvement. If they mention multiple moral systems within a community at all, it is only in passing.

My third claim, that alternative moralities ignore the issue of subjectivity, is also confirmed. The legacy of modernist moral philosophy dictates that psychological considerations be set aside if the moral theorist is to perform his [sic] task: the formation of universal moral principles. Gilligan's work challenges this legacy by arguing that the constitution of subjectivity and that of morality are intertwined. What sets Gilligan's approach apart is that she emphasizes this relatedness, by describing the constitution of the "different" moral voice in terms of the constitution of subjectivity. Again with some exceptions, the alternative moral theorists ignore this connection. Even when they do discuss it, they are much more likely to look for universal psychological characteristics than examine the particular constituents of moral subjectivity.

Feminist ethics

In 1989 Alison Jaggar published a short article in the *Journal of Social Philosophy* entitled "Feminist Ethics: Some Issues for the Nineties." Her article reveals much about the current status of discussions in feminist ethics. Most importantly, it reveals that "feminist ethics" has become a recognized philosophical concern. Books, journals, articles, and conferences have been devoted to its study; subgroups can be identified within the general category. But the article also reveals that exactly what feminist ethics is and what it should be doing are still very much at issue. Jaggar confidently defines feminist ethics as a commitment to rethinking ethics with a view to correcting male bias (1989: 91). She then goes on to present three lists: first, of what she thinks feminist ethics is *not*; second, of what it is; and third, of the key issues that it must confront. Jaggar's first and second lists indicate that there is disagreement among feminist ethicists as to what their task is; Jaggar herself has a different concept from that of the theorists she criticizes. The length of the third list reveals that, at least in Jaggar's view, there is much work yet to be done; indeed, the magnitude of the tasks facing the discipline is quite daunting.

Like Jaggar, I am interested in examining where feminist ethics is now and how it can build on existing theories. In the foregoing discussion of alternative moral theories I sought to establish that feminism should look elsewhere in its effort to reconstruct moral theory. Even a cursory examination of the literature on feminist ethics reveals that there is no single "feminist moral theory." It also reveals that all feminist moral theories are not predicated on the assumption that grounds my analysis: that feminist ethics should seek to radically restructure moral theory. It is the case, however, that some feminist moral theorists have defined a unique position in moral theory, a position that sets them apart from the tradition of modernist moral theory. The aim of the following discussion is not to survey contemporary feminist ethics but, rather, to focus on aspects of the literature that "jams the machinery" of modernist moral theory. The discussion is organized around three issues. First is the question of whether feminists should be talking about "ethics" at all. If the search for *the* moral or ethical theory has been a masculine preserve, rooted in a commitment to the disembodied subject who legislates abstract, universal principles, then, many feminists have argued, ethical theory is not for feminists. Marilyn Frye states this position very succinctly. She argues that if ethics is defined as "getting it right" in moral theory, then feminists do not need ethics at all (1991). She asserts that although women have a hunger for ethics because of having been forced to reexamine and reject masculinist moral rules, they should repress this hunger. She even suggests that the desire to "get it right" is the product of a particular class, race, and cultural situation (1990). What we need instead, she maintains, is a plethora of ethics that are class, race, and historically specific. A milder version of the same argument is advanced by Annette Baier, who asserts, against Kant, that moral philosophers must work with anthropologists, sociologists, and psychologists to find out what an actual morality *is* rather than dictate universal laws (1985a: 224).

As Jaggar notes in her article, this issue is essentially an epistemological one. If, as many feminists have contended, the search for objective, disembodied, ahistorical truth is by definition masculinist, then feminists must redefine this search, in ethics as in all other areas. As Jane Flax puts it, the issue is how to theorize after the abandonment of "truth" (1990: 4). For Jaggar the dilemma for feminist ethics is that feminists have challenged the universality of morality but do not want their position dismissed as simply another point of view (1989: 101). One of the most perceptive attempts to deal with this issue is that of Margaret Walker. Walker argues that we should define ethics not as an individual standing singly before the impersonal dicta of "morality" but as connected human beings searching for shareable interpretations of responsibility (1989: 20). But Walker, like many feminist ethicists, is not willing to jettison altogether the search for an "ethics." She argues that we can save some remnant of "ethics" by separating "theory" from "ethics." Her position is that we need a new ethics but not a new "theory" in the sense of theoretical judicial rules of conduct. Her new ethics involves a definition of morality as the "medium for bringing our moral resources to bear in determining how to go on" (1992: 34).

It would be misleading to assert that all feminist attempts to reconstruct ethics espouse the position outlined by Margaret Walker. There is no dearth of feminist theorists who follow the masculinist model of attempting to "get it right" in moral theory, of attempting to discover "the" feminist ethics that can counter the masculinist ethics of modernist moral philosophy. I believe that pursuing this strand of feminist ethics is self-defeating. Instead, I follow those feminist ethicists who, like Walker, argue that "getting it right" in moral theory, even from a feminist perspective, will not lead to the necessary reconstruction of moral theory. What we need to explore, rather, are the "truths" of morality, not its singular "truth." As Walker puts it, we must explore morality as the "logic of interpersonal acknowledgment" (1992: 33).

The second issue I want to explore is the nature of the alternative moralities that feminist moral theorists have advanced. In the first wave of discussions in feminist ethics, feminists were primarily concerned with specifying the nature of the masculinist bias in moral and political theory. Gilligan's critique of Kohlberg is in this tradition; philosopher Genevieve Lloyd's work on women's exclusion from the realm of reason is a major contribution (1984); Susan Moller Okin's work on the exclusion of women from the political realm is another (1979).[16] What all these theorists argue, albeit in different ways, is that the association of rationality and objectivity with masculinity effectively excludes women from both the political and the moral realms. More recently, feminist political theorists Carole Pateman (1988) and Zillah Eisenstein (1988) have elaborated this position by asserting that liberal political theory is rooted in a concept of the individual that is gendered rather than neutral. Arguing that the definition of the individual in our moral, political, and legal systems is inherently masculine, Pateman and Eisenstein conclude that women can achieve equality in this political world only by renouncing their embodiment as women. Against this, they argue for an equality that can encompass an embodied female, an equality based on multiplicity and diversity rather than conformity to a single standard.

A common understanding of the task of feminist ethics is that it represents an attempt to replace a masculinist absolutism with a feminist absolutism – that is, attempting to replace the justice voice with the care voice. On this definition, feminist ethics is epistemologically indistinguishable from the tradition of masculinist moral theory; like that tradition, it is attempting to formulate the one, true moral theory. This is an important argument in the present context, because Gilligan's work on the "different voice" is almost universally identified as the source of the argument for "the" feminist ethics. In my analysis of Gilligan I have argued that it is possible to interpret her work differently, as advocating an approach to moral theory that is pluralistic and nonabsolutist, that seeks the "truths" of morality, not a single truth. The feminist theorists who are frequently cited as heirs to Gilligan's "care voice" and also as the principal architects of absolutist feminist ethics are Sarah Ruddick and Nel Noddings. Ruddick's advocacy of "maternal thinking" and Noddings's "caring" are almost always interpreted as arguments for a superior feminine moral voice, as attempts to define the one, correct feminist ethics. Yet, particularly in their most recent publications, both Ruddick and Noddings have moved away from an absolutist stance, instead embracing a pluralistic, relativistic position that belies this interpretation. Ruddick cites Rorty, Lyotard, and Wittgenstein as her philosophical influences and asserts that her feminist standpoint theory does not constitute a claim of "Truth" (1989: 135). Likewise, Noddings asserts that we must avoid the error of supposing that all women are alike and that there is a universal women's standpoint (1989: 2). She specifically argues against the individualistic ethic of masculinist moral theory and for a relational ethic. The ethic of caring she advocates is based on a relational ontology which maintains that all human beings, not just women, are defined through relationships (1989: 236). It follows that Noddings's "caring for" resists the claim that morality must depend on a criterion of universalizability (Curtin 1991: 66).[17]

Discussions of the ethic of care, of the "different" moral voice of women, have been an important force in feminist ethics in the last decade. The task of articulating the ethic of care has provided a focus for feminist critiques of traditional, masculinist ethics, a standard around which to rally. But I think that continuing to discuss the relationship between the ethic of care and the ethic of justice as well as attempting to define the precise dimensions of "the" ethic of care is not the most fruitful path for contemporary feminist ethics. I have argued that Gilligan's work does not entail the articulation of an absolutist alternative to the masculinist moral tradition. Recent work by the theorists who first articulated the ethic of care seems to acknowledge this: Noddings and Ruddick are now defining their positions in nonabsolutist terms. What I am proposing is not that we should abandon discussions of the ethic of care but, rather, that we should avoid aping the absolutism of masculinist moral theory and instead discuss different moral voices, not "the" different voice.

One need not look far in the literature on feminist ethics to find support for this position, voices that argue for a displacement of the masculinist tradition. A significant number of feminist ethicists are defining their task as radically opposed to that of traditional ethical theory. Kathryn Addelson's recent book *Impure Thoughts* (1991) is an excellent example. Addelson argues that we need a new moral theory that is consistent with contemporary changes in philosophy and metaphysics, what she calls "post-analytic" philosophy (1991: 128). She argues for a moral theory that will illuminate patterns of moral thinking that analytic philosophy has made invisible (1991: 57). Our present moral theories, she claims, are radically mistaken about what men and women *do* morally, principally because they misrepresent human group life (1991: 190). As an alternative she proposes symbolic interactionism, a feminist morality that allows us to understand the process whereby we make ourselves and our societies (1991: 210).

One of the strongest voices in feminism today for a movement away from a masculinist, absolutist ethics is that of Sarah Hoagland. In commenting on Noddings's work, Hoagland states: "A truly radical ethics will challenge not only the masculine but also the feminine, for the feminine is born of a masculinist framework and so does not, at a deep level, represent any change. . . . In general, I do not find a society of mothers preferable to a society of fathers" (1991: 259). Her path-breaking *Lesbian Ethics* (1988) makes this position even clearer. At the beginning of the book she states her basic presupposition: "if I started with [traditional ethics] I would never get out of the framework" (1988: xiii). In the course of her work she opposes the grounding assumption of traditional ethics – that principles are necessary in ethical theory. Against this, she claims that her goal is to examine the function of our ethical judgments. She asserts that Anglo-European ethical theory promotes dominance and subordination and identifies the aim of her book as defining moral agency under oppression (1988: 2–13). Employing the concept pioneered by Weil and Murdoch, Hoagland argues that by "attending" to each other, we increase our own and each other's moral agency (1988: 115). The goal of such attending is not control or power but, rather, empowerment and enablement (1988: 137). Moral agency, she argues, does not involve making "free" choices but working within limits and acknowledging boundaries (1988: 231).

The intent of Hoagland's book emerges quite clearly: it is to formulate not an ethics for all women but an ethics specific to lesbians. She justifies this strategy by arguing that lesbians have unique ethical needs because they exist under heterosexist oppression. Although this may seem to render Hoagland's book of only parochial interest, I would like to suggest a different interpretation. Hoagland is elaborating a position that is appearing in an increasing number of studies of feminist ethics: the claim that we need many ethics to reflect the different situations of different women, not one true "feminist" ethic. Hoagland argues that the ethics that lesbians develop will necessarily differ from that of heterosexual women. It follows that heterosexual women will also speak in different ethical voices that are a product of their various situations. On this interpretation, Hoagland's work is compatible with what I have argued emerges from Gilligan's work: the call for a plurality of ethics that recognizes the diversity of women's moral voices.

The third issue that is prominent in contemporary discussions in feminist ethics is the claim that a revolution in morality necessitates a corresponding revolution in the concept of the subject. Hoagland's work also exemplifies this theme. Rejecting the concept of "autonomy" on the grounds that it implies separation, she seeks to articulate instead a self defined in terms of relations with others. She adopts the term "autokoenony," which she defines as self in community, to describe her approach (1988: 144–5). The concern to reformulate the concept of the subject that grounds traditional moral theory is a dominant theme in feminist ethics. Marilyn Friedman, for example, makes the formulation of an alternative concept of self the centerpiece of a recent article (1991). Placing her argument in the context of Nagel's dichotomy between partiality and impartiality, Friedman argues for a "complex self" that is both socially determined and capable of resistance.[18]

In the next chapter I explore the reconstitution of subjectivity in detail, attempting to articulate a concept of the subject that is compatible with a reconstructed moral theory. At this point, however, it is important to note that it is misleading to claim that feminist ethicists are in accord on the rejection of the autonomous, separate subject that grounds traditional moral theory. As will become evident, there are many different approaches to this subject among feminists, ranging from outright rejection to relatively minor modification. It is nevertheless the case that the modernist subject has been problematic for all feminist ethicists.

Many discussions in feminist ethics concerning the status of the autonomous subject of traditional moral theory are informed by Nancy Chodorow's path-breaking work in psychological theory. This in itself is significant. The autonomous, self-legislating moral agent is the centerpiece of traditional moral theory, thus the displacement of that subject could not have come from within the domain of moral theory itself. Chodorow's object-relations theory is the origin of Gilligan's different voice in moral theory and the subsequent interest in the ethics of care. Although *The Reproduction of Mothering* (1978) has received much criticism in the feminist community, Chodorow's influence is nevertheless still strong. In her more recent work Chodorow has attempted to correct what critics see as the deficiencies of her theory. Thus in her new collection of essays she argues that her theory in *The Reproduction of Mothering* was too monocausal and that it needs to be qualified both historically and culturally (1989: 6). The most pronounced theme of this work and several other recent articles, however, is the significance of the relational self of object-relations theory for feminist theory. In an article published in 1986 she puts the issue very bluntly: the problem of individualism and the self can be addressed by either reconstituting the traditional autonomous self or by reconstituting the relational self (1986: 199). Chodorow leaves little doubt as to which alternative she prefers. In several recent articles she develops significant arguments to advance her concept of the relational self. She maintains that the relational self offers the only possible basis for psychoanalytic theory and claims that this concept of the self can be found in nascent form in some of Freud's works (1986: 200). Most important, she argues that the relational self need not be seen as simply a "social dupe" but, rather, that a kind of "relational individualism" can be developed (1989: 162).

A representative attempt to develop the implications of the relational self for ethical theory is Catherine Keller's *From a Broken Web* (1986). Keller argues that the central assumption of Western philosophy is that selfhood requires separation and that women simply do not measure up in a society of separate selves (1986: 1–2). She urges women seeking empowerment not to follow the path of separation but instead to define selfhood through connection. Without denying that a self must be differentiated, Keller asks if there is some way to conceive differentiation other than through separation. Her answer is that differentiation can be achieved *in* relations and that selves can maintain connectedness without dependency (1986: 161). She advances the notion of a "composite selfhood," defined in terms of multiplicity without dispersion, that is very similar to Marilyn Friedman's "complex self" (1986: 163). The problem of the connected versus the separate self, as Keller is well aware, is central to the reconstruction of traditional moral theory. Keller's discussion also highlights the issue that provides the key to this effort to reconstruct the subject: agency. The problem is this: if we abandon the autonomous moral subject of masculinist theory, how can we have a moral agent at all? Must we retain some aspects of the modernist subject in order to retain the notion of agency? Or is it possible to redefine agency in a way that does not require recourse to the autonomy of the modernist subject? This is a problem that has broad ramifications: it is central to feminist ethics as well as to the attempt to challenge the hegemony of modernist epistemology in moral theory. It is this problem that I examine in detail in the next chapter.[19]

To conclude this discussion, I will look at two approaches to feminist ethics that are particularly germane to the theory I am advocating. These approaches both illustrate what I claim are the radical implications of some aspects of the feminist critique of moral theory and indicate the direction in which I want to take that critique in the next two chapters. The first is that of Iris Young in *Justice and the Politics of Difference* (1990). Young criticizes the definition of justice as universalizing, as abstracting from particulars, asserting instead that normative reflection must begin from particular circumstances (1990: 5). She defines justice as institutional conditions necessary for the development and exercise of individual capacities and collective communication and cooperation. By contrast, she defines injustice as oppression and domination (1990: 39). She objects to the ideal of impartiality in moral theory, on the grounds that it seeks to reduce differences to unity. It creates oppositions – public/private, reason/passion, universal/particular – that cannot be overcome. Worse, the ideal of impartiality is ideological, masking the domination of the hegemonic group (1990: 97). Against this, Young proposes an ideal of public fairness in a context of heterogeneity and partial discourse, a "radically pluralist participatory politics of need interpretation" (1990: 118).

The key to Young's "politics of difference" is an understanding of difference that eschews hierarchy. The politics of difference that she defines involves an understanding of group differences as ambiguous, relational, and shifting, rather than deviations from a given norm. The concept of justice she proposes is based not only on equality but also on the requirement of special rights for particular groups, the mutual recognition and affirmation of group differences (1990: 170–91). Young's attempt to define a politics of difference moves feminist theory beyond the sterile dichotomies imposed by modernist thought. What I am attempting here is compatible with her effort. My goal is to articulate the moral epistemology of the politics of difference and to explore the constitution of moral subjectivity that informs such a politics.[20]

Young wants to redefine the categories of traditional moral and political theory and to explode the dichotomies on which that theory rests. But the roots of these dichotomies lie deep within the epistemology of modernity. In order to displace them, it is necessary to challenge modernism's epistemological assumptions about knowledge and the subject. This is the task that Lorraine Code sets for herself in *What Can She Know?* (1991). Code advances a perspectival theory of knowledge that questions the fundamental distinction between subjectivity and objectivity. Her principal concern is theories of knowledge, but she draws out the implications of her approach for moral theory as well. She argues: "Perhaps the most radical effect of feminist moral critiques is their demonstration that moral theories close off more possibilities of discernment and action than they create" (1991: 107). Code's theory stresses two themes that, I believe, are central to a feminist reconstruction of moral theory. First, she argues that moral theory cannot be separated from the epistemological theory in which it is grounded. Subjectivity and agency, she claims, are even closer to the surface in ethical theories than in theories of knowledge (1991: 71). Second, she maintains that the feminist critique necessarily entails a radical restructuring of traditional moral and epistemological theory. Her goal, she says in her conclusion, is to "remap the epistemic terrain into numerous, fluid conversations" (1991: 309). My goal is to do the same for the moral terrain. I want to explore the plurality of moral voices that emerge from discursive relations. And, like Code, I want to link that discussion to epistemology and subjectivity, because what we know and who we are cannot be neatly separated.

The issue of the constitution of moral subjectivity is the topic of the next chapter. I begin that discussion by building on Gilligan's theory of the constitution of moral voices. The grounding assumption of my discussion is Elizabeth Spelman's point that children do not learn only how to become boys or girls. They also learn how to become certain *kinds* of boys and girls; the "girl" or "boy" part of the self cannot be separated from the "white," "black," or "middle class" part (1988: 101). She argues that "Selves are not made up of separable units of identity strung together to constitute a whole person" (1988: 158). My thesis is that moral voice is an integral and inseparable part of that whole person.

3
Subject Strategies

In her critique of mainstream moral development theory, Gilligan argues that moral voices and moral selves are inseparable. I have contended in the foregoing that this thesis is the central element in what amounts to a radical critique of moral theory. My claim is that by connecting morality and subjectivity, we can define a position that deconstructs the foundation of modernist moral theory: the autonomous subject. In the last chapter I further argued that it is this connection that separates Gilligan's approach from that of the "alternative moral theorists." My task in this and the following chapter is to outline a theory of subjectivity that can accommodate Gilligan's thesis of the connection between morality and subjectivity and to explore that connection. My goal is to articulate an approach that can accommodate a plurality of moral voices without denying the uniqueness of moral voice. The centerpiece of my argument is the claim that morality is not just one of the many language games that subjects pursue. It is central to the constitution of the subject itself and provides the grounding for the fundamental elements of subjectivity.

My discussion of contemporary theories of subjectivity is guided by the assumption that intellectual thought is witnessing a paradigm shift in the conception of the subject. In its most extreme form this entails the "death of man" that the poststructuralists and deconstructionists have proclaimed. At the very least, it means that the transcendent disembodied subject of the modernist tradition can no longer be taken for granted. My aim in what follows is to draw from some of the elements of this emerging concept of the subject in order to articulate what I call the "discursive subject." Although this concept of the subject, like any concept, is forged from elements of current theories, it cannot be neatly subsumed under any of the existing categories.

The relational self

The Cartesian understanding of the subject that forms the basis of modernist moral theory is one that specifically excludes any reference to psychological factors. The Cartesian subject is by definition autonomous, an ego that realizes its essential qualities divorced from contingent circumstances. Kant's explicit exclusion of psychology from the realm of moral theory has been strictly adhered to in modernist moral theory. The first step that led to the construction of the anti-Cartesian subject was taken, ironically, by one of the masters of modernist thought: Karl Marx. By positing a subject that is determined by historical contingencies, Marx laid the groundwork for what would become the twentieth century's constructed subject.[1] A second crucial step in this evolution was taken by Freud. Freud made the radically anti-Cartesian move of introducing a subject that was sexed. The modernist subject, by contrast, was disembodied; sex was a characteristic of women, not the neutered, disembodied self. Indeed, it was women's inability to divorce themselves from their sex that excluded them from the moral realm. For Freud, however, personal identity is sexed identity (Gatens 1991: 104). Freud's subject is also a constructed subject, a subject that emerges as the result of processes beyond its control. It represents a violation of the modernist subject in two significant respects: first, it is a subject that is constituted psychologically, and, second, it is a subject whose morality is connected to its psychological identity. In terms of the evolution of the anti-Cartesian subject, Freud's most crucial argument is that morality is produced by the suppression of sexual desire.

But neither Freud nor Marx banished the Cartesian subject outright. Both retained elements of this subject, Marx with his theory of the subject who transcends history and Freud with his biological essentialism. Even psychological theory did not quickly adopt the concept of the constituted subject. As is evident from the discussion in Chapter 1, the dominant concept of the self in psychological theory, and particularly in theories of moral development, is that of the separate self. Piaget and Kohlberg both assume that development toward autonomy and separation is the paradigm of healthy subjectivity. It is significant that the work of an early feminist psychologist, Karen Horney, should have been instrumental in moving psychological theory toward an acceptance of the constructed subject. Horney rejects Freud's theory of instincts, replacing it with a theory of the constitutive role of cultural forces (1967). Yet she retains elements of the modernist subject, defining the social self as annihilating the true, essential self that we all possess. Specifically, she argues that women must escape the devaluing associations of the feminine that are forced upon them by culture if they are to achieve true selfhood. Horney's concept represents an approach that has had much popularity in psychological theory, both then and now: the intersubjective self that is defined in terms of an interaction between a core, essential self and a socially conditioned self.[2]

The theory that provides the groundwork for a more radically anti-Cartesian concept of the subject, however, comes from another source: object-relations theory. Whereas Horney and other mid-century psychological theorists argued that the self is constructed in part through social relations, object-relations theorists argued that it is wholly a relational product. Object-relations theory seeks to describe a self that has no separate, essential core but, rather, *becomes* a "self" through relations with others. This concept of self jettisons the notion of a preexistent ego. But, more radically still, object-relations theory maintains that the separate, autonomous self that is the cornerstone of the modernist self is itself a product of relational forces. This point was central to Gilligan's deconstruction of the separate self. Nancy Chodorow, a feminist interpreter of object-relations theory, states this thesis as follows: "Differentiation is not distinctness and separateness, but a particular way of being connected to others" (1987: 257). This thesis definitely removes the separate self as the paradigm of subjectivity, defining it instead as the product of another paradigm: the relational self.

Both object-relations theorists and advocates of the relational self define their approach as a new paradigm in psychoanalytic theory, one that challenges the Freudian paradigm. This claim is, to a significant extent, accurate. Yet, elements of an essentialist, separate self remain. One of the founders of object-relations theory, John Bowlby, defines his theory as a description of "attachment behavior" and argues that it represents a Kuhnian-style paradigm shift away from Freud's drive theory (1988: 26). Bowlby's position reveals both the strength and the weakness of this approach. On the one hand, Bowlby understands that it constitutes a radical shift in theories of subjectivity. On the other hand, he wants to retain at least a tenuous connection to the "scientific" psychoanalysis established by Freud. Thus he argues that attachment behavior is a "biological function" aimed at protection and that psychoanalysis properly belongs in the natural sciences, not hermeneutics (1988: 27, 58). Bowlby's object-relations theory rejects Freudian theory by positing a relational self but retains the Freudian model insofar as it defines the other as the object of drives.

A similar ambiguity characterizes relational self theory. In 1988 Steven Mitchell published a book in which he tried to bring together the various aspects of a relational approach to psychoanalysis. In *Relational Concepts in Psychoanalysis: an integration*, Mitchell, like Bowlby, argues that a paradigm shift is under way in psychoanalysis. Labeling

Freud's theory "outdated," Mitchell tries to define an alternative by drawing together the various aspects of the relational model into a comprehensive theory (1988: viii). Mitchell rejects Bowlby's attempt to retain a quasi-scientific definition of psychoanalysis. Instead, he enthusiastically embraces a hermeneutic model, arguing that different theories arrange experience differently (1988: 90). He also explicitly connects this paradigm shift in psychoanalysis to that occurring in other disciplines. Referring explicitly to anthropology and linguistics, he defines the move from the individual to the interactional field in psychoanalysis as part of a broader epistemic shift (1988: 3–17). Mitchell's position here is similar to that of Foucault in *The Order of Things*. Both are predicting the demise of a concept of the subject that has held sway for several centuries. But unlike Foucault, Mitchell is reluctant to completely jettison reference to the "human experience" as a baseline for his theory. He argues: "Embeddedness is endemic to the human experience – I become the person I am in interaction with specific others. The way I feel it necessary to be with them is the person I take myself to be. The self-organization becomes my 'nature'" (1988: 276).

Object-relations theory and relational self theory claim to offer comprehensive alternatives to the Freudian paradigm. Yet there is a strange lacuna in this literature: an absence of specific applications to the experience of women. Despite the fact that women have long been identified as primarily concerned with relationships and are, in most cases, the primary nurturers of young children, neither Mitchell nor Bowlby accord women any particular attention in their theories. But several feminist psychoanalysts have recognized the significance of the relational theory of the self for a feminist understanding of psychological development. Judith Jordon, one of the editors of a collection of feminist applications of relational self theory, follows Bowlby and Mitchell in arguing that a new paradigm is emerging:

> Rather than a study of development as a movement away from and out of relationship, this approach posits growth through and toward relationship. Delineation of different kinds of relationships becomes important as a way of understanding what people are seeking in relationships and why certain relationships are a source of joy and meaning, while others become deadening and destructive. (1991: 81)

The articles collected in this volume seek to apply these insights specifically to the position of women, with the aim of countering the dismissal of relationships that characterizes the separate self tradition.

The most thoroughgoing feminist application of the relational self approach is that of Dana Jack. In *Silencing the Self* (1991) Jack addresses the "problem" of women's psychological development very explicitly.

She argues that women have been told that they must be autonomous and independent and, when they fail to become so, feel inadequate and devalued. Women's strength, their capacity to nurture and develop in relationships, is thus defined as a weakness and a liability. Jack's approach to this familiar story, however, is distinctive. She asserts that it is not relationships per se that are the source of women's problems, but the *quality* of the relationships in which they are engaged. Women are vulnerable to depression not because of their dependence on relationships but because of what happens to them *in* relationships (1991: 21). She maintains that women can conquer depression not by becoming more independent but by improving the quality of the relationships that structure their lives.

What Jack is promoting is a different way of theorizing about relationships that will, she claims, lead to a different way of defining reality. Like many contemporary theorists, she takes the position that no unbiased collection of data is possible, that the facts do not speak for themselves, but, rather, that reality is always ordered through the application of a particular framework (1991: 22). In her view, we need to "see" relationships not as a mark of dependency, a sign of a failure to attain some ideal of independence, but, rather, as defining aspects of subjectivity that can range from supportive and nurturing to destructive. Yet, despite Jack's enthusiastic application of relational self theory, her approach retains a residue of the concept of the intersubjective self and, consequently, of a concept of a "true" self. Following Horney, she refers to an "authentic self," which she contrasts with the "false" self that our culture demands of women (1991: 101). "Silencing the self" thus becomes, for Jack, silencing the "true" self that every woman possesses.

Jack's theory, like those of Bowlby and Mitchell, represents a significant step in the displacement of the concept of the separate self that has informed both psychological theory and the Cartesian concept of the subject that grounds modernist moral philosophy. Yet these approaches remain tied to that concept in a number of ways. First, references to the "authentic self" and the "reality of human development" reveal that none of these theorists is willing to take the decisive step of arguing that it is "relationship all the way down," that subjects are wholly constituted by discursive formation. In the case of Jack's theory, this amounts to a contradiction: on the one hand, she claims that theories constitute the reality they study; on the other, she posits a reality for the self that transcends the theoretical.

Second, all these theories fail to differentiate among the widely varying relational patterns experienced by different men *and* women. Both Jack and the authors of the articles collected in the Jordon volume posit "the" woman's developmental experience, ignoring differences of race, class, and culture or the possibility that marginalized men may share certain developmental similarities with some women. Two theorists who work with Carol Gilligan have attempted to remedy this deficiency by arguing that Afro-American girls face a developmental matrix that is distinct from that of white, middle-class girls (Robinson and Ward 1991). They argue that the process of identity formation that Afro-American girls experience is embedded in definitions of family and community that are differently constructed than those of white girls. The sense of "we" that Afro-American girls employ involves a recognition of individuals as connected to others and defines individualism as a threat to the black community. This recognition of diversity in development, that rests on race and class rather than gender alone is an important corrective to the theories of the relational self that are emerging in psychoanalytic theory.[3]

The relational self theorists claim that their position represents a paradigm shift in the concept of the subject in psychological theory. Despite the presence of these remnants of the separate self tradition, this is largely the case. But it is also the case that the impact of this theory is limited to psychology. The rise of "alternative moral theory" in recent decades notwithstanding, Kant's dictum that psychology is irrelevant to moral philosophy still holds sway for the dominant tradition in moral theory. A radical displacement of this tradition is likely to come not from psychology but from postmodern and feminist theories of the subject.

The postmodern subject

If it is indeed the case that a paradigm shift is occurring in our understanding of subjectivity, then it is also the case that the shift is represented most clearly by postmodernism. The belief that postmodernism has caused, or at the very least announced, the "death of the subject" is a pervasive one in today's intellectual climate. Yet, like many widely held generalizations, it is misleading. First, there is not one, single, postmodern theory of the subject but many. Theories ranging from the semiotics of Lacan to the deconstructions of Derrida to the genealogies of Foucault vary widely. Second, far from abandoning the subject, postmodern theories are better characterized as obsessed with subjectivity. Postmodern theorists devote as much attention to the nature of subjectivity as do modernist defenders of the Cartesian subject. They are not abandoning the subject but, rather, redefining it.

My intent in what follows is not to define the "essence" of "the" postmodern approach to the subject. It is, rather, to selectively appropriate aspects of postmodern theories in order to articulate a discursive concept of the subject that can address questions raised by a feminist reconstruction of moral theory. Some postmodern approaches to the subject overemphasize the instability of subjectivity, presenting the subject as a fiction or a fantasy; further, they deny that their position constitutes a "theory" of subjectivity at all. Other postmodern approaches, most notably that of Foucault, attempt to formulate a discursive concept of subjectivity; they argue for a new epistemological concept of the subject that can accommodate the situation of subjects in the contemporary world. It is these approaches that I want to build on in developing my own concept.

In *Language and Materialism* (1977) Rosalind Coward and John Ellis attempted to link the rise of the postmodern, or, more specifically, the semiotic, approach to the subject to other intellectual trends in the mid-twentieth century. Two elements of their analysis are noteworthy. First, they emphasize that the "new subject" that is emerging today has been made possible by a profound shift in theories of language. They see structural linguistics as having changed the focus of linguistic investigation to the relational composition interior to language itself (1977: 14). For these linguists, signification is defined as the play of differences within the signifying chain, not the work of a transcendent subject (1977: 23). What Coward and Ellis's analysis reveals is that language is at the center of our contemporary discussion of subjectivity for a good reason: that this discussion is the product of an epistemological shift in our attitude toward language itself. One of the principal objections to a discursive definition of the subject is the belief that subjectivity must somehow be more than "mere" language. Coward and Ellis's insights reveal the presupposition informing this critique: the belief that subjects necessarily transcend language, that they create meaning prior to language. The new theories of language reverse this formula by asserting that subjects are produced by, rather than produce, language.

Second, Coward and Ellis argue for a link between the postmodern subject and the revolutionary tradition of Marxism. They point out that Marx was the first to articulate a subject that was internal to the structure of language and society, a constructed subject. Yet Marx was enough of a modernist to simultaneously retain the notion of a subject that is outside the structure, a subject who changes society by perceiving its true reality (1977: 61). Postmodern theorists have discarded the vestiges of modernism in Marx's theory while building on his constructed subject. This link between the postmodern subject and the Marxist tradition is frequently ignored, yet it points to a significant dimension of postmodern approaches to the subject. It reveals that this subject has its roots in an attempt not to abolish subjectivity but to articulate it in terms appropriate to the conditions of modernity. Marx was the first to explode the fiction of the self-constituting subject, but he stopped short of a total deconstruction of the modernist subject. Postmodern theorists have taken the next step in this deconstruction by addressing the anomaly of the quasi-transcendent subject in Marx's work. The link between postmodernism and Marxism also reveals that, at its inception, the postmodern concern with the subject was tied to a concern with resistance. This is most evident in the work of the Marxist theorist Louis Althusser. Althusser's subject provides the necessary link between Marx's subject and the postmodern subject. Althusser's subject is one that is constituted by ideological (discursive) formations yet still retains the Marxist distinction between the "real" and the constituted. But in retrospect it is clear that Althusser's subject has more in common with the subject of Foucault than with that of Marx. The resistant subjects of Marx and Althusser provide the foundation on which the postmodern subject was built and which, at least in some approaches, it retains today.[4]

A major force in the creation of the postmodern subject has been the influence of semiotics and the related approach of psychoanalysis, especially the work of Lacan. The result has been to emphasize the linguistic constitution of the subject. By detailing the way in which language constitutes subjects, these theories have fostered the deconstruction of the transcendent subject. Semioticians describe subjectivity as the product of the play of meanings within language; Lacan articulates a theory of the subject divorced from consciousness. The most influential theorist in this tradition is Jacques Derrida. Derrida has continued both the semiotic and Lacanian impulses by rejecting the notion of a subject prior to language. He has revolutionized the discussion of the subject by introducing the concept of *différance*. "The movement of *différance*," he asserts, "is not something that happens to a transcendental subject. It is what produces it" (1973: 82).

Central to Derrida's concept of *différance* is his assertion that the modernist subject is constituted through the binary opposition of subject and object. In his effort to deconstruct this subject, he argues that this binary opposition can be displaced by an appeal not to yet another opposition but to a nonoppositional metaphor. This central aspect of Derrida's thought provides a bridge to some feminist concerns. One of the nonoppositional metaphors that Derrida utilizes is that of the hymen. The hymen is appropriate to Derrida's purposes because it is neither inside nor outside, neither present nor absent. This move, as Gayatri Spivak (1976) suggests, can be interpreted as a feminist gesture. Appeal to this feminine metaphor is a means of displacing the binary, of deconstructing the phallocentrism of the modernist subject. Julia Kristeva and other feminist theorists have developed a similar theory, arguing that "woman," not "essential woman" but the metaphor of the feminine, is one, if not the rhetorical, means of deconstructing the modernist subject.

Derrida's deconstruction, feminist appropriations of Lacanian psychoanalysis, and semiotics have played a central role in the paradigm shift in the concept of subjectivity that is now under way. An extensive literature exists that chronicles the role of these movements. Significant as they are, however, I think that pursuing the semiotic and psychoanalytic strands of the postmodern subject is unproductive, particularly for feminist attempts to redefine subjectivity. Three theoretical problems emerge in this literature. First, many of these theorists – Derrida in particular – argue that they are not offering an "alternative" theory of the subject, because to offer a theory is to succumb to the epistemological dictates of modernism and engage in the "tyranny of theory." This refusal to acknowledge that the postmodern approach to the subject constitutes a theory, a new paradigm of subjectivity, leads to a theoretical dead-end. It prevents these theorists from developing arguments for their position, because to do so would be "coercive." Second, the Derridian and semiotic strands of postmodernism encourage us to define subjectivity as play and to equate the subject with fiction and fantasy. Given this, it is small wonder that the postmodern approach to the subject has been accused of nihilism. Yet it is an important insight that the subject is constituted by the play of meanings within language. What the Derridian and Lacanian theories ignore, however, is that this "play" is a deadly serious business, whose end product has nothing to do with fictions and vacillations. The play of meanings within language produces real subjects with coherent subjectivities that constitute their identities. Subjects do not choose or change their identities as they do their clothes; rather, a particular definition of subjectivity provides the ground for meaning and value in a subject's life. A third problem characterizes the more explicitly psychoanalytic theories: a modified form of foundationalism. This is particularly evident in Julia Kristeva's account of subjectivity. Kristeva fails to transcend the founding assumption that the semiotic and the symbolic constitute the psychological grounds of subjectivity. This leads her to a form of essentialism that, although different from Freud's, still presupposes a preexistent psyche.[5]

Another way of putting these points is that, in the 1990s, it is possible to distinguish two distinct strands of postmodern theories of subjectivity. The first, represented by semiotics, Derridian deconstruction, and Lacanian psychoanalysis, is concerned with destabilizing the subject through an emphasis on play, fiction, and fantasy. It tends toward nihilism in its focus on the instability of subjectivity and its political quiescence. The second is concerned with redefining the subject of the Marxist tradition and articulating a subject that is both resistant and discursively constituted. This second strand of postmodernism, represented primarily by the work of Foucault, is much more appropriate to the political requirements of feminism. Far from being nihilistic, it is concerned with real subjects under real conditions and the question of how these conditions can be changed.[6]

In my discussion of Gilligan's work I argued that questions of moral subjectivity and epistemology are inseparable, that how the subject knows is necessarily linked to who that subject is. The same thesis informs Foucault's work. For Foucault, subjectivity and ethics form a cohesive unit that can be comprehended only in its entirety. Although Foucault, like many theorists who have been labeled postmodern, is often accused of denying subjectivity, even a cursory examination of his work reveals the fallacy of this charge. It is abundantly clear that throughout his scholarly career, Foucault's principal interest has been the "subject" in Western thought and practice. In his early work on the clinic, madness, and prisons, his aim was to detail the way in which the subjects of these institutions are scripted by the discourses that define them as subjects. In his influential *The Order of Things* (1971), Foucault takes on the question of the subject, or "man," even more directly. He examines how the scientific discourses of modernity have created "man" as both subject and object of analysis. In the conclusion to this work Foucault makes his now famous pronouncement that "man" as a concept is headed for extinction.

The series of books culminating in *The Order of Things* establishes a number of themes that are important to an understanding of Foucault's approach to the subject. First, it reveals Foucault's ongoing interest in subjectivity. Foucault's work is full of subjects; his analysis revolves around the examination of different constitutions of subjectivity and the discourses that inform them. It cannot even be said that he ignores the subject that has defined the modern era, the autonomous, transcendent Cartesian subject. On the contrary, he meticulously analyzes the constitution of this subject and its effect on Western thought. What he does not do, though, is treat this subject as given and transcendental; instead, he treats it, like any other subject, as a constituted entity.

A second theme that emerges from this work is the connection between power and knowledge. The tradition of modernity has insisted that, at least ideally, knowledge and power are two separate entities and that knowledge frees us from power. Against this, Foucault argues that "There is no point in dreaming of a time when knowledge will cease to depend on power. . . . It is not possible for power to be exercised without knowledge, it is impossible for knowledge not to engender power" (1980: 52). While for the Cartesian subject knowledge leads to freedom from power, for Foucault, knowledge, the subject, and power are inextricably intertwined: "The individual, with his identity and characteristics, is the product of relations of power exercised over bodies, multiplicities, movements, desires, forces" (1980: 74). Putting these two themes together suggests that the motivation for Foucault's interest in the subject is a pragmatic one: he is attempting to articulate a concept of the subject that is appropriate to the conditions of modernity, conditions defined by discourses of knowledge, power, and subjectivity. The modern world is not peopled by autonomous, Cartesian subjects, nor by Kant's self-legislating moral subjects. Rather, it is filled with subjects who are scripted by relations of power, subjects who are *subjected* rather than transcendent. What Foucault is trying to do, then, is

> to determine, in its diverse dimensions, what the mode of existence of discourses, particularly scientific discourses (their rules of formation, with their conditions, their dependencies, their transformations) must have been in Europe, since the 17th century, in order that the knowledge which is ours today could come to exist, and, more particularly, that knowledge which has taken as its domain this curious object which is man. (1991: 70)

In some of Foucault's more recent works this attention to the subject is even more pronounced. In *The History of Sexuality* (1978), *The Use of Pleasure* (1985), and *The Care of the Self* (1986) Foucault engages in what he calls the "genealogy" of the modern subject. How, he asks himself, have we come to define the subject, "man," in this particular way in the West? What is the connection between the subject and *eros*? between the subject and truth? The analyses in these books are subtle and provocative. They refocus Foucault's concern with subjectivity. But, for the purposes of my analysis, the significance of these works lies in the fact that Foucault establishes a position that is central to any discussion of the feminist moral subject: he deconstructs the basis of the Cartesian subject by tracing the historical and discursive origins of its defining characteristics. He shows that the characteristics that modernity as-sociates with subjectivity – agency, autonomy, separation – are not paradigmatic. Rather, he details how these characteristics evolved as constituted products of the discourse of the modern (Cartesian/ Kantian) subject. He shows that they are historical, discursive products, not given attributes of subjectivity itself.

This conclusion has important implications for moral theory in gen-eral and feminist moral theory in particular. It means that the notion of agency that is so closely identified with the modernist subject is not the only possible definition of agency but, rather, is a specific attribute of the Cartesian subject. This suggests that other definitions of agency can and, indeed, have been defined that are specific to other definitions of subjectivity. It means, further, that it is not necessary, as so many contemporary theorists have claimed, to "borrow" agency and au-tonomy from the Cartesian subject in order to construct the moral subject. Foucault's analysis suggests that other definitions of agency, rooted in other discourses of subjectivity, can be constituted and em-ployed in the moral realm. In an interview Foucault states this point succinctly:

I don't think there is actually a sovereign, founding subject, a universal form of subject that one could find everywhere. . . . I think on the contrary that the subject is constituted through practices of subjection, or, in a more anonymous way, through practices of liberation, of freedom, as in Antiquity, starting of course from a number of rules, styles and conventions that are found in the culture. (Quoted in Rajchman 1991: 110)

And:

What is important to me is to show that there are not on the one hand inert discourses, which are already more than half dead, and on the other hand, an all-powerful subject which manipulates them, overturns them, renews them; but that discoursing subjects form a part of the discursive field. . . . Discourse is not a place into which the subjectivity irrupts; it is a space of differentiated subject-positions and subject functions. (1991: 58)

Discourses, in short, define what can be said (1991: 63).

I would like to suggest that Foucault's theory of subjectivity, particularly as articulated in some of his more recent works, answers three principal objections that have been leveled against any "postmodern" approach to the subject.[7] The first is the charge that postmodern theories of the subject create "social dupes," wholly determined entities lacking free will and agency. Foucault's formulation deals with this criticism by reversing it, turning it against the Cartesian rather than the constituted subject. It is the Cartesian subject, he asserts, that is predetermined, in the sense that it is "given"; it is this subject that is incapable of moving beyond the rigid boundaries that define it. Once we abandon the Cartesian subject, however, subjects become not social dupes but acts of self-creation: "From the idea that the self is not given to us I think there is only one possible consequence: we have to create ourselves as a work of art" (quoted in Dreyfus and Rabinow 1982: 287). On Foucault's account, this self-creation is accomplished through a kind of discursive mix. At any given time we find ourselves confronted with an array of discourses of subjectivity, scripts that we are expected to follow. We can accept the script that is written for us or, alternatively, piece together a different script from other discourses that are extant in our particular circumstances. It is important to note that this concept of subjectivity does not involve an appeal to a core, or essential, self. It is not a matter of "finding" our true, authentic self. Rather, we employ the tools (scripts) available to us in our situation. Furthermore, our application of these tools is a creative act; it can even be an act of resistance. What emerges from Foucault's theory, then, is that subjectivity is a potential to be realized, not a truth to be deciphered (Donzelot 1991: 271).

The second charge frequently leveled against the postmodern approach to subjectivity is that it fosters nihilism, because it precludes any consideration of moral or ethical issues. This charge is particularly salient in this context: it would negate the relevance of Foucault for feminist theory in general and feminist moral theory in particular. The answer to this charge, however, lies once again in turning the question around, so that it reveals the weakness of the Cartesian concept of the subject. Foucault's statement concerning the subject as a work of art provides the answer: *because* we cannot assume that subjectivity is a given, therefore we must take moral responsibility for the construction of ourselves as subjects. Despite significant differences, there is a parallel here between Foucault's ethics and that of Max Weber. Weber argued that the lack of meaning in the world, its "disenchantment," entails that we must assume ethical responsibility for the meaning and values we choose to bestow on it. Although Foucault would reject the existentialist individualism implicit in Weber's account, there are strong similarities between the two positions. Each tries to grapple with the loss of meaning in the modern world and attempts to fashion an ethics that addresses this loss.

In his more recent work Foucault has a good deal to say about ethics. The goal of his last three books is to trace the connection between ethics and the subject that has dominated Western thought. These works provide a sustained argument for the relevance of Foucault's work for ethical inquiry. In an article devoted to the issues of ethics and freedom, Foucault summarizes these arguments and deals directly with critics who accuse him of having no ethics. He argues that to assert, as he does, that relations of power are everywhere is not to assert that there is no freedom (1987a: 124). Power produces not only domination but also resistance to domination – freedom. Appealing to the Greek notion of *ethos*, Foucault asserts that ethics is always a practice, a way of being. For the Greeks a man with a good ethos was a man who was practicing freedom (1987a: 117). It is this notion of ethics that Foucault wants to explore, a notion of ethics as a way of living with others rather than some abstract notion of "freedom." He asserts: "It seems to me that to use this ethical problem of the definition of the practice of freedom is more important than the affirmation (and repetitions, at that) that sexuality and desire must be set free" (1987a: 114). Coming back to the question of practices of power, he concludes: "The problem is not of trying to dissolve them in the utopia of a perfectly transparent communication, but to give one's self the rules of law, the techniques of management, and also the ethics, the *ethos*, the practice of self which would allow these games of power to be played with a minimum of domination" (1987a: 129). Foucault's argument that ethics is a practice embedded in social life and history precludes the common definition of freedom as liberation. He argues that the problem with "liberation" movements is that they presuppose an essential human subject that must be liberated. Foucault argues instead that, in order to be ethical beings, we must figure out the practice of freedom and how to employ it.[8]

Far from precluding a feminist perspective, Foucault's account is remarkably appropriate to feminist concerns. His perspective on ethics is compatible with Wittgenstein's understanding of language games, which I will use to develop a reconstructed feminist moral theory in the next chapter. Foucault suggests that ethics is both a discourse and a practice, because language is a way of life embedded in history and culture. Foucault's perspective is also compatible with Gilligan's approach. Gilligan details the way in which women have been excluded from the discourse of morality, marginalized to the edges of ethics. Yet women today are employing subjugated discourses to claim a moral space and define a practice of freedom, an ethics appropriate to their needs. They are doing so by employing the discursive tools available to them, not by appealing to some abstract notion of freedom and liberation. Furthermore, in order to analyze the practice of ethics, feminist moral theorists have set themselves the task of examining what we actually *do* when confronted with moral dilemmas. This is particularly evident in Gilligan's work: her goal is to examine moral practices and listen to moral voices. The moral voices she hears have been heard before: the inferiority of women's moral voice has been documented for centuries. By interpreting these voices in a new way, however, by defining them as valid and equal to the dominant moral voice, Gilligan has revolutionized our understanding of morality and defined a new practice of ethics.[9]

The third charge frequently leveled at a postmodern theory of the subject is that it obviates the possibility of resistance. Foucault's definition of the subject as an act of self-creation provides an answer to this charge as well. The self-creating subject, the subject that pieces together elements of subjectivity from the discursive tools available, is a subject capable of resistance. The resistant subject is one that refuses to be scripted by the dominant discourse and turns instead to subjugated knowledges to fashion alternative discourses of subjectivity. Foucault's understanding of the resistant subject is informed by his concept of "local resistance." Against those who claim that his approach entails political quiescence, Foucault argues that it is not necessary to appeal to universalistic concepts of truth and knowledge in order to ground political action (1980: 81). He even goes so far as to assert that universalistic concepts actually impede political action rather than foster it (1991). He argues instead that resistance arises at the site of repression. It is necessarily local, because repression itself is always specific and local. The same applies to the subject. The resistant subject need not appeal to a given subjectivity or an abstract notion of freedom to ground resistance. Rather, resistance can be constructed from the discursive mix, particularly from marginalized subjectivities, that is available locally.

Bakhtin's theory of language provides a linguistic explanation of how Foucault's theory of resistance operates. Bakhtin identifies the heteroglossia of language as the site of the possibility of resistance:

> Thus at any moment of its historical existence, language is heteroglot from top to bottom: it represents the co-existence of socio-ideological contradictions between present and past, between different socio-ideological groups in the present and the past, between differing epochs of the past, between different socio-ideological groups in the present, between tendencies, schools, circles and so forth, all given a bodily form. These "languages" of heteroglossia intersect each other in a variety of ways, forming new socially typifying "languages." (1981: 291)

The "new socially typifying 'languages'" that result from this process can be languages of resistance. The emergence of a feminist language of resistance is an excellent example of how this process occurs. But, like any other language of resistance, it is not created *ex nihilo*. Rather, "something created is always created out of something given" (Bakhtin 1986: 120). The resistant discourses of feminism and the resisting feminist subject were fashioned from our discursive configurations; they could arise in no other way.

The "discursive subject" that I am formulating here draws heavily on these elements of Foucault's theory. Ultimately, the question of whether this discursive subject or Foucault's subject is "postmodern" is unimportant. Engaging in contentious debates about the modern versus the postmodern subject in feminist theory is neither necessary nor fruitful. By advancing the concept of the discursive subject, I am not siding with the postmoderns against the moderns but, rather, advancing an argument from a feminist perspective that I would like other feminists to consider on its own merits.[10]

Feminist theories of the subject

How to formulate a theory of subjectivity has always been problematic for modern Western feminism. The reason for this is not hard to identify: the Western philosophical tradition that has defined women as inferior and excluded them from the political and moral realms is grounded in a concept of the subject that is inherently masculine. Thus, in their ongoing attempts to fit women into this tradition, feminists have been stopped at every turn by the insuperable obstacle of the masculine subject. In the early years of the modern feminist movement, feminists were eager to appropriate both the liberal and the socialist

subject for their purposes. That these appropriations would be unsuc-
cessful, however, was evident from the beginning. Reading Mary
Wollstonecraft or John Stuart Mill, for example, reveals the awkward-
ness of their effort to fit women into the rational, autonomous definition of the subject that liberalism articulated.[11] These texts reveal that
women are excluded from these discourses because they lack the basic
criterion of admission: masculine subjectivity.

The discovery of this exclusion led feminists to attempt to articulate
a specifically feminine subject, to define "woman" in universal terms
that could counter the universalism of the masculine subject. Radical
feminists in particular have argued that we must revalorize the
feminine, to challenge the masculine values that inform the modernist
subject with the superior feminine values of "essential woman." Most
recently, with the advent of poststructuralist and postmodern critiques
of the modernist subject, feminist theories of the subject have taken
another turn. The attack on any essentialist concept of the subject,
whether the allegedly neutral subject of modernity or the essentially
feminine subject of radical feminism, has generated a heated debate
among feminists. The questions raised in this debate go to the very
heart of the feminist enterprise. Is essentialism a useful or a dangerous
tactic for feminist theory? Is it premature or foolish to abandon the
concept of a fixed subject when women have never reaped the benefits
of such a subject? Does abandoning the modernist subject entail abandoning the autonomous agency that is the hallmark of that subject? If
so, does it also preclude a political agenda for feminism?

I will not attempt to answer all these questions in what follows.
Instead, I will argue for what I am calling the "discursive subject" as the
best tactic for addressing these issues in feminist theory. The principal
advantage of the discursive subject is that it moves out of the epistemological space defined by the modernist subject, an epistemological
space that excludes women. The discursive subject as I am articulating
it here necessitates a redefinition of agency and political action, one that
eschews the categories of the modernist subject. But it is a redefinition
that many feminists have been reluctant to accept. They insist that we
must retain elements of the modernist subject, specifically agency and
the possibility of principled political action, in order to provide the
grounding for feminist politics. In defense of the discursive subject, my
central argument is that it is not necessary to "borrow" agency and a
concept of political action from the modernist subject. Rather, I am
arguing that agency and action are themselves discursive products, not
the exclusive attributes of the modernist subject. Hence other discursive formations define these concepts differently and thus can provide
feminism with more appropriate tools for resistance.

My discussion of feminist approaches to subjectivity focuses on two
main issues: "essential woman" and what I have called the "dialectical"

subject. The contemporary debate within feminist theory with regard to essentialism revolves not so much around whether there is an essential feminine subject but whether *any* argument can be advanced for an essentialist concept of "woman." The feminist debate regarding essentialism was decisively altered in 1988 with the publication of Elizabeth Spelman's *Inessential Woman*. Spelman presents a powerful argument against adopting an essentialist concept of woman by asserting that such a concept necessarily results in a hierarchical ranking of categories of "woman": some women are defined as conforming to the category "true woman," while those who fall short of this ideal are ranked as inferior. Arguing that we must jettison any concept of "true woman," Spelman asserts that feminists must take differences among women seriously, that gender cannot be isolated from class and race and theorized separately (1988: 16). She also articulates the point that I made in the first chapter with regard to psychoanalytic theories of development: that in childhood girls learn not just how to be women, but how to be certain *kinds* of women; race and class enter in, as well as gender (1988: 85).

Persuasive as Spelman's argument is, doubts remain about the utility of positing an essential feminine subject. In *Essentially Speaking* (1989) Diana Fuss maintains that essentialism in feminist theory is an issue that refuses to die. She asserts that essentialism is neither inherently good nor inherently bad but, rather, is a concept that can be used either progressively or conservatively (1989: xi). She also makes the telling point that the dichotomy between essentialism and constructionism is a product of the binary thinking that is the cause of the problem that feminists face. She argues that deconstructionists who vehemently attack essentialism are themselves held captive by the essentialism/constructionism dichotomy that they seek to displace. Thus, although she appears to be offering a qualified defense of essentialism, in effect, she is offering an even more radical deconstruction of the concept. She claims that the deconstructionists have not moved beyond the epistemological boundaries of the essentialist subject, whereas her own analysis succeeds in accomplishing this goal.

One of the most persuasive arguments for retaining a concept of essential woman is that it is politically expedient to do so. Denise Riley (1988), Gayatri Spivak (1987), and Rosi Braidotti (1989) all offer compelling arguments for retaining essentialism as at least a provisional interventionist strategy. They maintain that although feminist theorists may understand all too well the liabilities of an essentialist feminine subject, it is nevertheless necessary for the present politics of women's liberation to retain this concept. These are powerful arguments that cannot be dismissed lightly. But two serious objections call them into question. First, their position conjures up the vision of an elite cadre of feminist theorists who comprehend the folly of an essentialist

argument but nevertheless dictate to the feminist political operative an
essentialist politics. The implicit assumption is that the rank and file are
not capable of understanding the epistemological nuances of their
position. Second, it assumes that women can only be united politically
through nature; that is, that unless women share a common nature,
they cannot share a common politics. That this assumption is false has
been illustrated by the experience of racial politics. It is widely accepted
by both scientists and members of minority racial groups that race is
not a "natural," or biological, fact but, rather, a social construction. Yet
this has not prevented a strong sense of identity and solidarity among
people of color. Nor has it prevented effective political action on the
part of racial minorities. The same can certainly be true for women. As
Donna Haraway (1985) argues, women can – and even should – be
linked through affinity and choice, not through identity and nature.

A consensus appears to be emerging on the issue of essentialism in
feminist theory: that we need to think seriously about differences,
rather than continuing to concentrate on essences. It may be that
feminist theory has reached a critical juncture, a point at which we can
discuss women's differences with greater confidence. Whereas in previous decades the discussion of women's differences was potentially
divisive and threatening, this is no longer the case; feminist theory
and politics have matured to the point that differences can be
acknowledged and explored. This conviction informs my discussion
of women's "different" moral voice. Once we have established that
there are different moral voices and have deconstructed the unitary
paradigm of modernist moral theory, we can go on to discuss the
differences among a plurality of moral voices. Nothing would be
gained in this discussion by conceptualizing the different voice as
"essentially female," nor by assuming that it is characteristic of all
women. Furthermore, having established the relational constitution
of moral voices, it would be exceedingly odd if we then concluded
that gender is the only variable in their formation. Feminist theory
can benefit enormously from examining how moral discourses are
constructed and what factors, gender among them, constitute moral
subjectivity.

The second issue that is central to contemporary discussions of
the subject in feminist theory is that of the "dialectical subject."[12] The
dialectical subject has arisen primarily as an attempt to deal with a
problem that has concerned feminist theorists of the subject since the
rise of postmodern and poststructuralist critiques: agency. Although
the issues raised in this discussion are complex and wide-ranging, the
basic question is quite simple: does positing the agency of the subject,
particularly moral and political agency, necessarily entail recourse to
some version of the Cartesian, modernist subject? A recent book on
gender identity by Tamsin Lorraine (1990) provides a representative

statement of this issue. Lorraine argues that there are two contemporary views of the subject: the humanist subject – a unified, rational, self-interested agent – and the postmodern or poststructuralist subject – a constructed self with no coherent account of freedom, responsibility, or authenticity (1990: 2). Lorraine attempts to deal with the problem of these two opposing concepts by positing a subject that combines elements of both. What emerges is what I am calling the "dialectical subject." Lorraine characterizes this subject as an entity that is both produced by and produces social codes. She defines these forces in dialectical terms, claiming that social codes influence human subjects and human subjects influence social codes (1990: 3). The definition of agency that arises from this concept privileges the producing side of the dialectic. For Lorraine, an intentional agent requires a subject that perceives itself as having some degree of autonomy and efficacy in the world (1990: 15).

Lorraine's attempt to integrate elements of the Cartesian, modernist subject with the constructed subject that is identified with post-modernism or poststructuralism has become increasingly popular in recent feminist theory. Two key assumptions ground this approach. First, theorists who argue for a dialectical subject assume that agency is the sole province of the modernist subject and, conversely, that the constructed subject is a social dupe. Thus they assume that if feminists are to retain any vestige of autonomy in the subject they theorize, they must retain at least some elements of the modernist subject. The second assumption informing this debate is that the relationship between the modernist and the constructed subject is a binary opposition that must be resolved dialectically. Dialectical logic dictates that opposites be synthesized in a new, truer concept that embraces the truths of each side of the opposition – hence the dialectical subject.

I think that this debate is wrong-headed for a number of related and complicated reasons. In my discussion of the debate my goal is to specify those reasons and hence to shift the focus of the debate. My primary objection to the debate is that the logic that informs it is thoroughly modernist. The dichotomy that is its centerpiece – the constituting versus the constituted subject – is a modernist dichotomy that presents an impossible choice for feminist theory: a choice between transcendent subjects and social dupes. Furthermore, the dialectical logic that fuels the debate is likewise modernist. It dictates that the opposites be synthesized, their contradictions resolved. One of the results of this dialectical logic is that all postmodern theories of the subject are seen as defining a constituted subject, a social dupe, and are hence rejected. In other words, the postmodern subject is defined in terms of this modernist dichotomy.

This characterization of the postmodern subject ignores the paradigm shift that this subject effects. The modernist and the postmodernist subject are not opposites, because they do not inhabit the same epistemological space. The epistemology informing the modernist subject assumes that knowledge is either absolute or relative and action either autonomous or determined. The epistemology informing the postmodern subject displaces, rather than takes issue with, this opposition. It assumes that knowledge is a product of discourses that are historically and culturally constituted; it defines action as produced by agents who utilize the discursive tools available to them. Another way of putting this is that modern and postmodern approaches to the subject represent two irreconcilable paradigms. Competing paradigms cannot be synthesized, resolved into a more final truth, for they represent incompatible ways of seeing the world. A corollary of this thesis is that agency is not the sole province of the modernist subject, the transcendent presupposition of all subjectivity but, rather, that agency is a function of discursive formations. The disembodied agency of the Cartesian subject is not the paradigm of all agency but merely one of its manifestations. Other discourses produce other kinds of agency, specific to the discourse in question. My position, then, is that we should stop arguing endlessly about whether feminist theory should adopt a constituting or a constituted subject or some synthesis of the two. Rather, we should embrace the new paradigm that is emerging and explore questions of agency and action within the parameters of that paradigm.

In order to illustrate the problems implicit in the dialectical approach to the subject in feminist theory, I will look closely at three representative formulations of this position. Feminist constructions of the subject that can be labeled dialectical are by no means monolithic. Whereas some feminists who construct a dialectical theory of the subject emphasize the modernist pole of the dichotomy, others produce accounts that are heavily weighted in favor of the constructionist pole. A theorist who is representative of the first group is Diana Meyers. In her book *Self, Society and Personal Choice* (1989) Meyers's stated goal is to articulate a position between the two extremes of an essentialist, pre-social concept of the subject (the disembodied self of the Kantian tradition) and a wholly constructed subject incapable of agency. Her aim is to describe a subject that is a dialectical compromise between the two extremes. Meyers employs both essentialist and constructionist language in her description: she states that the "true self" is not immune to social influences yet is "someone who lives at least part of the time by his or her own lights" (1989: 20); similarly she declares that the "free agent" is not untainted by social influences (1989: 42). In all these formulations Meyers's goal is to reject the modernist understanding of a pre-social core self, opting instead for a concept that involves an interaction between social experience and personal choice (1989: 96). This goal is most clearly expressed in her notion of a "life plan." No sane person, she insists, is without a life plan (1989: 51). Persons are able to formulate life plans by means of what she calls "autonomy competency." This concept, she claims, avoids the problem of a static, authentic self. Autonomous people are those who are capable of fashioning their lives with the means at their disposal (1989: 55). "The authentic self is the evolving collection of traits that emerges when someone exercises autonomy competency" (1989: 76).

Although Meyers's aim is to construct a compromise subject that effects a dialectical interaction between the constituted and the constituting subject, the balance between the two shifts as her argument progresses. In the latter half of the book, the constituting subject, in the guise of a quasi-Kantian subject, increasingly obscures the constituted subject. Pivotal in this shift is Meyers's emphasis on autonomy as the essence of the subject she advocates. She rejects out of hand the feminist notion that autonomy and the self-respect it generates are masculinist concepts (1989: 208). Instead, she appeals to Kant to establish a counterargument: only the morally autonomous person is worthy of self-respect (1989: 224). The key to the definition of the subject, she argues, hinges on the existence of choice. She applies this insight specifically to the case of women: women who cannot choose their social roles cannot attain autonomy or self-respect (1989: 232). The Kantian tenor of Meyers's argument leads her to an objectivist stance on moral judgments, specifically to a discussion of "deficient values" (1989: 225). What we are left with at the end of the book is a "feminist" subject defined almost exclusively in terms of autonomy, self-respect, and personal choice, a subject who, although influenced by social forces, lives by her "own lights" and, most important, *chooses* her social role.

Meyers's subject is an extreme example of the dialectical subject, but it nevertheless illustrates some of the characteristic problems of this concept for feminist theory. First, Meyers has in effect abandoned her own dialectical approach in the course of her argument. The subject she articulates amounts to only a slight variant of the Kantian subject on which she relies to express her central themes. It is a subject that is only marginally affected by social forces, a subject that must overcome those forces to achieve autonomy. Second, and more important, Meyers fails to address feminist criticisms of this subject. She almost cavalierly dismisses the feminist claim that autonomy is a masculinist characteristic, assuming instead that autonomy is central to all definitions of the self. The argument that autonomy, like rationality, has been defined as exclusive to the masculine realm in Western thought is a powerful one, buttressed by work in philosophy (Lloyd 1984) as well as psychology (Chodorow 1978). At the very least, Meyers should make an attempt to refute these arguments. Third, she stresses personal choice in a way that denies autonomy, her criterion for true subjectivity, to most, if not all, women *and* men. Clearly, none of us chooses her social role in complete freedom; all choices are socially constrained. Just as clearly, some choices of social role are more constrained than others, with male upper- and middle-class whites in the West having the most choice. Meyers's concept, then, is both ethnocentric and class-bound, restricting true subjectivity to this privileged group. Finally, the status of the subject she articulates, a subject who is "influenced" by social forces, is unclear. If this self is not the pre-social core of the Kantian tradition, then who is she, or he? Meyers insists that, in order for an interaction between the true self and social forces to occur, there must be a "true self" to do the interacting. But she does not adequately define the nature of this "true self."

Another feminist theorist who tries to establish a dialectical interaction between elements of an essential subject and a constructed subject is Linda Alcoff (1988). Unlike Meyers, however, Alcoff is concerned to bridge the gap not between the modernist (Kantian) subject and a constructed subject but between the essentialist feminine subject of what she calls the "cultural feminists" and the subject of postmodernism. Central to her argument is her identification of the postmodern subject as wholly constructed. She thus rejects the "nominalism" of postmodernism, which, she claims, denies gender, subjectivity, and hence agency. But she is also critical of feminist essentialism, which, in her view, denies the effect of social influences and posits an untenable unitary female essence. Alcoff's means of bridging the gap between these two subjects is to posit an interaction between what, following Teresa de Lauretis, she calls inner and outer worlds: the inner world of subjectivity and the outer world of social forces. This compromise allows her to define femininity as constituted yet agentic: feminine subjects rearticulate their subjectivity from the historical experience of women through political practice (1988: 424). She concludes by arguing, against the essentialists, that "woman" is not a fixed set of attributes but a particular position in historical reality. Against the postmoderns, she argues that woman *does* have an identity, but an identity that she creates from the elements available to her in a social context (1988: 433–4).

Although on the surface Alcoff, like Meyers, claims to be articulating a dialectical subject that includes elements of essentialism and constructionism, the tone of her argument differs significantly from that of Meyers. Unlike Meyers, who emphasizes the constituting subject, Alcoff moves toward the opposite pole, the constituted subject. She argues that woman creates her identity from the mix of discursive forces available to her in her historical situation. While Alcoff retains a quasi-essentialist concept of subjectivity in her assertion of an "inner world" and thus follows the dialectical pattern, there is another sense in which her approach is moving into a different epistemological space. This movement is significant. Although her theory ostensibly remains within the parameters of dialectical logic, elements of it violate that logic and call into question dialectical epistemology. As a result, it is possible to posit an alternative reading of Alcoff that sees her as edging toward a new concept of creativity and agency that is not tied to the constituting subject. Likewise, her attempt to articulate a concept of feminine identity as formed from the elements of a given historical situation can be interpreted as a way of defining identity apart from the concept of a fixed essence. The concept of agency that Alcoff employs is a "rearticulation" within a concrete historical experience. This is a far cry from the quasi-abstract autonomy posited by Meyers.

The concept of a dialectic between inner and outer worlds that Alcoff employs originates in the work of Teresa de Lauretis. Like Alcoff, de Lauretis is explicitly arguing for a dialectical subject. But, also like Alcoff, de Lauretis is at the same time moving beyond a dialectical approach. Her dialectical definition of the subject is expressed in various ways: as an interaction of inner and outer worlds (1984: 182) and as each individual's "personal subjective engagement" with the world forming the basis of her identity (1984: 10). But the emphasis on dialectics is not the only component of de Lauretis's work; other components challenge the rigid dichotomies of modernist thought. Her emphasis, like Alcoff's, is on the constituted pole of the constituting/constituted dichotomy. Yet her discussion of the constituted subject violates the logic of the dichotomy she claims to espouse. She argues that "the social being is constructed day by day as the point of articulation of ideological formations, an always provisional encounter of subject and codes at the historical (therefore changing) intersection of social formations and her or his personal history. While codes and social formations define positions of meaning, the individual reworks those positions into a personal, subjective construction" (1984: 14).

In a somewhat later work de Lauretis asserts that her aim is to construct a new notion of identity, one that is "multiple and self-contradictory and shifting." Identity, she claims, is "reclaimed from a history of multiple assimilations" (1986: 9). The feminine subject is thus one that is constituted across a number of discourses, discourses that frequently conflict with one another (1987: x). De Lauretis defines feminist theory as residing both inside and outside its own social and discursive determinations (1990: 116). Identifying the feminist subject as "eccentric," she argues that it is "attained through practices of political and personal displacement across boundaries between sociosexual identities and communities, between bodies and discourses" (1990: 145). The "new" subject that she articulates in these passages appears to be one that breaks away from the modernist dichotomy of constituted/constituting. Like Alcoff, de Lauretis is exploding the boundaries of this dichotomy, despite her nominal adherence to it. In effect she is exploring what subjectivity might look like from outside modernist dichotomies.

She does not embrace the postmodern project of the deconstruction of modernist discourse, however. She clearly states her reason for rejecting the postmodern move: like Alcoff and Meyers, she sees postmodernism as advocating a passive nonsubject that is unaccept- able to feminism. She argues that postmodernism entails a denial of identity for women and hence a denial of political agency. She expresses a particular animosity toward Foucault, who, she claims, excludes the notion of gender from his theory altogether (1987: 3) and, by failing to provide for political agency, ends up as a "paradoxical conservative" (1984: 94). The conviction that postmodernism obviates subjectivity prevents de Lauretis from fully exploring a new paradigm of subjectivity that would displace the modernist dichotomy of consti- tuting/constituted. It also prevents her from exploring a concept of agency that is not defined by this dichotomy and explains why she retains, albeit minimally, a concept of the constituting subject. Even though she has taken significant steps away from the modernist sub- ject, a residue remains in her attachment to the modernist concept of political agency.

This discussion of Meyers, Alcoff, and de Lauretis suggests two conclusions. First, it reveals the ongoing appeal of a notion of an "inner self" that is the legacy of the modernist tradition of the subject. The dialectical approach that these theorists articulate is a compromise that retains a notion of this inner self (severely modified in the cases of Alcoff and de Lauretis) but does not abandon it altogether. Second, it reveals the deep distrust of many feminist theorists of a "postmodern" approach. Meyers, Alcoff, and de Lauretis fault postmodernism for failing to provide a coherent concept of the subject and hence of politi- cal agency. That postmodern approaches to the subject are perceived as both a threat and an opportunity for feminism is evident in the intense debate they have generated in feminist theory.

I would like to suggest that we refocus this debate. My first reason is that much of the debate is misconceived. Most of the participants equate postmodern theories of subjectivity with the constituted subject of modernist epistemology. This entails that much of the debate revolves around a straw man (or woman?): the allegedly passive postmodern subject. My position, by contrast, is that postmodern theories of subjectivity displace modernist epistemology. My second reason is that even those who understand that the postmodern theory of subjectivity constitutes a new paradigm are reluctant to embrace that paradigm because of the range of theories classified as "postmodern." As a counter I suggest that we stop arguing about whether feminism should adopt a "postmodern" theory of subjectivity and instead look at individual theories on their own merits. This is my goal in what follows. I contend that some, although not all, theories of subjectivity that fall under the "postmodern" label are useful for feminism. I want to make a case for employing these theories in the definition of a feminist, discursive subject.

For many Anglo-American feminists, their first introduction to postmodern themes came from so-called French feminists. This in itself has created a great deal of confusion. There are significant differences among the theorists who fall under this label and, to complicate things further, several of them refuse the label "feminist." More important, perhaps, persistent misinterpretations of these theorists have prejudiced many Anglo-American theorists against any approach labeled "postmodern." But, despite the difficulties, these French theorists, particularly Irigaray, Cixous, and Kristeva, have established a number of themes that have transformed discussion of the subject in feminism. These themes also provide the basis for a new approach to the moral subject.

The first and most central theme of these theorists is the significance of discourse and the link between discourse and subjectivity. Hélène Cixous puts this point most eloquently:

> What I call "feminine" and "masculine" is the relationship to pleasure, the relationship to speaking, because we are born into language, and I cannot do otherwise than to find myself before words; we cannot get rid of them, they are there. We could change them, we could put signs in their place, but they would just become closed, just as immobile and petrifying as the words "masculine" and "feminine" and would lay down the law to us. So there is nothing to be done except to shake them like apple trees all the time. (1988: 15)

Julia Kristeva also has much to say about discourse. She avoids the pitfall of searching for woman's identity by speculating instead on woman's discourse. But the theorist who has done most to revolutionize discussion of the feminine subject is Luce Irigaray. Irigaray maintains that, first and foremost, our task as feminists is to interrogate philosophical discourse, to uncover the coherence of discursive utterance (1985b: 74). Discourses, she claims, both produce and reproduce subjects. But the discursive mechanism that she uncovers in her analysis defines women as a lack, as a deficiency. What is necessary, then, is to destroy this discursive mechanism; not to create a "theory of woman" but to secure a place for the feminine within sexual difference (1985b: 159). The discursive mechanism as we know it can define the feminine only in terms of the masculine, as "lack." What is needed instead, Irigaray declares, is to seek a nonhierarchical articulation of the masculine/feminine opposition in language (1985b: 162). But she also identifies the principal difficulty of this approach: a feminine syntax will not be easy to articulate because it must necessarily reject the subject/object dichotomy on which our present syntax is founded (1985b: 134).

The exploration of the feminine subject by these theorists has taken different forms. Irigaray emphasizes woman's *jouissance* as a way of refusing the binary discourse of masculine subjectivity (1985a: 230). Kristeva focuses on the semiotic/symbolic distinction and the realm of the maternal to define the feminine subject (1988: 23). One of the elements shared by all these approaches provides a second theme of these accounts: an emphasis on psychoanalysis and, specifically, a condemnation of the psychoanalytic tradition for failing to provide an understanding of the feminine. Irigaray is particularly vehement in her attack on Freud's construction of feminine subjectivity. She concludes her diatribe against psychoanalytic theories of the subject by arguing that *any* theory of the subject is inherently masculine. When women submit to such theories, she argues, they give up their own relationship to the imaginary; women as *not* subjects provides the ground for the masculine subject (1985a: 133).

The vehemence of Irigaray's attack on the masculine discourse of the subject indicates a third theme of this literature: a redefinition of the nature of resistance. In a now famous passage that has become a sort of call to arms for her followers, Irigaray declares: "In other words, the issue is not one of elaborating a new theory of which woman would be the *subject* or the *object*, but of jamming the theoretical machinery itself, of suspending its pretensions, to the production of a truth and a meaning that are excessively univocal" (1985b: 78). What we must do, she maintains, is to engage in "disruptive excess," to cast phallocentrism loose from its moorings and open up the possibility of a different language (1985b: 80). We must "Turn everything upside down, inside out, back to front. *Rack it with radical convulsions*" (1985a: 142).[13] In a similar vein, Kristeva (1984) argues that linguistic (discursive) change *is* social and political change – they are two sides of the same coin.

The French feminists have had a mixed reception among Anglo-American feminists. It is significant that their critics have characterized them in diametrically opposed terms. On the one hand, the French feminists have been accused of being "essentialist," of attempting to replace phallocentrism with gynocentrism, particularly by equating the feminine with the maternal.[14] On the other hand, these same theorists have been accused of obviating the possibility of defining "woman" at all, by emphasizing the discursive constitution of the feminine. The contradictory nature of these criticisms is revealing. It indicates that these theorists have significantly changed the terms of the debate, that they have quite effectively "jammed the theoretical machinery" not only of the masculinist tradition but also of previous feminist theory.

The work of Cixous, Irigaray, and Kristeva has thus changed the discussion of the feminist subject in significant and positive ways. Through their emphasis on psychoanalysis, they have encouraged feminists to define the subject in developmental and constitutive terms. In their theories subjects do not spring full-blown from some essential core of subjectivity. Rather, they are discursively and culturally constituted, a product of societal forces. Furthermore, these theorists have succeeded in defining a concept of resistance that is not rooted in the Cartesian, autonomous, agentic subject. For the modernist, resistance is predicated on a subject that is both agentic and autonomous, a subject that speaks from an Archimedean point of objectivity. Against this, these feminist theorists have argued that resistance is simultaneously discursive and political and that these two elements cannot be neatly separated. Resistance involves appealing to the discursive tools available to us and, most important, reshuffling them to suit our purposes. The French feminists have only begun the difficult task of identifying this non-Cartesian definition of resistance. The value of their work is that, like that of Foucault, they have encouraged us to think about discursive resistance as "real" resistance, not "mere words."

If, for many feminists, postmodern themes first came to their attention through the work of these French feminists, it is no longer the case that the latter define the agenda of what might be called postmodern feminism. Feminists inspired by postmodern themes have produced a diverse array of analyses. Some have turned to the Foucaultian theme of biopower and have examined the way in which the discourses of femininity are inscribed in the female body (Diamond and Quinby 1988). Others have adopted the psychoanalytic themes of the French feminists to develop a distinctive approach to feminist theory (Flax 1990). What unites these diverse analyses is the emphasis on discourse. All these theorists reject the foundationalism implicit not only in modernist concepts of the subject but also in essentialist feminist concepts. An analysis of these approaches reveals that the feminist convictions of these theorists lead to a transformation of the postmodern themes they adopt. It is not the case, as some critics have claimed, that feminists who employ postmodern themes subsume feminism under the "male voice" of postmodernism (Brodribb 1992: xvi). Rather, feminist theorists have put postmodern themes to distinctly feminist uses. This is particularly evident in feminists' attempts to deal with a criticism frequently leveled at postmodern approaches: nominalism, the claim that postmodernism reduces everything to "mere" discourse. While many postmodern thinkers, as their critics have noted, make no attempt to connect their abstract analyses to any practical political positions, feminist theorists are very concerned to make this connection. This is a central aspect of the transformation of postmodern theories by feminist thinkers.

Postmodern themes appear in feminist arguments in a variety of forms. Susan Jarratt's (1990) position is one of the most sweeping: she asserts that rhetoric and feminism have shared the status of "other" since the beginnings of Western thought and that today's feminists are sophists in that they describe rhetorical (discursive) solutions to the problem of defining a feminist theory with the power to change women's lives. Feminist literary critics, in theorizing about women's autobiographies, have turned to theories of discourse to explain how subjectivities are created, even in the act of writing one's own life (Brodzki and Schenck 1988). Political theorist Kathy Ferguson has argued that deconstructing gender through discursive and genealogical processes "loosens the hold of gender on life and meaning" (1989: 5). This process, she claims, calls not for the end of the subject but for a new form of subjectivity (1989: 35). In her most recent work she argues for what she calls "mobile subjectivities": "mobile subjectivities locate themselves in relation to the moving trajectories of power and resistance via circumstances of proximity and distance, restlessness and rootedness, separation and connection" (1993: 161); they "ride on the ready-made conversations/contestations" among the different approaches to feminist theory (1993: 154). Film critic Kaja Silverman (1988) takes the line that a discursive approach to feminism does not entail nominalism or the denial of the body. Rather, it entails that, although the body is prior to discourse, it can only be articulated through discourse as male or female.

Finally, the emphasis on discourse has led feminist theorists to focus on differences among women as well as the constitutive power of discursive formations. The discourses of femininity are multiple. Women are scripted not only as "woman," although this does occur, but as women of a particular type: white, nonwhite, lesbian, middle-class (Spelman 1988; Fraser 1991c: 178). Nancy Fraser nicely illustrates the point I am making here. Sorting through the various aspects of postmodern thought, she catalogs those that feminists have found useful, as well as those they have rejected. She concludes:

> Complex, shifting, discursively constructed social identities provide an alternative to reified, essentialist conceptions of gender identity, on the one hand, and to simple negations and dispersals of identity on the other. They thus permit us to navigate safely between the twin shoals of essentialism and nominalism, between reifying women's identity under stereotypes of femininity, on the one hand, and dissolving them into sheer nullity and oblivion on the other. (1991c: 191)

The appropriation of postmodern concepts for distinctively feminist purposes is perhaps most evident in feminist theorists' attempts to address the central problem raised by postmodern theories: the alleged political quiescence of postmodern thought.[15] Against this charge, feminist theorists who employ postmodern concepts have maintained that although some aspects of postmodern thought are nihilistic and even misogynist, this does not entail that all approaches labeled postmodern are antithetical to feminist goals. Several feminists have adopted the argument I have presented here: that Foucault's discursive strategies provide a possible basis for a feminist theory of resistance (Sawicki 1991; Diamond and Quinby 1988). Teresa Ebert's (1991) argument is particularly relevant in this context. Although she rejects Foucault's approach, she accepts the argument that postmodernism is not all of a piece. She distinguishes two strands of postmodernism: ludic postmodernism, which defines reality as a theater for free-floating play, and resistance postmodernism, which defines language as acquiring meaning through its place in the social structure. She argues that whereas ludic postmodernism dismantles politics itself, resistance postmodernism has within it the potential to define a postmodern feminism in more social and political terms, a "postmodern materialist feminist theory" (1991: 886). Central to her argument is the claim that postmodern strategies, by destabilizing the identity of "woman," can expose the illusions of patriarchy (1991: 896).[16]

The path-breaking work of Donna Haraway and Judith Butler illustrates the advantages of employing postmodern approaches to the question of the feminist subject. Haraway is best known for her innovative work in feminist philosophy of science, but her interest in the epistemology of science has led her to consider the question of the subject as well. This move is by no means mere happenstance. Haraway's work offers a graphic illustration of the thesis which I am defending: that subjectivity and epistemology are inextricably intertwined. Haraway's philosophy of science consists of a sustained critique of positivist science, its absolutism and universalism and the misogynism it has produced. Her approach to questions of subjectivity is informed by this critique. She attempts to deconstruct the "Western self" and replace the transcendent, absolute, unitary subject with a "split and contradictory self" (1988: 586).

The connection that Haraway posits between the epistemology of science and subjectivity is most evident in her famous essay "A Manifesto for Cyborgs" (1985). Her goal in this essay is to build an "ironic political myth" faithful to feminism, socialism, and materialism (1985: 65). She posits a "cyborg," half man and half machine, creature of a post-gender world. Cyborg politics, she insists, resists translating everything into a single code, it rejects the ideal of perfect communication (1985: 95). What is evident in this analysis is that Haraway's feminist critique of positivist science is inseparable from a critique of the transcendent subject that makes that science possible. The "cyborg" she posits is not only post-positivist, it is post-Cartesian as well.

Haraway further develops her definition of a post-Cartesian feminist subject in a later essay that also posits a connection between epistemology and subjectivity. In "Situated Knowledges" (1988) her goal is to define a concept of objectivity for feminism that is not universal and transcendent; central to that effort is the articulation of an alternative to the transcendent subject. She defines feminist objectivity as situated, perspectival knowledge, a limited location rather than an Archimedean point. This situatedness also informs her definition of the subject. The "split and contradictory self" she advocates is about "heterogeneous multiplicities that are simultaneously salient and incapable of being squashed into isomorphic slots" (1988: 586). She concludes: "Subjectivity is multidimensional. . . . The knowing self is partial in all its guises, never finished, whole, simply there and original; it is always constructed, situated together imperfectly, and *therefore* able to join with another, to see together without claiming to be another" (1988: 586).

There are several noteworthy aspects to the approach Haraway outlines here. First, it is clear that she is redefining, not abandoning, subjectivity. Many critics of postmodernism claim that all postmodern approaches entail a subjectless position because they present the subject as a "fiction." Haraway's approach confounds this criticism. For, although Haraway uncovers the fiction of the Cartesian subject and the falsity of the claim that this subject is the paradigm of all subjectivity, she does not claim that subjectivity itself is a fiction. On the contrary, her situated subject is still very much a subject. Second, Haraway's subject is one that is suited to the political needs of feminism. Even though she argues that there is no "essential woman," she claims that situated subjects can join together into a collective subject for political purposes. Central to her argument is the claim that feminists need not rely on "nature" or "essence" to act together politically. Finally, for Haraway, both knowledge and subjects are situated: epistemology defines subjectivity. She thus illustrates very clearly the paradigm shift that I am describing. Deconstructing one aspect of the edifice of modernity necessitates deconstructing all the other aspects: situated knowledge entails situated subjects; it obviates the possibility of the Archimedean point that produces not only objective knowledge but the "moral point of view" as well. It is significant that Haraway uses the phrase "the view from somewhere" in describing her subject, thereby implying that "the view from nowhere" that constitutes the necessary basis of modernist moral theory rests on very different epistemological grounds.

Articulating a concept of subjectivity that reveals the fiction of the Cartesian subject while at the same time addressing the political needs of feminism is the project of Judith Butler's work as well. In her influential book *Gender Trouble* (1990a) and a number of related essays,

Butler addresses the issues that are central to many feminists' criticism of postmodernism. One of the most pivotal of these is the claim that we need a concept of "woman" if we are to effect the liberation of women. Butler counters this with the assertion that gender coherence is a regulatory fiction, not the common point of our liberation (1990b: 339). She presents an argument that parallels Foucault's criticism of universal concepts in political theory. She asserts that relying on the category of "woman" or gender coherency takes feminism away from its proper aim: the critical genealogy of gender constructs (1990a: 5–6). Her argument entails that unless we deconstruct the category "woman," we cannot even begin the task of loosening the hold of gender categories on our thought. In her view, the deconstruction of "woman" is the necessary beginning of feminist politics, not its destruction. She goes on to attack the notion that feminism needs any grounding at all, whether in "natural sex," the body, or "woman." She even opposes one of the long-standing pillars of feminist theory, the sex/gender distinction. Gender, she claims, is the discursive/cultural means whereby "natural sex" is produced (1990a: 7). The body is not a given entity, but the "theater of gender," the site of received cultural meaning (1989: 258). Gender is always a doing, but not by a subject ("woman") who precedes the deed (1990a: 25). In an argument that resembles Foucault's claim that subjectivity is a work of art, she asserts that gender is a project, a skill, a pursuit, an enterprise (1989: 256).

The aspect of Butler's work that is most relevant to my concerns is her discussion of agency. The debate over agency, Butler realizes, is tied to the long-standing issue of free will and determinism. Within the parameters of modernist epistemology, the claim that a subject is constructed entails that it is incapable of free will and hence of agency. Butler attempts to deconstruct the dichotomy between the constituting agentic subject and the constituted nonagentic subject by redefining agency. To claim that a subject is constituted, she asserts, is to claim not that it is determined but, rather, that the constituted character of the subject is the precondition of agency (1991: 157). Challenging the notion that agency must be grounded in a pre-discursive "I," Butler claims instead that "There is no self that is prior to the convergence or who maintains 'integrity' prior to its entrance into this conflictual cultural field. There is only a taking up of the tools where they lie, where the very 'taking up' is enabled by the tools lying there" (1990a: 145). And, further, "Construction is not opposed to agency, it is the necessary scene of agency, the very terms in which agency is articulated and becomes culturally intelligible" (1990a: 147).

The work of Butler and Haraway demonstrates the usefulness of employing postmodern concepts to construct a feminist subject. The subject they articulate is situated but no social dupe. Rather, she is a subject who refuses to play the role scripted for her. She is a resistant subject, a subject who is capable of political actions with other women, even though her subjectivity may differ from theirs. It is my goal to build on this concept of the subject in my attempt to define moral subjectivity. Central to this concept is the redefinition of agency. Along with Butler, I define agency as a product of discourses, a definition that strips it of its transcendental trappings and its necessary connection with the modernist subject. Agency is not the transcendental presupposition of subjectivity but, rather, a discursive product that varies from discourse to discourse. This thesis is particularly significant when applied to the question of moral subjectivity and moral agency. Modernist discourse links moral agency to the Cartesian subject. The approach described here suggests instead that different moral discourses define different kinds of moral agency. On this conception, moral agency is not restricted to the "justice voice" of the modernist moral tradition; rather, it is expressed in many different moral voices. Gilligan has shown that gender plays a major role in the constitution of moral voice; I have argued that factors such as race and class are also constitutive. These speculations open up exciting new possibilities for moral theory. They suggest a new array of definitions for moral voices and a new approach to the articulation of moral subjectivity.

Race, ethnicity, and subjectivity

During the last decade, feminist theory has been revolutionized by an issue that is still at the forefront of feminist discussions: the intersection of gender and race/ethnicity. The issue first arose in the political arena, with the claim by women of color that the feminist movement was dominated by white, middle-class women. Subsequently this political protest came to affect theoretical discussions as well. Women of color have claimed that feminist theory is about white, middle-class women and that their own voices have been silenced in both theory and practice. Many of these arguments have been directed specifically at the influence of postmodern theories. While some feminist theorists have claimed that postmodern theories are particularly suited to issues of race and ethnicity, feminist theorists of color have countered that the adoption of such theories is yet another form of colonization, one more effort to subsume women of color under a white male discourse.

The stage was set for the current discussion of the intersections of race, ethnicity, and gender in feminist theory by Edward Said's path-breaking *Orientalism* (1978). Although Said is discussing the European "invention" of the Orient, the terms of his discourse are directly relevant to theorizing about women in general and women of color in particular. Said's thesis is that Orientalism is a created body of theory and practice that is parasitic on the cultural hegemony of the West. In this discourse the West is the actor, the Orient the passive reactor; as such, the Orient is identified as feminine, silent, and supine (1978: 138). Said explicitly links the concept of the Orient with concepts identified as "Other" in the hegemonic discourse: women, the insane, the poor (1978: 207). His point is that there is no "essence" of the Orient, but that it is both a discursive construct and a necessary product of the hegemony of the West.

Said's thesis both illuminates and complicates the current feminist dispute about women of color and feminist theory, especially as it relates to postmodernism. On the one hand, Said reveals that the "otherness" of women of color is a constructed, not an essential, category and that it is parasitic both on the hegemonic discourse of white society and on the discourse of white feminist theorists. The very term "women of color" makes no sense without the corresponding concept of "white women." One of the conclusions that seems to follow from this insight is that it would be in the interests of women of color to deconstruct the discourse that marginalizes them, to displace the discourse of center and periphery, self and other. Thus, it would seem that postmodern theories are uniquely applicable to the situation of women of color, women who have been doubly marginalized: by white males in the larger society and white women in the feminist movement. The problem with this neat solution, however, is that in order to effect this displacement, women of color would have to rely on the theoretical constructs of the white European males who created postmodernism. Many women of color find this option unacceptable.

What the question comes down to, then, is whether women of color should employ nonindigenous theories in general, and postmodern theories in particular, in order to foster their resistance. The negative position is clearly expressed in Audre Lorde's famous statement: *"The master's tools will never dismantle the master's house. They may allow us temporarily to beat him at his own game, but they will never enable us to bring about genuine change"* (1981: 99). This sentiment has been frequently reiterated. Cherrie Moraga states: "No one can or will speak for us. We must be the ones to define the parameters of what it means to be female and mestiza" (1983: 139). Similarly, Lugones and Spelman (1983) argue that women of color do not recognize themselves in the theories of white feminists. They argue that women with different racial and ethnic identities should not try to fit themselves into these theories but, rather, should work together with white women to jointly create feminist theory. Barbara Christian (1987) takes this line specifically in relation to literary criticism. She claims that the literary world has been taken over by Western philosophers, who have changed literary criticism to suit their own purposes, devaluing and dispriviledging those who do not follow in their footsteps. As a result, black and Third World critics have been co-opted "into speaking a language and defining their discussion in terms alien to and opposed to our own needs and orientation" (1987: 52). She argues that women of color can and must theorize, but asserts, like Moraga, that it must be in ways that are specific to them:

> For people of color have always theorized – but in forms quite different from the Western form of abstract logic. And I am inclined to say that our theorizing . . . is often in narrative forms, in the stories we create, in riddles and proverbs, in the play with language, since dynamic rather than fixed ideas seem more to our liking. (1987: 52)

She concludes that what will emerge from this process will not be a "set" theory, a "black feminist literary criticism," but a language that arises from black feminist texts themselves.

Christian's target is theory in general, but other feminist theorists concerned with questions of race and ethnicity have attacked postmodern and poststructuralist theories in particular. Paula Gunn Allen (1986), in her work on the American Indian tradition, specifically criticizes the use of postmodern literary theory in American Indian literary criticism. She claims that American Indians' rejection of Western theory is distinct from that of postmodernism, because the former does not constitute a reaction against Western tradition. Rather, she argues that the tropes of American Indian literature are unique – they do not constitute an alternative to Western tropes. Thus, in the "surrealism" of American Indian literature, dreams and visions do not represent departures from Western rationality but are an integral part of a separate oral tradition (1986: 81–91). Likewise, Joyce Joyce (1987), in an argument with Henry Louis Gates on the use of poststructuralism in black literary criticism, argues that treating blackness as a metaphor violates the integrity of black literary criticism. She argues instead that black creative art is an act of love that sustains the black community.

But there are also theorists concerned with race and ethnicity who see an affinity between discursive, postmodern approaches and theories of race and ethnicity. Henry Louis Gates makes a strong case for the convergence of postmodernism and black literary theory. In 1985 Gates, like many black critics, argued that blacks must turn to the black tradition itself in order to develop theories of literature indigenous to black culture (1985: 13). But in his influential *Figures in Black* (1987a) he espouses a method that he labels "critical bricolage," which borrows heavily from postmodernism. Addressing the question of whether black literary critics should be "theoretical," he argues strongly for the creation of text-specific theories arising from the particularities of black literature. He urges black literary critics to invent their own theories, to name indigenous black principles of criticism, to explicate the black tradition in detail (1987a: xviii–xxii). But Gates makes it clear that in this process of inventing, the goal is not to define the "essence" of blackness; for " 'Blackness' is not a material object, an absolute, or an event, but a trope; it does not have an 'essence' as such but is defined by a network of relations that form a particular aesthetic unity" (1987a: 40).

In his argument with Joyce, Gates makes his position more explicit. He defends theory in general, and postmodernism in particular, as appropriate to black literary criticism. He contends that it is only through critical activity that the literary profession in general can redefine itself away from a Eurocentric, male canon and sustain a pluralistic notion of literature. Where he most takes issue with Joyce, however, is in his claim that literature cannot be approached *without* a theory (1987b: 351). Although he recognizes that the notion of a black "essence" is a "healthy political gesture," he nevertheless rejects it (1987a: 53). In the end he argues for a kind of middle ground: "The challenge of the critic of comparative black literature is to allow contemporary theoretical developments to inform his or her own readings of discrete black texts but also to generate his or her own theories from the black idiom itself" (1987a: 58).[17]

Feminist women of color have a particular stake in this dispute. On the face of it, rejection of the hegemonic discourse informing postmodernism would seem to be a welcome theoretical refuge for marginalized groups. This is precisely what Jana Sawicki, a (white) postmodern feminist argues. Sawicki's view is that Foucault's politics of difference is particularly applicable to women of color and lesbians because he assumes that difference is not an obstacle to effective resistance (1986: 32). Mae Henderson (1992) argues that Bakhtin's dialogism is an appropriate model for understanding black women's writing, because it defines each group as speaking in its own "social dialect," its own language, values, perspectives, and norms. Gayatri Spivak is perhaps the best-known feminist theorist to unite postmodernism and ethnicity. Despite her advocacy of postmodernism, however, Spivak is ambivalent about the convergence of postmodernism and theorizing ethnicity. In her analysis of the Subaltern Studies Collective (1987: 197–221) she acknowledges an affinity between the imperialist subject and the humanist subject and hence the relevance of the critique of humanism for subaltern studies. Yet she qualifies this by adding that subaltern studies mixes discourse theory with traces of essentialism. What her position comes down to is another version of Gates's "cultural bricolage."

Bell hooks offers one of the most positive arguments for uniting postmodernism and theories of ethnicity. Hooks labels her recent work, *Yearning*, as postmodern, because of its "polyphonic vocality" and its critique of essentialism (1990: 228). In the book she explicitly addresses the charge that postmodernism does not relate to the realities of the lives of black people. Although she concedes that postmodernism unfortunately directs its critical voice primarily to a specialized audience, she nevertheless insists that it is also the contemporary discourse that speaks most directly to questions of heterogeneity and difference. Avoiding theory altogether, she claims, will simply result in the perpetuation of racism. She advocates the employment of postmodern techniques while at the same time conceding that postmodernism lacks a political program. In the course of presenting her position, she outlines how postmodernism might be employed to address the marginality of black women. Staying on the margins, she argues, nourishes one's will to resist:

> This is an intervention. A message from that space in the margin that is a site of creativity and power, that inclusive space where we recover ourselves, where we move in solidarity to erase the category colonizer/colonized. Marginality as a site of resistance. Enter that space. Let us meet there. Enter that space. We greet you as liberators. (1990: 152)

Bell hooks also addresses a question that is central to a consideration of the intersection of postmodernism, ethnicity, and feminism: subjectivity. The issues here are complex. If Said is correct, then it is modernist theories of the subject that have constituted the "otherness" of racial identity, by constructing the marginalized other as inferior. Thus it would seem that embracing racial/ethnic identity, declaring that there is an essential subject that is, for example, black, native American, or Chicana, will perpetuate rather than defeat the modernist hegemony of self and other. But the postmodern move of deconstructing identity has its dangers as well. What is left, many theorists ask, if we deconstruct the otherness of the other? Isn't it necessary to posit a concrete identity on which to build identity politics?

Hooks argues that this is a danger that can be met and overcome. Like Spivak, she connects essentialist concepts of the self with racism and looks to postmodernism to deconstruct these notions. She argues that the postmodern critique of essentialism provides possibilities for the construction of self and agency that avoid the strictures of essentialism. Furthermore, postmodernism can help define black subjectivity as not unitary but plural (1990: 28–9). In *Talking Back* (1989) hooks illustrates her thesis by describing how she came to be "bell hooks." She explains that as a child she rejected the good little black girl she was supposed to be and, instead, adopted the persona of her outspoken and rebellious great-grandmother, bell hooks. What is significant here is that hooks does not argue that she "discovered" her "real" or "authentic" self in taking on the identity of "bell hooks" but, rather, that she used the elements of subjectivity available to her in her cultural setting. Gates expresses a similar attitude toward subjectivity in his attack on the notion of a transcendent black subject. He maintains that the assumption of an "unassailable integral black self" is false to the black experience (1987a: 115–16). Like hooks, he argues that we must deconstruct this essential self.

Although she wants to claim that there is no essence to black subjectivity, hooks nevertheless argues that the construction of the black subject is distinctive. This in itself is an important point. It means that abandoning the concept of essence and arguing for a discursively constituted identity do not necessarily entail abandoning a distinctive definition of identity. Hooks asserts that the sense of self in black community is a self in relation, a self dependent on others (1989: 30–1). This thesis is echoed in the work of several other black writers. Patricia Collins alleges that, for black women, "Self is not defined as increased autonomy gained by separating oneself from others. Instead, self is found in the context of family and community" (1990: 103). She maintains that black women have fashioned an independent standpoint regarding the meaning of black womanhood, a standpoint that arises out of their common experience. In discussing Afro-American autobiographical writing, Selwyn Cudjoe argues that it avoids "excessive subjectivism and mindless egoism" (1984: 9). She concludes that "the Afro-American autobiographical statement emerges as a *public* rather than a *private* gesture, *me-ism* gives way to *our-ism* and superficial concerns about the *individual subject* usually give way to the *collective subject* of the group" (1984: 10).[18]

The question of difference and identity is central to the construction of the self for all women. But, given the hegemony of the Self/Other discourse of the West, it is a particularly crucial issue for nonwhite women. The question of how this identity can be constructed is problematic. There appear to be advantages, particularly in politics, to defining the subject in essentialist terms: an essentialist subject can be opposed to the hegemonic subject of the dominant discourse. But these writers make a persuasive case that the disadvantages of this move outweigh the advantages. First, positing an essentialist subject denies the multiplicity of subjects that are constructed by the different experiences of nonwhite women. The experiences of nonwhite women, "women of color," are not monolithic: many differences divide them; they are subject to different kinds of oppression. Subsuming all nonwhite women under one concept of identity would deny the specificity of their oppression and impede the political process of overcoming it (Moraga 1981). Second, an essentialist subject is parasitic on the hegemonic discourse that defines "women of color" as "Other" (Minh-ha 1989: 99); it constructs identity using the master's tools. What these writers are suggesting is that identity need not be abandoned if difference is embraced. Rather, as Elizabeth Meese puts it, wholeness and identity require continual negotiations in the field of difference (1990: 48). Difference does not annul identity but, rather, is beyond and alongside it (Minh-ha 1989: 104).

The key issue in this dispute over identity is politics. Feminist women of color seek to posit a subject that can resist the hegemony of the white, middle-class subject, both masculine and feminine. Spivak expresses a common fear in her rejection of the "disappearing subject" of postmodernism on the grounds of political inadequacy (1987: 209). Hooks, Meese, and Minh-ha, however, argue that defining subjects as differently constructed does not negate identity but, rather, fosters it. They assert that recognizing that subjects are differently constructed by race, class, and gender does not preclude the movement to end oppression (hooks 1989: 23). Instead, it recognizes that there are different *kinds* of oppression, as well as different subjects that are oppressed. What is required is a "differential consciousness" (Sandoval 1991) that can transform the dominant discourse.

The issues raised in this discussion are directly relevant to the question of the constitution of the moral subject. Gilligan's work has made us aware that moral voice is constituted rather than discovered. She emphasized the role of gender in this constitution. Introducing the influences of race, class, and culture complicates this picture, but it is a necessary and useful complication. Many feminist theorists are beginning to explore these complications. Sandra Harding maintains that "in cultures stratified by both gender and race, gender is always a racial category and race a gender category" (1986: 18). Both Harding and Patricia Collins claim that the ethics of care that Gilligan identifies has striking similarities to the African or African-American world view (Harding 1987; Collins 1990: 215). Other theorists have sought to complicate the Chodorow/Gilligan narrative of the constitution of self and moral voice by discussing differences caused by race (Carothers 1990; Manning 1992; Stack 1990). These arguments entail that just as there is more than one "different voice" for all women, so there is more than one different voice for "women of color." Acknowledging these differences does not silence the various voices – unless, of course, we acknowledge the existence or legitimacy of only one voice. It is only within the confines of the hegemonic discourse that constitutes them as "Other" that "women of color" appear unified. The different forms of oppression that afflict women of color call for different forms of resistance. This demands a pluralistic approach, not a unitary one.

Pursuing the question of the relevance of postmodern theory to the construction of nonwhite subjects is, I think, unproductive. All the furor over postmodernism masks what is really at issue here: whether an essentialist concept of identity is necessary for the theory and practice of race/ethnicity. I have argued that it is not and that what I am calling the discursive subject is appropriate to questions of subjectivity, race, and ethnicity. This is a concept tailored to the specific needs of feminist subjectivity, not one defined exclusively by white male theorists. A discursive, multiple concept of subjectivity is appropriate to both the theoretical and the political issues faced by nonwhite women. Far from abandoning the identity necessary to political resistance, it creates possibilities of resistance by recognizing diversity of oppressions. To embrace a discursive approach to the subject is not to "lose" subjects altogether but, rather, to acknowledge their variety and to begin to fashion resistances to the multiple oppressions. To deny that multiplicity would be to silence the plurality of voices that speak as women today.

The discursive subject

My goal in this analysis of contemporary theories of the subject has been to articulate a concept of the subject that is appropriate to the task of a feminist reconceptualization of moral theory. I have argued that the contemporary reaction against the modernist/Cartesian subject is evidence of a paradigm shift that is occurring in theories of subjectivity. My examination of the relational self, the postmodern subject, feminist theories of subjectivity, and theories of race and ethnicity is designed both to describe and to argue for the efficacy of that paradigm shift. It is also designed to piece together elements of what I am calling the discursive subject. The discursive subject is neither relational, feminist, postmodern, nor a product of theories of race and ethnicity, yet it borrows from each of these discourses. In this sense it illustrates the principle that Judith Butler articulates in her discussion of the subject: it employs the tools available to fashion a concept that is both unique and a product of the resources at our disposal.

In the following chapter I employ this concept of the discursive subject in my reconceptualization of moral theory. The discursive subject is particularly suited to this task, because it redefines three key elements of subjectivity that are central to moral subjectivity: identity, agency/creativity, and resistance. In order to present an argument for this concept of the discursive subject I will address what I take to be the central objections to this definition of the subject on these three issues. First, for the Cartesian subject, identity is disembodied, given, transcendent. It is what the subject "discovers" as he [sic] "finds" himself. For the discursive subject, by contrast, identity is constituted, multiple, and fluctuating. The subject is a work of art, fashioned from the discursive tools at the disposal of the situated subject. A common objection to the discursive concept of identity I am advocating is that if we abandon the Cartesian subject and instead embrace a subject that is constituted, multiple, and fluctuating, we will be unable to talk about "woman" at all. For how can we formulate an agenda for the liberation of women if we cannot identify "woman"?

The best answer to this charge is to point to the historical evolution of concepts of the subject. The Cartesian subject, the subject that has been reified into the paradigm of all subjectivity, is, despite such claims, itself a historical product. It was first articulated in the seventeenth century and is a consequence of clearly identifiable historical, political, and philosophical influences. Its key characteristics – autonomy, separateness, rationality, disembodiment, and agency – are products of the evolution of a particular discourse, not transcendent elements. What we are witnessing now appears to be a paradigm shift in the concept of the subject that will lead to the establishment of a new concept. This new concept of the subject, however, will also be a discursive product, rooted in the historical and cultural influences extant in our situation. The concept of "essential woman" can be viewed similarly. It has been around since at least the time of Aristotle, yet its definition has varied greatly, a product of fluctuations in the concept of the feminine. The effort on the part of some feminists today to embrace this concept ignores both its historicity and its key role in establishing and maintaining the subordination of women.

Another way to address the question of identity and subjectivity is to argue that the multiplicity of subjects and identities is an inescapable feature of our world and that it is incumbent on us to fashion concepts that can account for this diversity. This is a corollary of Lyotard's argument with regard to the multiplicity of knowledges in the postmodern world. Martha Minow, in her important book *Making All the Difference* (1990), adopts such an attitude to the diversity of subjects. She advocates a new legal approach to the issue of difference, one that emphasizes social relations and defines difference as an expression of the variety of human experiences. Minow's approach is particularly relevant to the question of moral voice. One of the key elements that divides people is, quite obviously, different moral perspectives. Minow argues that "Denying the multiplicity of moral perspectives and demands does not make them go away; instead it marks a rigid either/or thinking that constrains moral understanding" (1990: 222). There is not just one subject called "woman," but many; there is not just one different moral voice, but many. What is needed is a theory that can encompass this multiplicity.

The objection most likely to be raised against a discursive concept of agency and creativity is that it obviates the possibility of both. My reply is that the discursive subject redefines what constitutes agency and creativity. For the discursive subject, agency is defined and circumscribed by the discursive formation; it is not a given condition but a constituted element of subjectivity. The Cartesian subject posits a particular kind of agency, a disembodied, autonomous, abstract agency. It is an agency that has little relevance for most subjects in the contemporary world, particularly those marginalized by race, class, and/or gender. For these marginalized subjects Cartesian agency is an abstraction; to attempt to convince these subjects that they are, in a Kantian sense, essentially free and transcendentally self-constituting would be insulting. The challenge, rather, is to redefine agency in non-Cartesian terms. Judith Butler puts the point most succinctly: construction is not opposed to agency. Discourses script agency differently, but in all cases agency is a discursive resource.

The issue of creativity is closely related. If subjects are wholly constructed, the argument goes, how can they be creative? In the discourse of the modernist subject, determination precludes creativity. The best response to this view is to refer to the process of language acquisition. Speakers who acquire languages are restricted by the vocabulary, rules, syntax, and grammar of the languages they speak. Yet any competent speaker of a language is capable of creativity, of devising unique sentences out of the discursive mix available to her. The same is true of subjectivity. Subjects have a diverse array of subjectivities available to them. This is particularly true in the case of women. Although there is strong pressure to conform to the subjectivity labeled "feminine" in our society, other subjectivities are available as well. The history of the women's liberation movement is a history of women who have claimed the right to adopt subjectivities formerly restricted to men, subjectivities that grant them equality, rights, and justice before the law. Further, women have adopted what Foucault calls subjugated knowledges (for example, "the personal is political") and have introduced them into the political world in order to fashion resistance to the subjectivity of femininity. Employing a diverse array of strategies, women have refused to accept the script handed to them, to play their assigned role. But they have done so by appealing to other elements in the discursive mix of subjectivities, not by "discovering" their "true selves."

Finally, critics of the discursive subject might argue that it precludes the possibility of resistance, particularly political resistance. To refute this charge, I appeal to a variant of the argument I advanced in defense of a Foucaultian theory of resistance. For the Cartesian subject, resistance necessarily involves an appeal to abstract, universal principles that establish the justice of the resistance and the injustice of the oppression being resisted. In order for the subject to arrive at these abstract principles, he [sic] must be able to abstract himself from the particular conditions of injustice, remove himself from his own connection to the situation. For the discursive subject, resistance is framed in radically different terms: discursive subjectivities other than the one that is scripted for the subject provide the possibility of resistance. The feminist movement in the latter half of the twentieth century provides an illustration. The feminist movement has been about resisting the subjectivity of the "feminine." Feminists of many different persuasions have offered a variety of new scripts: a new concept of the relationship between women and nature (ecofeminism), bringing the personal into the public sphere, the "different" moral voice, a "feminist" science. Feminists of color have resisted the script of "woman" that white, middle-class feminists have written. Other examples abound. What these resistances have demonstrated is that resistance does not require reference to a core, disembodied, autonomous self who appeals to universal principles. Rather, resistance can be crafted in the subjugated knowledges that we already possess. As Page Du Bois puts it: "Efforts of subversion . . . are conceived within culture, within the languages which speak us, which we must turn to our own purposes" (1988: 188).

That all these issues are relevant to moral subjectivity should be obvious. The different moral voices I am positing possess identities supplied by the discourses that define them as moral subjects. Thus identity coexists with difference; it does not negate it. These moral subjects, likewise, are capable of agency, but an agency supplied not by a true, authentic, or core self but by the moral discourse itself. Different moral discourses will define different kinds of moral agency. The paradigm of agency supplied by the discourse of the Cartesian subject is not the only possibility; nor is it the paradigm of all moral agency.

The moral subjects I am positing are also capable of resistance. They can and do take moral positions against oppression; they make moral judgments and advance moral arguments. But such moral judgments and arguments are not based on universal absolutes, on disembodied and abstract moral principles. Rather, they are a product of the moral discourse that gives rise to them, what I call in the next chapter moral language games. Wittgenstein's reflections on language as an activity encourage us to listen to moral voices, to be attentive to what we *do* when we make moral arguments. Gilligan has begun this process; I am attempting to take up where she left off, to explore the many paths to moral truth. The best argument in defense of this position, finally, is the pragmatic one offered by Minow and Lyotard. We live in a pluralistic world, a world of many knowledges and many moral voices. There is no master narrative that can command the allegiance of all the moral voices that assail us. To try, falsely, to impose such a narrative can result only in rigidity and in silencing those moral voices that fail to conform to the norm.

4
Back to the Rough Ground: Theorizing the Moral Subject

In her discussions of the "different voice" Gilligan listens to a moral voice that has been silenced in the Western moral tradition. It is a moral voice constituted by relational experiences in childhood, a voice that is the expression of a subject that defines all morality in relational terms. It has been my intent in the foregoing to develop the radical implications of this conception. I have attempted to show that the concept of both morality and the subject entailed by Gilligan's work constitutes a distinctive epistemological break with the Western tradition of moral theory. More is entailed by Gilligan's work than a turn to "alternative moral theory," relativistic morality, or a communitarian approach. It entails, rather, a deconstruction of the epistemological foundations of the tradition itself. Central to this deconstruction is the displacement of the Cartesian, modernist subject. The discursive subject that I developed in the last chapter is the centerpiece of the alternative approach I am advancing. It is a subject constituted by the play of linguistic forces, a subject whose moral agency is a function of that constitution.

The most difficult challenge for this thesis, however, remains: connecting this discursive subject to an understanding of moral voice that is consistent with the linguistic constitution of subjectivity. I believe that Gilligan has begun this task, but that more work remains to be done. What is needed is an explanation of the relationship between subjects and moral voices and how moral voices can be diverse and plural while at the same time avoiding the arbitrary and the anarchic. My argument is organized around two theses. The first is that moral voices are central – even integral – aspects of what it means to be a subject, that becoming a subject and developing a moral voice are inseparable. To put it another way, we do not recognize someone as a subject unless she/he possesses a moral voice. Second, moral voices are unique, in that they are not subject to the vagaries of preferences that characterize other choices that subjects make. What makes a moral voice *moral* is its connection to who we are and the certainty that entails.

I rely on a variety of contemporary sources to develop this theory. My principal source is one that has rarely been employed for feminist purposes: Wittgenstein's later philosophy. I believe that Wittgenstein's understanding of language games and his rejection of the possibility of an ideal language provide tools for a reconstruction of moral theory along feminist lines. Wittgenstein's explicit statements about ethics are few, but they suggest that he embraces an individualistic – even an idiosyncratic – approach to ethical issues. Although I reject such an approach to ethics, I nevertheless employ his understanding of language games in order to develop a theory of an entity he never discusses: the moral language game.

The moral language game: constituting the moral subject

In his presidential address to the American Political Science Association in 1992 James Q. Wilson addressed the issue of "The Moral Sense" (1993a). He argued that people everywhere have a natural moral sense that is not a product of convention, a "directly felt impression of some standards by which we ought to judge voluntary action" (1993a: 1). The first moral judgment of a child, he alleges, is the claim "That's not fair," a claim that soon begins to take on the quality of a disinterested standard (1993a: 5). The following year Wilson published a book with the same title as the address. It received a great deal of attention in both the academic and the popular presses and was widely reviewed. Wilson's argument is not in itself unique; it is consistent with the long-standing tradition of Western moral theory. I refer to his work to illustrate the continuing influence of the universalistic, disembodied concept of morality that defines modern moral theory. Wilson is not a philosopher; he is not interested in the complex epistemological ramifications of his position. But his view exemplifies the power of the hegemonic moral discourse of Western society. His work embodies two widely held assumptions that ground that discourse: that morality both is and must be universal, rather than conventional, and that it must be disinterested/disembodied if it is to count as morality.

The work of the later Wittgenstein provides an important resource for the project of reconceptualizing this discourse. In turning to Wittgenstein's work in my attempt to articulate a theory of moral discourse, my aim is not to determine the "correct" interpretation of his approach or to extrapolate from his position what he might have said about ethics. My intent, rather, is to employ certain aspects of his approach for my own feminist purposes. Wittgenstein's understanding of language games supplies a useful tool for theorizing about the diversity of moral voices and subjects; it provides the inspiration for the model that I employ to describe moral discourse. Wittgenstein's extended polemic against the attempt to construct an ideal language, furthermore, provides salient arguments for my critique of a related attempt in moral theory. The attempt to formulate the one, true form of moral theory, a form characterized by universality and abstraction, is the centerpiece of modern moral theory; it entails silencing the other moral voices that I am questioning. Likewise, the articulation of an ideal logical language that supersedes and corrects the messiness of everyday language was the centerpiece of logical positivism; it entailed depriving everyday language of its validity and relegating it to an inferior status. Wittgenstein's critique of an ideal language offers useful arguments against the possibility of *any* such language, logical *or* moral.

Wittgenstein's actual statements on ethics, however, not only fail to support my approach but, quite possibly, contradict it. Wittgenstein's approach to ethics, to the extent that it can be discerned at all, was individualistic and existential. Like Max Weber, he saw a world devoid of value and believed that it was incumbent on the individual to assume an ethical stance. The view I will present here is very different, but I do not think that it violates the spirit of Wittgenstein's philosophy. In *Philosophical Investigations* (1958) Wittgenstein states that his goal is not to spare other people the trouble of thinking but, rather, to stimulate his readers to thoughts of their own. The theory of moral discourse that I am presenting may not be consistent with Wittgenstein's view of ethics, but it was stimulated by his thoughts concerning the role of language in human life.

Central to Wittgenstein's later philosophy is the concept of the language game. This concept is the focus of my effort to define moral discourse as a multiplicity of voices. Most significantly, it emphasizes that there is no neat division between words and actions, but, rather, that language is something we *do*. For Wittgenstein, language is a form of life, not "mere words" that can be contrasted with "real life." Further, Wittgenstein emphasizes that, as with a form of life, the justification for a language game is internal to the practice itself, not an external standard. Fundamental to his argument is the assertion that, at some point, justification must stop and we say, "This is simply what we do."

For my purposes, however, there is one significant liability to the concept of language games: the connotations of the word *game*. Wittgenstein's reason for using this word is clear: he is drawing a parallel between the use of language and the rules of a game. But in the context of a discussion of morality, the connotations of the word are unfortunate. Central to my argument is the claim that moral language games are not "games" in the sense that they are activities that are frivolous and arbitrary. Rather, I argue that moral discourses are a deadly serious business, that they are inseparably linked to our conception of ourselves as subjects and our conceptions of the world in which we live. I think that Wittgenstein's concept of language games provides an excellent way of talking about moral discourse understood in these terms and that abandoning the word "game" would obscure the connection I am seeking to establish. Thus I will continue to employ his concept despite this liability.

At the beginning of *Philosophical Investigations* Wittgenstein states his aim in a deceptively simple manner. What we need, he asserts, is "a clear view of the aim and functioning of words" (1958: §5). That this is far from simple is obvious to anyone familiar with Wittgenstein's earlier philosophy. In the *Tractatus* Wittgenstein stated the same goal and, in the course of attempting to realize it, enunciated what would become the definitive statement of logical positivism. Wittgenstein's repudiation of his earlier view is embodied in the concept that defines his later philosophy: the language game. "Getting a clear view of the aim and functioning of words," for the later Wittgenstein, no longer means seeking an ideal language that will supersede the inexactness of everyday language. Rather, it involves plunging into the messiness of that everyday language, because, as he puts it, "to imagine a language means to imagine a form of life" (1958: §19). His definition of "language game" reflects this thesis: "Here the term 'language *game*' is meant to bring into prominence the fact that the *speaking* of a language is part of an activity, or a form of life" (1958: §23).

In *The Blue and Brown Books* (1960) Wittgenstein describes what might be called the methodology of language games that he employs in the *Investigations*. "Language games are the forms of language with which a child begins to make use of words. The study of language games is the study of primitive forms of language or primitive languages" (1960: 17). In this and other passages Wittgenstein presents language games as a kind of proto-language: thus, "Children are taught their native language by means of such games" (1960: 81) and "When we look at such simple forms of language the mental mist which seems to enshroud our ordinary use of language disappears" (1960: 17). But he also asserts that language games are not incomplete parts of language but, rather, complete systems of human communication (1960: 81).

He acknowledges at the outset that "this line of investigation" will be "difficult." What stands in our way is our "craving for generality," the desire to define an "essence" of words and find clear boundaries between them (1960: 17). This is a not-so-subtle reference to Wittgenstein's own previous effort to do precisely this – to construct an ideal language that will avoid the confusions of ordinary language. Wittgenstein is now arguing that we must abandon this goal, that we must embrace the complexities and contradictions of ordinary language, to describe what it is we actually *do* with words. Our culture's preoccupation with the method of science has led us to try to reduce everything to a series of laws. One of the results of this is that we have been disdainful of the particular (1960: 18), subordinating individual cases to universal laws. Wittgenstein is now claiming that we must take particular cases seriously.

The logical positivists believed that philosophy must mimic the method of science; what this meant was that the task of philosophy was to find the precise definitions of words, to uncover what is common to all uses of a word. This goal, Wittgenstein asserts, stems from our tendency to "sublime the logic of our language" (1958: §38). What Wittgenstein is now claiming is that there is no essence to words, but that we use them in different ways. We can, nevertheless, define what Wittgenstein calls a "family resemblance" among the different uses of a word. Such uses, while they may not share a single common element, are related to each other much as members of a family share a resemblance. It is impossible to define precisely a family resemblance, but that does not mean that it is not apparent in, for example, family pictures. To illustrate his concept, Wittgenstein refers to the word *game* itself. Although it is impossible to specify the essence of the concept *game*, it is nevertheless the case that games form a family the members of which resemble one another in certain ways (1958: §64–71).

Wittgenstein's description of language games focuses on grammar. Just as games have rules, so language games have grammar (1974: 60). "Our investigation," Wittgenstein declares, "is therefore a grammatical one" (1958: §90); "Grammar tells us what kind of object anything is" (1958: §373). But the analogy between grammar and the rules of a game goes only so far. Rules of games are, in most instances, precisely stated. Grammar, on the other hand, can create confusions; knowing "our way about" can be difficult (1958: §664). These and other comments on language games lead to the conclusion that the new method that Wittgenstein is proposing is in sharp contrast to the exact method of the logical positivists. It involves much messing around in what Wittgenstein calls the "toolbox" that constitutes both language games and language itself. The toolbox metaphor is central to Wittgenstein's approach. Knowledge is no longer identified as the product of an idealized logical language. Rather, "Knowledge is the hypothesized reservoir out of which the visible water flows. . . . It is as if I get tools in the toolbox of language ready for use" (1974: 49). The rules (grammar) by which we decide which tool (word) to use will not be exact, but variable. The reason for this is that, as Wittgenstein puts it, for a large class of cases, although not for all, "the meaning of a word is its use in the language" (1958: §43). Which tool we select will depend on the use to which we are to put it.

The difficulty here, as Wittgenstein makes abundantly clear, is that we are looking for a kind of certainty that is not possible and, more important, the search for this certainty will lead to serious error. The logical positivists sought absolute certainty, an ideal language with precise definitions that articulated the "essence" of its subject. Against this, Wittgenstein proposes diversity and relativity. He urges us to keep the multiplicity of language games always in view; this will keep us from asking unanswerable questions like "What is a question?" (1958: §24). In an unpublished manuscript dating from the 1930s, Wittgenstein draws a parallel between his views and relativity theory, claiming that "we have here a sort of relativity theory of language before us" (quoted in Hilmy 1987: 155). Translated into the language of postmodernism, Wittgenstein is claiming that there is no meta-narrative that can be used to justify the claims of a language game. Justification and certainty are always internal to the language game.[1]

But Wittgenstein goes beyond the rejection of meta-narratives to develop a position that is missing in postmodern thought: the claim that the ultimate justification for language games is found in our "form of life." This position is particularly relevant to my theorizing about moral language games. Wittgenstein claims that our language is grounded not in the universal meta-narrative of logic but, rather, in our activity. The ultimate justification for our claims to knowledge is not logic but simply "what we do." "It is what human beings *say* that is true and false; they agree in the *language* they use. That is not agreement in opinions but in forms of life" (1958: §241). Our concepts rest not on "a kind of seeing on our part; it is our *acting* which lies at the bottom of the language game" (1969: §204). Since Plato, philosophers have looked for ultimate justifications, complete explanations. What Wittgenstein is advocating, by contrast, is an end to justifications not in logic but in human activity itself: "What people accept as a justification is shown by how they think and live" (1958: §325); "the chain of reasons has an end" (1958: §326). "Our mistake is to look for an explanation where we ought to look at what happens as a 'proto-phenomenon.' That is, where we ought to have said: *this language game is played*" (1958: §654).

At a crucial point in his argument Wittgenstein appears to go beyond a description of human activity as the justification for our knowledge and to appeal once again to a universalistic grounding. His discussion of "general facts of nature" and "natural history" seems to imply that he is not content with the contextual account he has given and is looking for more reliable, universal criteria. But a careful reading of the relevant passages suggests a different conclusion. For Wittgenstein, our "natural history" includes not just our biological or "natural" activities but our linguistic activities as well: "Commanding, questioning, recounting, chatting, are as much a part of our natural history as walking, eating, drinking, playing" (1958: §25). Our language games are as natural to human life as our biological life. Most important, language games literally *give* us a world in which to live; our concepts are part of the fabric of our form of life. Wittgenstein's point in his famous statement "If a lion could talk, we could not understand him" (1958: §223) is not that our biology differs from that of lions but, rather, that a lion's concepts would create a world that we could not comprehend. Wittgenstein summarizes thus:

> I am not saying: if such and such facts of nature were different, people would have different concepts (in the sense of a hypothesis). But: if anyone believes that certain concepts are absolutely the correct ones, and that having different ones would not mean realizing something that we realize – then let him imagine certain very general facts of nature to be different from what we are used to, and the formation of concepts different from the usual ones will become intelligible to him. (1958: §230)

Wittgenstein's theory of language games provides a model for a feminist discussion of moral discourse that addresses many of the problems raised by the deconstruction of modernist moral theory. He emphasizes the multiplicity and diversity of language games, the internal character of justification, and, most important, the rootedness of language games in forms of life. It is even possible to interpret Wittgenstein's theory as an extension of Gilligan's discussion of the different moral voice of women. Joining the two approaches has interesting results: a theory that identifies the "care voice" as a distinct moral language game rooted in the particular experiences of most women in our culture. The logic and justification of this language game are different from those of the justice voice, but, as with the justice voice, the criteria of rightness are internal to the language game. The difference between the two moral discourses can be attributed to the fact that the "form of life" experienced by most women in our culture is distinct from that of men. Women do most of the nurturing, caring work in our culture. Men, on the other hand, are dominant in the public realm, in which questions of abstract justice figure prominently.

There is a significant problem with this theory, however. This appropriation of Wittgenstein's approach appears to be inconsistent with what Wittgenstein himself has to say about ethics. For, although he has very little to say on the subject, what he does say, particularly in the *Tractatus* (1961), is completely consistent with the logical positivist relegation of ethics to the realm of the inexpressible. In his introduction to the *Tractatus* Russell states this quite explicitly, adding the description "mystical." And this is indeed a plausible interpretation of Wittgenstein's approach to ethics in the book. He states that ethics and aesthetics are "one and the same" (6.421) and that "the limits of my language mean the limits of my world" (5.6). Ethical statements, it seems clear, are beyond that limit.

But although Wittgenstein's approach to ethics has certain similarities to the logical positivists' view, there are important differences as well. Wittgenstein begins the *Tractatus* with the famous statement that "what can be said at all can be said clearly and what we cannot talk about we must pass over in silence." References to this silence recur throughout the book: "The sense of the world must lie outside the world" (6.41); "God does not reveal himself *in* the world" (6.432); and, most fully, "We feel that even when *all possible* scientific questions have been answered, the problems of life remain completely untouched. Of course, there are no questions left, and this itself is the answer" (6.52). These passages suggest an interpretation that represents a significant departure from that of the logical positivists. For logical positivism, ethics is the realm of nonsense; only scientific (philosophical/logical) statements can make sense. Thus the whole point of philosophy is to construct and examine such statements. Wittgenstein does not make his very different position clear in these passages. But in a letter he wrote to Ficker about the *Tractatus*, he states explicitly what is only implicit in the book:

> The book's point is an ethical one. . . . My work consists of two parts: the one presented here plus all that I have *not* written. And it is precisely this second part that is the important one. My book draws limits to the sphere of the ethical from the inside as it were, and I am convinced that this is the ONLY *rigorous* way of drawing those limits. (Wittgenstein, in Engelmann 1968: 143)

I would like to advance two theses with regard to Wittgenstein's approach to ethics: first, that although Wittgenstein retains the logical positivists' definition of ethics as linked to aesthetics, he does not share their repudiation of ethics; and, second, that although Wittgenstein's attitude toward language in general changes radically from his earlier to his later work, his attitude toward ethics appears to change hardly at all. In his "Lecture on Ethics" (1965), which clearly belongs to his later period, Wittgenstein reaffirms the similarity between ethics and aesthetics that he advanced in the *Tractatus*. He also restates the rigid dichotomy between facts and values that characterized his earlier work. In this later lecture, ethics is once more defined as running up against the boundaries of language, a realm excluded from the province of science. He also reaffirms the respect for ethics that characterized his earlier work, defining it as documenting "a tendency in the human mind which I personally cannot help respecting deeply and I would not for my life ridicule it" (1965: 12).

What is peculiar, if not outright contradictory, about this attitude toward ethics is that, although in his later philosophy he advances a rigorously social concept of language, he excludes ethics from this concept. For the later Wittgenstein, language is exclusively a social activity: meanings are defined by use; justification is conventional and relative to language games; private languages are impossible. Yet ethics does not seem to have any place in this social world. For Wittgenstein, ethics remains personal, individual, and idiosyncratic.

His position is perhaps most reminiscent of Weber's well-known ethic of responsibility. Like Weber, Wittgenstein seems to be espousing an individualistic existentialism in which endowing the world with meaning is a mystical act.

It is even possible that Wittgenstein shares another famous Weberian belief: that the disenchantment of the modern world is regrettable and that it is this unfortunate state of affairs that is the cause of the modern privatization of ethics. A short passage in *Culture and Value* suggests that Wittgenstein believes that a privatized ethics is not the ideal relationship between individuals and ethical beliefs: "A culture is like a big organization which assigns each of its members a place where he can work in the spirit of the whole. . . . In an age without culture, on the other hand, forces become fragmented and the power of an individual man is used up in overcoming opposing forces and frictional resistances" (1980: 6). This passage suggests a number of theses: that our culture *should* supply us with an ethics, an ethical language game that will be a central element of our form of life; that our culture's failure to do so is a result of the "disenchantment" of the modern world; and, finally, that it is only in such a disenchanted world that the individual is forced to choose an ethics without social guidance.

This interpretation of Wittgenstein's approach to ethics, however, is highly speculative. The interpretation I would like to advance is a more modest one. Although Wittgenstein's approach to language underwent a sea change from his earlier to his later work, this change did not apply to his view of ethics. Wittgenstein offers no discussion of morality as a language game, even as a unique language game with special qualities. There is evidence that he saw beliefs, even religious beliefs, as constituting a form of life, a perspective on the world that provides a context for knowledge and its justification. On religious belief he states: "Hence, although it's a *belief*, it's really a way of living, or a way of assessing life. It's passionately seizing hold of *this* interpretation" (1980: 64). But for Wittgenstein ethics does not constitute a belief. Thus he does not extend his identification of belief as a form of life to the ethical realm.[2] It is precisely this extension, however, that I want to pursue.

A central aspect of Wittgenstein's concept of a language game is the claim that the justification for knowledge claims is internal to the language game itself, a function of the fact that language games are activities, forms of life. He does not apply his understanding of how knowledge claims are justified to the issues of ethics and morality, but his position is particularly relevant to some of the questions that have been raised in moral philosophy. Modernist moral philosophers have been obsessed with the question of justification; they have insisted that unless moral claims have unimpeachable foundations, unless they are disembodied and universal, they cannot be counted as moral at all. Wittgenstein's approach to the question of justification offers an effective deconstruction of this position.

His most extended discussion of the relationship between justifications and language games is found in *On Certainty*. His principal concern in the statements collected in this book is the central role of science and education in our form of life. His thesis is that the concepts fundamental to science and education form the ground of our form of life. They are not in themselves provable but, rather, provide the means whereby anything at all is proved and even the definition of proof itself. Wittgenstein never refers to ethics or moral philosophy in these statements. Yet much of what he says is relevant to the dominant language game of moral philosophy, especially as it has been articulated since Kant. He emphasizes that the absolute certainty that science seeks is an impossible goal. As he puts it, "At the foundation of well-founded belief lies belief that is not founded" (1969: §252). He also asserts that justifications must come to an end because "at the end of reasons comes persuasion" (1969: §612). Most important, the end we reach is not an absolute, unimpeachable reason but, rather, the activity that grounds our language games. Thus, as early as the *Philosophical Investigations*, he writes: "If I have exhausted the justifications I have reached bedrock, and my spade is turned. Then I am inclined to say 'This is simply what I do'" (1958: §217).

These points can quite profitably be brought to bear on the attempt to deconstruct modernist moral philosophy. Wittgenstein reveals the impossibility of the goal of that tradition: grounding moral judgments in absolute certainty. For him, the goal of absolute certainty is an epistemological impossibility. He maintains that, instead of looking for absolute grounds, we should look at what it is we actually *do*; our certainty comes from our form of life, not epistemology. Wittgenstein's approach here is closely related to what Gilligan does in her exploration of moral voices. Gilligan asks us to look at what we *do* morally and stop seeking certainty akin to the certainty of science in moral matters. Wittgenstein claims that philosophers "are like savages, primitive people, who hear the expressions of civilized men, put a false interpretation on them, and then draw the queerest conclusions from it" (1958: §194). The philosophers whom Wittgenstein has in mind here are the logical positivists, who abstract from the concreteness of ordinary life and language in order to formulate an ideal language. But what he says applies just as well to modernist moral philosophers, who attempt, with concepts such as Kant's categorical imperative and Rawls's original position, to abstract from moral practice to the realm of the universal and absolute. Both Wittgenstein and, in a different way, Gilligan encourage us to avoid this error by attending to linguistic practice.

One of the most vivid metaphors employed by Wittgenstein to make his point is that of the riverbed (1969: §§96–8). He argues that our language games, our forms of life, are like water flowing through a riverbed. The riverbed determines the direction of the water that flows through it, just as the fixed beliefs that are central to our form of life determine what we mean by an argument, proof, and evidence. The riverbed may shift over time; propositions that were once fluid may harden, and others that were hard may become fluid. But despite these changes, it is nevertheless the case that at any given time the riverbed provides the ground of our language games, our form of life. When, driven by the philosophical quest for certainty, we search for the indubitable ground of our reasons, the riverbed is the hard rock that we hit, causing our spade to turn; it is the end of reasons. Thus:

> All testing, all confirmation and disconfirmation of a hypothesis takes place already within a system. And this system is not a more or less arbitrary and doubtful point of departure for all our arguments: no, it belongs to the essence of what we call an argument. The system is not so much the point of departure, as the element in which arguments have their life. (1969: §105)

And later: "As if giving grounds did not come to an end sometime. But the end is not an ungrounded presupposition: it is an ungrounded way of acting" (1969: §110). It follows that "If language is to be a means of communication there must be agreements not only in definitions but also (queer as this may sound) in judgments" (1958: §242). The tradition of modernist philosophy since Descartes and Kant has been driven by what Wittgenstein calls the "illusion" that the point of investigation is to grasp "one comprehensive essence" (1970: §444). What Wittgenstein suggests as a counter to this is that we accept what looks like a preliminary solution, our form of life, as *the* solution: "The difficulty here is: to stop" (1970: §314).

Wittgenstein's attack on the possibility of absolute certainty is closely related to his attempt to deconstruct the idea that the goal of philosophy is to articulate an ideal, logical language in which statements can be made with absolute clarity and precision. The aim of such a language is to clear up the ambiguities and confusions of ordinary language, make the truth and falsity of statements apparent, and reveal the single comprehensive essence of things. Against this, Wittgenstein proposes that we "go back to the rough ground," return to the messiness of ordinary language. It should be obvious from the foregoing discussion of modernist moral theory that the attempt to formulate an ideal language is not limited to the epistemological investigations of logical positivists. From Kant to Kohlberg, the tradition of modern moral philosophy has been to define the essence of morality, to reduce moral discourse to its one true form, to exclude all other forms as not truly moral, and to define, as Kohlberg puts it, what morality really *is*.

Wittgenstein's argument against the logical positivists is twofold: he challenges both their definition of truth and their concept of the task of philosophy.[3] For the logical positivist, truth is pure and singular. It involves abstraction from the confusions of everyday life and language, disdain for the particular, and the privileging of the universal and the abstract. Wittgenstein rejects this definition of truth in its entirety. He bids philosophers return to the particular, the ordinary, the everyday. He claims that in their attempt to define the pure essence of truth, philosophers have abstracted themselves from the very thing they are seeking to explain: the complexity of human life. By abstracting words from their context, philosophers have lost their way. When the words that philosophers study are cut loose from their moorings in ordinary language, language goes on holiday: it thereby loses any connection to the phenomena it studies.

Wittgenstein's solution to this problem is to return to the ordinary language that philosophy has rejected. In another compelling metaphor he argues: "We have got on to slippery ice where there is no friction and so in a certain sense the conditions are ideal, but also, just because of that, we are unable to walk. We want to walk: so we need *friction*. Back to the rough ground!" (1958: §107). This metaphor goes a long way toward explaining Wittgenstein's later philosophy. The smooth, icy ground of the ideal language is so perfect that it is useless. It has no connection to the concrete roughness and ambiguity of the phenomenon it seeks to explain: human life. The logical positivists thought that they could get a clear view of things by abstracting from the concreteness of everyday life. Wittgenstein's reply is that "a main source of our failure to understand is that we do not *command a clear view* of the use of our words" (1958: §122). And for Wittgenstein, "getting a clear view" entails not abstraction but connection.

He does not shy away from the conclusion that this new definition of philosophic truth entails a radically new definition of the goal of philosophy itself: "No, for the task of philosophy is not to create a new, ideal language, but to clarify the use of our language, the existing language. Its aim is to remove particular misunderstandings; not to produce a real understanding for the first time" (1974: 115). The logical positivists' desire to formulate an ideal language was motivated by the desire to find the one, true *explanation* of reality. Wittgenstein rejects this goal in favor of a new definition of the philosophical enterprise: *description*. "Philosophy may in no way interfere with the actual use of language; it can in the end only describe it. For it cannot give any foundation either. It leaves everything as it is" (1958: §124).

The parallels between Wittgenstein's attempt to bring philosophy back to the rough ground of ordinary language and Gilligan's attempt to listen to the moral voice of women are striking. Modernist moral philosophers' attempts to define the one, true morality, the one correct

moral discourse, are motivated by the same desire as the logical positivists' attempts to define an ideal language: to get it right once and
for all. By contrast, Gilligan, like Wittgenstein, is attempting to get back
to the rough ground, to return to the complexities of everyday language; she explicitly calls for the need to account for the "messiness" of
human life. The attempt to define something like Kant's categorical
imperative or Kohlberg's Stage 6 as the "essence" of morality closely
parallels the logical positivists' attempt to define an ideal language.
Gilligan's attempt to listen to moral voices, to see what it is we
do, likewise parallels Wittgenstein's turn to ordinary language.
Wittgenstein attacks philosophers' craving for generality, their desire
to reduce everything to abstract principles. Gilligan attacks the same
impulse in moral development theory; her work entails that moral
discourse is something about which we cannot fashion a single set of
rules. Wittgenstein's work suggests a similar conclusion for all the
topics that philosophers study. One commentator has suggested that
Wittgenstein's style, his rejection of the linear, doctrinaire method of
philosophy, is a symptom of his rejection of the linear tradition in
philosophy itself (Hilmy 1987). Gilligan's reliance on musical metaphors – theme, fugue, counterpoint – also evinces a rejection of the
linear.

Wittgenstein argues that language games are inseparable from forms
of life; that language is an activity, a doing that is part of our natural
history. Gilligan's work also parallels this aspect of Wittgenstein's
theory. If we assume that moral discourse constitutes a language game
(which Wittgenstein does not), then it would seem to follow that different moral discourses constitute different forms of life. And this, of
course, is exactly what Gilligan found. She found that the care voice is
thematically feminine – that is, that it is spoken not only by women but
is associated with culturally defined feminine values. Most significantly, it corresponds with women's form of life, the fact that, in our
society, women usually fill the role of care-giver. She also found that
the justice voice is associated with qualities that our culture defines as
masculine and that this voice defines the public realm, the realm that,
until quite recently, excluded women. The private realm, by contrast, is
the realm of women, the realm of the moral voice of care and connection. In Wittgensteinian language, Gilligan has defined two language
games of morality rooted in two different forms of life. Yet one of these
language games is hegemonic and holds sway as the only "truly moral"
discourse.

The goal of my consideration of Wittgenstein's work is to employ
some of his central concepts – language games, certainty, the ideal
language – to construct an approach to morality that is appropriate to
feminist concerns. My argument revolves around two theses: first, that
moral language games are unique in that they are inseparably tied to

subjectivity itself – that we recognize a subject as fully human only if she can participate in moral discourse – and second, that moral language games negotiate the boundary between the conventional and the nonarbitrary in a unique way. It is beyond question that moral language games are cultural products, that they are multiple and varied, and that they differ even within cultures. I refer to this as the *content* of the moral language game, a content that is always contextual, historical, located. What makes moral language games unique, however, is that their *form* is neither conventional nor arbitrary. To put forward a moral argument is to claim not that such-and-such is right for me or for my culture but that it is right, period. Moral language games provide internal criteria of justification. Thus, within the parameters of a particular moral language game, I can say with certainty that my moral judgment is right. In the context of a different language game – that of anthropology or moral philosophy, for example – I may acknowledge that the morality of my culture is a historical product and that other moral language games exist. But when I am actually engaged in moral argument and/or action, the discourse provides clear standards of right and wrong.

The point of departure of my argument is a consideration, once more, of subjectivity. Although Wittgenstein never discusses the subject as such, the concept of the subject implicit in his ordinary language philosophy offers a sharp contrast to the Cartesian subject. His discussion of language games, certain knowledge, and, most significantly, the status of "private" sensations implies a subject much closer to the discursive subject theorized here than to the transcendent, self-constituting subject of the modernist tradition. His deconstruction of the very foundations of Western/modernist philosophy necessarily entails the deconstruction of the centerpiece of modernism, the Cartesian subject. In a sense, Wittgenstein does not need to discuss the subject because its deconstruction is implicit in his whole philosophical project.[4]

The question that I want to address is in what sense this subject can be said to be moral. My argument is that morality is a practice – a habit in Oakeshott's sense – that members of cultures teach their children. Although habits/practices vary widely among cultures and even within cultures and the content of the moral practices that are taught varies, the teaching of moral practice appears to be common to all human cultures. Being taught a moral practice is not an optional aspect of childhood education; rather, it is central to the process of becoming a person. Another way of putting this is that in every culture that we have knowledge of, to become a person is to become a moral person. Furthermore, in any culture, and most particularly in ours, the ability to employ moral arguments, to discriminate between right and wrong, is definitive of mature adulthood. Our legal system provides an excellent example of this point. We exclude juveniles and the mentally defective from the full force of the law precisely because they are unable to make moral judgments. The ability to make moral distinctions thus constitutes *the* criterion of full legal and political personhood in our society.[5]

The second aspect of my thesis involves the claim that the content of moral language games is culturally relative, whereas the form of their employment is not. By "form," however, I mean something quite different from a standard such as Kant's categorical imperative. Kant argued that there is a universal standard for moral rightness and that the content of this standard is invariable. By contrast, I am maintaining that standards of moral rightness are internal to moral discourses and thus their content varies, but that moral discourses are similar in form: they all make the claim to rightness. My thesis can best be illustrated by comparing two language games that exemplify the extremes of my argument. If I were to assert that I like chocolate ice cream and that I prefer it to any other flavor of ice cream, it would be compatible with this assertion to accept the arbitrariness of my preference. I might admit that it is mere chance that I prefer chocolate, that I have not always liked it, or even that I may lose my taste for it in the future. The language game of taste preferences can accommodate all these statements. If I were to assert, on the other hand, that I believe in Jesus Christ as my personal savior, it would be compatible with this statement to acknowledge that not everyone has this belief and even that the Christian religion has its roots in a particular culture. But it would not be compatible with this statement to say that my belief is arbitrary, that I might just as well believe in another God, or that if I had been born into another culture, I would believe in another God. For me, my belief in Christ is absolute and true; he *is* the savior, even if that fact is not universally acknowledged. Furthermore, my belief makes me the kind of person I am: a Christian. Being a Christian constitutes a way of life for me. The language game of religious belief, unlike that of taste preferences, does not include vacillation or willy-nilly choice.

The moral language game has more in common with the religious language game than with that of taste preferences. Although moral and religious language games are not identical, they share an important attribute: nonarbitrariness. In any culture, growing into personhood means growing into moral personhood. I can acknowledge that other cultures have different moral systems, but it does not follow that my beliefs are arbitrary. My moral beliefs constitute who I am as a person. When I make a moral statement, I am not saying that I believe this is right but could just as well believe that something else is right. I am asserting that this *is* right; I would be a different kind of person if I believed differently. Wittgenstein's famous lion statement is relevant here. If I had different moral beliefs, I would be a different person; I cannot fully understand what my form of life would be if I had a different set of moral beliefs, because moral beliefs are so central to who I am.

Making this point in Kuhnian language might help to clarify my argument. I am asserting that moral beliefs are *a*, if not *the*, paradigm of mature subjectivity. Our moral beliefs define us as persons; they give us a world to inhabit and endow that world with meaning. Although moral beliefs vary both across and within cultures, it does not follow that they are fickle. A change in moral beliefs entails a profound change in world view – a conversion, in other words. It entails inhabiting a new world. Very few, if any, other language games are similarly fundamental. Changing my taste in ice cream will have little effect on my perception of myself as a person; changing my moral language game, however, will make me a very different person.

In articulating what he calls his "discourse ethics," Habermas asserts: "Individuals who have been socialized cannot take a hypothetical attitude toward the form of life and the personal life history that shaped their own identity" (1990: 104).[6] This statement is true in the sense that my moral beliefs constitute me as a person and provide me with an identity that I cannot just decide to set aside. But it is false in the sense that, quite obviously, human beings can and do examine and sometimes change their moral beliefs, compare moralities across cultures, and discuss the process of moral education. But when they do so, they are engaged in a *different* language game, the language game of philosophical analysis or epistemological doubt or anthropological investigation. Language games, Wittgenstein reminds us, are activities. When I am engaged in the moral language game – that is, in moral action – I am not at the same time examining my moral beliefs or involved in cultural comparison or critique. Rather, I am engaged in moral judgment, a quite different activity. Although I can reflect on my moral judgments, my reflections take place within the parameters of the language game; they presuppose that "This is what I believe."

Two recent commentaries on Wittgenstein's moral theory address this question directly. Iris Murdoch argues that human experience compels us to assert that morality has an absolute and necessary claim on us, that there is something about moral value that must go "all the way" to the base (1992: 418–26). She thus rejects the use of the concept of "language games" to describe religion or ethics because of its alleged relativism (1992: 413).[7] Paul Johnston, like Murdoch, tries to construct a Wittgensteinian approach to morality that can account for the special status of moral beliefs. Like Murdoch, he argues that moral beliefs cannot be conceptualized as arbitrary, because this leads to the "error" of relativism. But Johnston, much more clearly than Murdoch, states the key problem here. The greatest difficulty in understanding ethics accurately, he states, is construing its claim to correctness (1989: 202).

Both Johnston and Murdoch attempt to address the issue of correctness implicit in moral discourse by positing a form of moral objectivism. Murdoch presents a fairly traditional metaphysics, and Johnston argues for the objectivity of moral judgments as opposed to moral facts. But I believe that there is another option. Johnston is correct in his assertion that the description of moral language games must account for the claim to correctness. But this requirement can be met, I think, by focusing on the form of moral arguments rather than their content. When I make a moral argument, I am making a claim to correctness; I am asserting that my moral statements are not arbitrary. This claim is rooted in the centrality of my moral beliefs to my status as a person: I am the kind of person I am because I have certain moral beliefs. Neither my subjectivity nor my morality is arbitrary; both are my way of being in the world. But they are not "correct" in a universalist sense, because, quite obviously, other kinds of persons and other kinds of moral beliefs exist in the world. My understanding of my own world, however, is substantially constituted by my necessarily moral subjectivity; I cannot fully understand any other kind of world. My "understanding" of other beliefs and other subjectivities is of a different order: it is an intellectual understanding constituted by the language game of cultural critique.[8]

One further issue must be addressed to complete my outline of the moral subject. In the foregoing I have argued both that there are multiple moral language games within any culture and that moral agents are capable of piecing together elements of the various moral language games available to them in order to fashion new moral discourses. Both claims are central to my argument as to how resistance to hegemonic moral discourses occurs. Yet they also raise a disturbing question: if moral agents are capable of employing different moral discourses, why is it necessary to recognize multiple discourses? Would it not be simpler to adopt the tactic recommended by modernist moral theory – requiring everyone speak in the same moral voice? Although she never confronts it directly, this problem arose in Gilligan's research on moral voices. Gilligan discovered that both women and men can speak in both the justice and the care voices; she dealt with this finding by positing what she called the "focus" phenomenon. But this solution does not address the underlying issue uncovered by her research. Specifically, it does not address the question of why, if women can and do speak in the justice voice, we should be so concerned with theorizing about the care voice.

There are two replies to this objection. First, moral voices are constitutive of, not peripheral to, subjects. Each subject will possess a particular moral voice, a voice rooted in her social, historical, linguistic, and cultural situation. Although she may be able to employ other moral voices for specific purposes, forcing her to adopt a moral voice not her own, a voice that is not a product of her situatedness, would be like forcing her to speak a foreign language. Although she could learn a "foreign" moral voice, just as anyone can learn a foreign language, this would radically change – and impoverish – her moral life. Second, as Gilligan discovered, defining the moral realm as constituted by only one moral voice, severely restricts the dimensions of moral discourse. If the moral realm is defined exclusively in terms of the justice voice, for example, the care voice is silenced, and the issues raised by the care voice are defined as outside the moral realm. By defining the moral realm as a multiplicity of voices, we not only broaden and enrich it, we also allow subjects to speak in the moral voices that define them as subjects.

It is this concept of the moral subject that is the basis for the feminist moral theory I am proposing. It addresses the issues raised by feminist critiques of masculinist moral theory in two central respects. First, it highlights the connection between morality and subjectivity. It emphasizes that to be a subject is to be a moral subject, to have a moral voice. It entails that different kinds of subjects will have different moral voices and that there is not one paradigm for either morality or subjectivity. Second, it focuses on the plurality of moral language games and facilitates the analysis of hegemonic and marginalized moralities. It can also accommodate the nonarbitrariness of moral language games, the claim to correctness that is implicit in moral judgments, and hence the uniqueness of the moral language game.

There are, nevertheless, two serious lacunae in the Wittgensteinian outline I have presented here. First, since Wittgenstein does not define morality as a language game or discuss the issue of subjectivity, his theory leaves these issues open. To fill this gap I attempt to develop a way of talking about the plurality of language games that is compatible with feminist concerns. The work of Gadamer, Oakeshott, and contemporary theorists of narrative is particularly useful in this regard. Although these writers are rarely used for feminist purposes, their perspectives are compatible with feminist goals. The second lacuna is political. Wittgenstein, again quite obviously, does not address any specifically political issues.[9] But I think that the theory of moral language games I have developed here can accommodate political issues. In the course of establishing this aspect of my thesis, I will review the work of a number of contemporary thinkers who have attempted to formulate a "postmodern" ethics/politics. My claim is that aspects of this literature, most notably the work of Foucault, provide an outline of a politics that eschews universalistic foundations. This outline is useful for the task of formulating a feminist moral and political theory.

Paths to moral truth

In *Truth and Method* (1975) Hans-Georg Gadamer attacks the exclusive association of truth with the scientific, empirical method that has characterized modern philosophic thought.[10] Against this, Gadamer argues that there are many paths to truth, that the single path identified by empiricism is too narrow a conception, and that we "experience" truth in different ways. Gadamer's explicit target in this book is scientism, or something akin to the logical positivism that Wittgenstein opposes in his later philosophy. Like Wittgenstein, Gadamer argues that restricting "truth" to the products of scientific method seriously impoverishes thought, reducing it to logical calculi that deny the richness of human experience. Most important for Gadamer, it denies the vital role of tradition, the prejudgments that, he claims, constitute our understanding.

Gadamer's emphasis on tradition would seem to preclude his relevance for feminist theory. Central to the tradition of the West has been the subordination of women, a practice buttressed by countless theories in philosophy, science, and religion that supposedly establish the inferiority of women. But to dismiss Gadamer's relevance for feminism because of his emphasis on tradition is both to misunderstand what he means by "tradition" and to overlook the broader implications of his approach. There is an important parallel between Gadamer's questioning of the singular path to truth and Gilligan's questioning of one true moral voice. Gadamer argues that scientific truth is not the sole paradigm of truth, but only one of the paths to truth, even perhaps an aberrant one. Gilligan argues that the dominant moral tradition, the justice voice, is not the paradigm of all morality. She documents the existence of another moral voice and argues that it is equally valid as moral expression. Gadamer makes much the same argument in epistemological terms. These similarities are significant; the two theories reinforce each other in important ways. But Gadamer also supplements Gilligan's approach on a salient issue: he argues that there is not just *one* alternative to the unitary definition of truth, but many. In the foregoing I have argued, similarly, that there is not just one alternative to the justice voice, but many; that moral voices are multiple and relational. Gadamer's approach can be useful in developing this perspective, in providing a way of exploring the radical implications of Gilligan's critique.

Gadamer's principal argument against the Enlightenment's exclusive identification of truth with the products of scientific method is that all understanding is hermeneutical. What he means by this is that all understanding occurs in language, in the complex web of meanings that constitute our linguistic activity. At the beginning of *Truth and*

Method Gadamer appeals to art as an experience of truth that is distinct from that of scientific method. He asks, "Must we not also admit that the work of art possesses truth?" (1975: 39). Aesthetic understanding not only poses a clear alternative to scientific truth; it also reveals an aspect of understanding that is obscured by scientific method: understanding is always self-understanding; it relates to the whole of our existence.

The centerpiece of Gadamer's attack on the Enlightenment concept of knowledge is his concept of prejudice. He states that "the fundamental prejudice of the enlightenment is the prejudice against prejudice itself" (1975: 239–40). For Gadamer, "prejudice" is the pre-understandings that inform our language and make meaning possible. Another way of putting this is to say that all understanding is historical; all knowledge is connected knowledge, located in place and time. Scientific method seeks to deny the located, hermeneutic character of knowledge by defining abstraction from locatedness as the paradigm of all knowledge. This argument provides Gadamer with his most effective charge against the Enlightenment's concept of knowledge. If locatedness, "prejudice," is *the* central characteristic of all knowledge and scientific knowledge attempts to deny this characteristic, then it cannot be seen as the paradigm of all knowledge. On the contrary, Gadamer asserts, it is an aberrant form of knowledge (1975: 106).

The parallels between this argument and that of Gilligan are significant. Gilligan's intent in *In a Different Voice* is to demonstrate that the abstraction of the justice voice is an aberration. She argues for the validity and "truth" of the connected, hermeneutical, located moral voice of women. The arguments she puts forward to establish her position, furthermore, are very similar to those of Gadamer. Connection, Gilligan argues, is an essential aspect of the human condition. It follows that the striving for abstraction that characterizes the justice voice, the attempt to formulate moral arguments that eschew connection, is an "adolescent ideal" (1982: 98). She too turns to art to make her argument. Her discussion of novels and life narratives emphasizes that connection is fundamental to the human condition, that the "truth" of human life lies not in abstraction from relationships but, rather, is constituted by them.

Yet the attempt to ally Gadamer and Gilligan raises a significant question: how can a feminist deconstruction of moral theory rely on an approach that foregrounds tradition, when it is precisely the tradition of women's moral inferiority that is the target of that deconstruction? There are several possible answers to this objection. First, Gadamer argues that the dominant "tradition" of the Enlightenment is seriously flawed, because it denies the connectedness of all human understanding. One way of reading this is that Gadamer is arguing for what amounts to a "feminine" concept of knowledge – "feminine" in the sense that the feminine has been defined in terms of locatedness and connection, as opposed to the masculine qualities of abstraction and autonomy. Second, and more important, Gadamer does not define the prejudice that grounds all understanding as inflexible, dogmatic, or fixed; his definition of the word eschews the negative connotations that we have attached to it. For Gadamer, prejudice defines the rootedness of language, its dependence on the hermeneutic context or "horizon" of thought. For him, this hermeneutic horizon is flexible and open; it allows – demands, even – critique and examination. As he puts it, there cannot be "an enclosure in language" because every language is unlimited. "Precisely the experience of finitude and particularity of our being – a finitude manifest in the diversity of languages – opens the road to the infinite dialogue in the direction of ontological truth" (1976: 15–16).

There is a sense in which Gadamer's thesis regarding the openness of language supplies an explanation for the feminist critique of moral theory. Discourses are open to reinterpretation. It is just such a reinterpretation in which Gilligan is engaged; her reinterpretation has opened the way for feminist moral theorists to develop the "ethic of care." Understanding, Gadamer asserts, is an adventure: "But when one realizes that understanding is an adventure then it affords unique opportunities as well" (1981: 109). A Gadamerian definition of tradition is one that can serve feminism well. It involves seeing tradition as the necessary ground of our understanding and as an open-ended and potentially critical medium that we can employ for our own purposes. "Tradition" in Gadamer's sense provides us with tools that we can use to criticize and reflect on our discourses; it is opportunity, not enemy.[11]

Michael Oakeshott is another theorist of tradition whose work can be turned in feminist directions. Gadamer does not discuss morality, politics, or power in his epistemological ruminations on tradition; but Oakeshott, whose work is similarly rooted in a definition of tradition, discusses all of these issues. He is also interested in certain issues that I have already discussed: acquiring a moral voice, agency, and change. The most forceful presentation of his approach is found in his essay "The Tower of Babel" (1962). Reading this essay across Gilligan and the issues she raises yields some startling conclusions. It is not implausible to interpret Oakeshott's meaning in this essay as more radical than that of Gilligan. Whereas Gilligan wants to put the justice voice on the same level as the care voice, Oakeshott presents a strong case for disprivileging it.

Oakeshott's subject in "The Tower of Babel" is the form of moral life in contemporary Western civilization rather than ultimate moral values. He begins by defining moral life itself: "The moral life is human affection and behavior determined not by nature but by art. It is conduct to which there is an alternative. This alternative need not be consciously before the mind; moral conduct does not necessarily involve the reflective choice of a particular action" (1962: 60). We are all born into societies, Oakeshott argues. It follows that we are not given a *choice* as to the form of moral life we will adopt. Elsewhere he makes this even more explicit: "Indeed, strictly speaking, there is no such thing as 'moral choice'" (1975: 79). He goes on to claim that our society exhibits two contrasting definitions of morality. It is the first that occupies most of his attention: morality as the habit of affection and behavior; not reflective thought, but conduct. This form of moral life, he maintains, depends on education. Moral education does not involve memorizing rules and precepts; rather, "by living with people who habitually behave in a certain manner we acquire habits of conduct in the same way we acquire our native language" (1962: 62).

Oakeshott's defense of this understanding of moral life is close to impassioned. He argues that moral education is not a distinct aspect of education, one of the "subjects" covered, but is part of all activities.[12] The result of moral education is the ability to *act*, not the ability to explain our behavior in abstract terms. Oakeshott readily concedes that this concept of moral life – what Wittgenstein would call a form of life – is not recognized as a system, since it has no principles that can be analyzed. But he sees this as an advantage rather than a disadvantage. It means that it is not subject to sudden collapse; it is stable and elastic rather than fixed. It changes, but in a more evolutionary way: "The sort of change which belongs to this moral life is analogous to the change to which a living language is subject: nothing is more habitual and customary than our ways of speech and nothing is more continuously invaded by change" (1962: 65).

Oakeshott's assessment of the second form of moral life is much less positive. This form is characterized by the reflective application of moral criteria, and its key value is self-consciousness. What Oakeshott is describing here corresponds to Kohlberg's Stage 6. Moral ideas are more important than moral action in this form of moral life; education in it requires intellectual training, and thus only philosophers will do it well. Finally, this form of moral life changes by revolution, not evolution. Oakeshott concludes his assessment by arguing that this form of moral life is dangerous in an individual and disastrous in a society (1962: 66–70).

Like Gilligan, Oakeshott wants to join these two forms of life because, he argues, each on its own is inadequate. But, unlike Gilligan, he does not want to accord equality to the two forms. What is wrong with our society, Oakeshott claims, is that we have privileged the morality of rules over the morality of habit. He concludes: "What should be subordinated has come to rule, and its rule is a misrule" (1962: 75). By subordinating the morality of habit to the morality of rules, he claims, we have built a tower of Babel: "we exaggerate the significance of our moral ideals to fill the hollowness of our moral life" (1962: 74).

Oakeshott is well aware that in privileging moral habits over moral ideals, he is opposing what he calls the "moral inheritance of Western Europe," both classical and Christian. His challenge to this inheritance is twofold: to question the tradition's privileging of moral ideas over moral habits and to argue that the habitual moral life also partakes of rationality. Habitual morality can be called rational if we define rationality as "the certificate we give to any conduct which can maintain a place in the flow of sympathy, the coherence of activity, which composes a way of living" (1962: 109). There are echoes of both Gadamer and Wittgenstein in this formulation. Like Gadamer, Oakeshott is claiming that tradition is neither dogmatic nor fixed but, rather, is a flexible and constantly changing living entity. Like Wittgenstein, he is claiming that standards of rationality are internal to our form of life. Although Wittgenstein did not define morality as a form of life, had he done so, it would probably look much like Oakeshott's discussion of moral education.

Oakeshott expands on the understanding of morality as a practice that he presents in "The Tower of Babel" throughout his work. Two themes of this work are particularly relevant to the arguments I have advanced here. The first is Oakeshott's insistence that we understand morality as a language. Gilligan talks about moral voices and analyzes the language that constitutes the different moral voice of women. Oakeshott asserts that morality, like language, is an instrument of understanding and a medium of intercourse (1975: 62). A practice, Oakeshott argues, is a language of self-disclosure. It comes to the speaker as "various invitations to understand, to choose, to respond . . . It is an instrument to be played upon, not a tune to be played" (1975: 58). He concludes: "A morality, then, is neither a system of general principles nor a code of rules, but a vernacular language. General principles and even rules may be elicited from it, but (like other languages) it is not the creation of grammarians; it is made by the speakers" (1975: 78).

This emphasis on language also informs Oakeshott's discussion of a related issue: the possibility of change. He argues that moral practices, like languages, are subject to change, but that this change is not due to the dictates of an authority who changes the rules. Moral practices do not change because moral philosophers decree new moral principles, any more than language changes as a result of linguists' decrees. Rather, in both cases change occurs because speakers change their practices.

In the foregoing I claimed that morality and subjectivity are inseparably linked. Oakeshott presents a similar argument in his discussion of a second theme: moral agency. He asserts that moral practices define both moral agency and subjectivity and that it is impossible to conceive of an agent outside the jurisdiction of a moral practice (1975: 61). It follows that morality is intimately tied to subjectivity. Being a subject means being a moral subject, engaging in a moral practice; subjects without moral practices are not recognizable as subjects. Oakeshott brings all this together in his discussion of agency. For children, he claims, learning agency is inseparable from learning a moral practice: "There is no agency which is not the acknowledgment of a moral practice, and no moral conduct which is not the exercise of agency" (1975: 63).[13] A corollary of this is that moral practices are necessarily multiple rather than singular and that each practice defines a specific form of moral agency. Moral practices, Oakeshott argues, "postulate" free agents; they do not discover them (1975: 79). The plurality of moral practices, furthermore, is not a "regrettable divergence from a universal moral language" but "intrinsic to their character" (1975: 80). Moral practices vary across cultures and even, Oakeshott argues, among women and men within a culture (1975: 65).

There is much in Oakeshott's approach that is unacceptable from a feminist perspective. Issues of power and hegemony never surface in his discussions. Nor does he consider the possibility that moral practices privilege the dominant group over marginalized groups. And neither gender nor race enters in. Oakeshott imagines himself participating in the "conversation of mankind" yet fails to acknowledge the gender and race hierarchy implicit in this phrase and the practice it describes.

Despite these liabilities, however, Oakeshott's theory offers a number of useful insights. He extends Wittgenstein's notion of language games and forms of life to a consideration of morality. The result of this extension is significant: the disprivileging of the abstract, rule-bound concept of morality, a morality that has silenced women's moral voice, defining it as inferior. The contextual morality that Oakeshott advocates is very similar to Gilligan's care voice. Their common emphasis on the language of moral life provides a discursive understanding of morality that goes a long way toward deconstructing the dominant tradition. Another significant advantage is Oakeshott's emphasis on the connection between morality and subjectivity, his argument that subjects are necessarily moral subjects. At the center of his theory is the claim that, as subjects, moral persons possess agency, a capacity that is a product not of transcendent givens but of moral practices. This position effectively deconstructs the claim that only the Kantian/Cartesian subject possesses agency. It defines both morality and agency as discourse-specific. Finally, Oakeshott's argument that moral practices change like languages provides a definition of those practices as flexible and evolving, rather than fixed and dogmatic. In sum,

Oakeshott's theory offers what amounts to a philosophical justification of Gilligan's approach. What he adds is an extension and articulation of some key elements of that approach.[14]

Oakeshott asserts that what we ought to do is connected to who we are, because what we are is what we believe ourselves to be (1962: 248). Or, to put it another way, we are told stories about who we are and hence what we ought to do. Our belief in these narratives provides us with both an identity and a moral practice. Several contemporary theorists have focused on the concept of narrative to explain the phenomenon of subjectivity in general and moral subjectivity in particular. Understanding identity and morality in terms of narrative, on the face of it, appears to be inherently conservative. The most prominent contemporary theorist of narrative, Alasdair MacIntyre, certainly turns the narrative approach to conservative ends. But other contemporary theorists of narrative have shown that this approach can be a significant tool for change.

The most exciting attempt to use narrative as a means of deconstructing traditional categories is that of Donna Haraway. In *Primate Visions* (1989) Haraway examines the complex narratives that constitute the field of primatology. She argues that the rational discourses of science in this field, far from transcending politics, are actually primary forces in the decidedly political construction of the narratives of race and gender (1989: 196). This in itself is a significant undertaking. But more relevant to my project is Haraway's other accomplishment: revealing how new stories can be formulated that shake up the old verities, that destabilize the traditional narratives.

Haraway argues that, in history, "All units and actors cohere partially and provisionally, held together by complex material – semiotic – social practices. In the space opened up by such contradictions and multiplicities lies the possibility for reflexive responsibility for the shape of narrative fields" (1989: 172). Feminism, she argues, like primatology, is a storytelling practice, even if they tell radically different stories:

> Both feminist and scientific discourses are critical projects built in order to destabilize and reimagine their methods and objects of knowledge in complex power fields. Addressed to each other, western feminist and scientific discourses warp each other's story fields and redraw possible positions for claiming to know something about the world, including gendered social space and sexed bodies. (1989: 324)

The importance of Haraway's approach lies in the fact that she identifies the theoretical use of narrative as a potentially destabilizing, rather than an exclusively conservative, force. Stories can be retold and reinterpreted. New stories can be fashioned from elements of old stories. It is also significant that she avoids the temptation to claim that the story told by primatology is wrong and that it is now up to feminists to "get it right." Instead, she argues that she and other feminists are telling a different story. The goal of her book, she states, is to tell and retell stories, in order to "shift the webs of intertextuality" and facilitate new possibilities (1989: 377).

Haraway's thesis is that narratives can be used for social change. Another application of narrative theory for this purpose is found in the work of two theorists who have worked closely with Gilligan. Tappan and Brown (1989) employ the narrative method to articulate an alternative approach to moral development. They argue that narratives are the primary vehicle of moral development, because narratives always moralize. Subjects develop morally by authorizing their own stories; thus, constructing a narrative involves moralizing and thereby claiming moral authority. Like Haraway, they define the narrative approach as a vehicle for change, multiplicity, and plurality. They see Gilligan's approach to moral development as itself a narrative method, claiming that what Gilligan is doing is collecting narratives of moral life. It is an approach, they assert, that fosters pluralism but not individualism.[15] This is an important distinction. The position I am advancing counters the universalistic, unitary narrative of the dominant moral voice with a plethora of moral narratives that give voice to other stories of moral responsibility. But the concept of moral pluralism inevitably raises the specter of moral anarchy, the fear that each individual will decide her/his own moral values and that moral chaos will follow the demise of universal moral standards. The emphasis on narrative counters this tendency. Narratives are necessarily social and communal. They are the glue that holds our society together; they furnish clear standards and concrete values. They are neither inflexible nor arbitrary. Rather, they provide us with a definition of who we are and how we can act as moral agents.

My aim in exploring the approaches of Gadamer, Oakeshott, and the narrative theorists is to suggest that there are powerful forces in contemporary thought that can be used to foster the goal of a feminist reconstruction of moral theory. Gadamer's epistemological critique of Enlightenment knowledge, Oakeshott's extension of Wittgenstein's theory of language games to the moral realm, and theories of the narrative self provide theoretical resources for the argument for a plurality of moral voices. They provide the basis for defining a new paradigm for knowledge in general and moral knowledge in particular. For these theorists, knowledge is situated and contextual. This provides a way of defining moral knowledge that counters the abstract, disembodied approach of modern moral theory. In this new paradigm, moral knowledge need not be abstract in order to count as knowledge. Rather, knowledge is defined as situated yet critical, plural yet providing standards of truth. Feminists can profitably use these theories to tell a different story about moral voices.

A postmodern ethics/politics?

Postmodernism has become an unavoidable issue in the present intellectual climate, particularly in discussions of feminism and social and political theory. It is impossible to avoid taking a position on the issue of postmodernism or to escape being labeled pro- or anti-postmodern. In my discussion of contemporary theories of subjectivity I argued for the selective use of postmodern approaches. I adopt the same tactic in my discussion of postmodern ethical/political theories. I do not argue for or against a "postmodern" approach to feminist ethics and/or politics, because I do not think that such an argument is possible or meaningful, given how many differences there are among approaches labeled "postmodern." Instead, I argue for the selective use of such approaches for the construction of feminist moral theory. I divide postmodern thought into two categories: apolitical and political postmodernism. What I call "apolitical postmodernism" comes close to making a mockery of ethical and political issues. Although several of the authors whom I place in this category claim to have a political agenda, their claims are almost laughable when seriously examined. What I call the "political postmoderns," on the other hand, have much to contribute to feminist moral theory. Thus I rely heavily on the theories of Foucault and Lyotard in my effort to reconceptualize moral theory.

Apolitical postmodernism

The most prominent representative of apolitical postmodernism is Derrida. That Derrida's work has been immensely influential in defining postmodernism in recent decades is undeniable. That aspects of his work are useful for feminism is at least arguable.[16] The strength of Derrida's work lies in his radical challenge to the epistemology of Western thought. By deconstructing the central dichotomies of Western thought, Derrida effectively undercuts the gendering of these dichotomies and the consequent disprivileging of the feminine. As noted earlier, Derrida uses feminine metaphors to attack the binary logic of Western thought. He seeks a new inscription of difference that is not based on the masculine/feminine binary, one that will yield a multiplicity of sexual voices. This is the basis of his claim that deconstruction is not merely a negative method, a destruction of all that went before, but is rather an intervention and a displacement.

These are not inconsiderable advantages. Displacing the binaries of Western thought is, in my view, essential to the program of feminism, and Derrida's thought is instrumental in achieving this goal. I do not want to deny these advantages. What I do want to deny, however, is the success of Derrida's forays into ethical and political questions. I do not think that Derrida can be of much use in the task of constructing a feminist ethics and politics; indeed, his efforts in this regard have given the whole notion of a postmodern ethics/politics a bad name.[17]

A few examples from Derrida's recent publications will suffice to make my point. In two publications whose aim is explicitly political, Derrida adopts a tactic that anyone interested in practical politics must find at least irritating and at worst offensive. In a discussion of nuclear war (1984), he devotes most of his attention to analyzing the concept of "deterrence," asserting that it entails deferral or *différance*. He argues that the problem with the "logic" of deterrence is that it is a logic of deviation and transgression, chance and luck (1984: 29). Nowhere in the article is there any discussion of the practical politics of the problem or even of a theoretical position that might conceivably have practical effects. He takes much the same tactic in *The Other Heading: Reflections on Today's Europe* (1992), concentrating his analysis on the logic of the concept "heading" and relating this to the current reconfiguration in European politics. Again, there is nothing to indicate that the topic is a practical political problem, not merely a linguistic exercise. The complex – even clever – conceptual analyses that constitute the centers of these works are insightful in certain respects. But if one considers the subject matter that Derrida is addressing – the possibility of nuclear war and the fall of Communism in Europe – his cleverness borders on insult. His conceptual analyses, however brilliant, fail to even touch on the pressing political questions raised by these revolutionary events.[18]

I am not arguing here that political theories must address the "real world" of politics, a realm distinct from the realm of "mere words." Such a claim would fly in the face of the Wittgensteinian conviction that guides my discussion: that language is an activity constitutive of human life. What Derrida does in these articles, however, is turn the language of politics into a parlor game, a clever linguistic exercise. He removes the language of politics from the very political activity that gives it its meaning. He in effect denies that political language is a *political* activity.

An even more disturbing tendency is evident in his 1990 essay "Force of Law." On the face of it, it would seem that deconstruction is uniquely suited to legal analysis. The law is, after all, all text, text that must be carefully interpreted and applied. Derrida does not make such an obvious point in his analysis, however; for what he wants to talk about is the relationship between law and justice. Justice, he claims, always exists outside the law; it is not itself deconstructible. "Thus," he concludes, "deconstruction is justice" (1990: 945). Without trying to explain the logic of this "thus," he goes on to assert that deconstruction takes place between the undeconstructability of justice and the deconstructability of law. He concludes that even though deconstruction may seem like a move to irresponsibility, it actually entails an increase in responsibility (1990: 952).

It is perhaps foolhardy to try to decipher this at all. But at least one probable interpretation of this text yields some startling results. A central theme of Derrida's philosophical project is his rejection of traditional metaphysics, what he calls the "metaphysics of presence."[19] Portions of "Force of Law"reflect this thesis. Thus, he specifically rejects what he calls the "classical emancipatory ideal" associated with justice (1990: 971). Yet, in his references to the "undeconstructibility" of justice, he seems to be slipping metaphysics in through the back door. It is difficult not to interpret his distinction between law and justice, his claim that justice lies outside the law, in anything but metaphysical terms. This suggests that although Derrida rejects what he calls the metaphysics of presence, he admits that some form of metaphysics is necessary to explain a concept like justice. What this metaphysics might be, how it might relate to the metaphysics of presence, or how it might translate into political terms, however, is left unclear.

Derrida has made bold claims for the political relevance of deconstruction. He asserts that deconstruction is *always* political: "the strategic re-evaluation of the concept of text allows me to bring together in a more consistent fashion, in the most consistent fashion possible, theoretico-philosophical necessities with the practical, political and other necessities of what is called deconstruction" (1986a: 168). He claims that those who deny its political relevance do so because they "only recognize politics by the most familiar road signs" (quoted in Bernstein 1987: 108). But the road signs that Derrida has given us are not sufficient to mark his political position. Derrida's forays into political and ethical analysis are characterized by two tendencies: detailed conceptual analysis that bears little relationship to practical political issues and quasi-metaphysical speculations. The first tendency is frustrating to those who seek political guidance; the second implies that politics without some form of metaphysics is impossible and, ironically, suggests a return to a modernist conception of politics grounded in metaphysics.

What I see to be the liabilities of this strand of postmodern thought are most clearly illustrated in the work of another thinker who is a representative of apolitical postmodernism, Peter Sloterdijk. His *The Critique of Cynical Reason* (1987), despite its daunting length, became a best-seller in Germany and has been widely read in the United States. Sloterdijk's thesis is that we must confront the "cynical reason" that dominates our age, a pattern of thought that is a product of the naive critique of ideologies. In its place he proposes what he calls *kynismos*, a kind of "argumentation" composed of "irrelevantly provocative gestures (farting, nose-picking, masturbation), the use of the animal body in the human and its gestures *as* arguments" (1987: 101–3). The elementary kinical organ, Sloterdijk claims, is the ass (1987: 148). He traces the origin of kinical "thought" to Diogenes, who practiced it in the marketplace. Kinical "reason" culminates in nihilism, an attitude that, Sloterdijk claims, we cannot have enough of (1987: 194). Central to his argument is the contention that posing any kind of answers, theories, or values incurs the danger of falling back into the "serious thinking" that has been the ruin of philosophy. In short, we cannot speak; we can only fart.

Sloterdijk expresses a thesis, if we can call it that, that is common to apolitical postmodernism. If, the argument goes, the error of modernism was to advance universal theories grounded in absolute knowledge, then the task of those who oppose it is to advance no theories at all. To advance a theory is, first, to fall back into the epistemological errors of modernism and, second, to incur the coercion and tyranny that characterize absolutist thinking. I see this argument as seriously flawed and, ultimately, contradictory. Despite Sloterdijk's valiant effort to free himself from the clutches of modernist epistemology, he has not succeeded in doing so. He is assuming, consistent with modernist thought, the validity of the dichotomy between grounded and ungrounded knowledge. Since modernist knowledge is grounded, its counter must, by definition, be ungrounded. What he and the postmodern thinkers who adopt this thesis refuse to consider is a different kind of ground for knowledge, a discursive ground rooted in language games, forms of life, "prejudices." In their desperate attempt *not* to offer an alternative to modernist knowledge, *not* to articulate a new paradigm of knowledge, these thinkers end up reaffirming the epistemological grounds of modernist knowledge. Their assumption that no grounding exists except an absolute grounding is, ironically, a modernist assumption.

Further evidence of this tendency to return to modernist thought while ostensibly rejecting it is Sloterdijk's turn in a quasi-mystical direction at the end of the book. In an effort to sum up kinicism, Sloterdijk writes:

> What is left to say? Experiences would now come into play that one can only refer to mysteriously without being able to call on the aid of proofs. That about which one cannot argue should be told at a more opportune time. It is a matter of experiences for which I can find no other word than the exuberant experience of a well-spent life. . . . Every conscious second eradicates what is hopelessly past and becomes the first second of an other history. (1987: 547)

Jonathan Culler once described deconstructionists as theorists who saw off the theoretical branch on which they are sitting (1982: 149). Sloterdijk's version of this is that he cannot get enough of nihilism. There is nothing to stop the free-fall if one takes this theoretical route: everything is fiction, fantasy, play. It is significant, however, that neither Derrida nor Sloterdijk appear to be able to totally accept the free-fall they describe. Derrida seems to be moving back to metaphysics, while Sloterdijk seems to be embracing mysticism.[20] Both these moves entail a tacit acceptance of modernist epistemology. Ultimately these theorists find themselves in an untenable situation. They refuse to discuss an alternative concept of knowledge, a new paradigm, claiming that any alternative theory would necessarily entail the coercion of modernist thought. Yet they also seem unable to accept the full extent of the nihilism their position entails. I am arguing that another option is possible; that another paradigm can be, and is being, articulated. Some postmodern thinkers, along with Wittgenstein and Gadamer, have defined another kind of grounding for knowledge: the language games that constitute our form of life. Language games are neither fictions nor fantasies but, rather, the riverbed through which the thought and action of our culture flow. This perspective rests on the assumption that our form of life is neither a groundless ground nor an arbitrary construction but, rather, provides the very possibility of thought and meaning.

Political postmodernism

In *The Postmodern Condition* Jean François Lyotard argues that, like it or not, we live in a world devoid of meta-narratives, lacking a groundless ground for knowledge. This in itself is hardly a startling insight; it is the basic thesis of most postmodern writers. What is significant about this book, and all of Lyotard's work, however, is that he then goes on to ask the question that the apolitical postmoderns ignore: the question of what kind of knowledge *does* exist in this world, and how we can be said to *know* anything. In *The Differend* (1988) Lyotard pursues this inquiry in a specifically ethical context, asking how we can live in the postmodern world as moral beings. He assumes the impossibility of avoiding conflicts and the absence of a universal genre of discourse. But he goes on to ask how, given this situation, we can save the "honor of thinking"? His answer is that thought, cognition, ethics, and politics are in play when one phrase is linked to another. The key to knowledge and ethics in the postmodern world, then, is the free examination of phrases (1988: xiii–xiv). On the face of it, this answer appears to be yet another instance of the nihilistic strand of postmodernism I discussed above. An indication of Lyotard's very different approach, however, is his reliance on the thought of Kant and Wittgenstein. Like Wittgenstein, Lyotard believes that discourses have rules and that there exist genres of discourse that fix the rules of linkages for other discourses (1988: 29). Following Kant, he argues that it is the task of philosophy to act as the critical tribunal of thought (1989: 410).

What this means for ethics and politics is most fully developed in *Just Gaming* (Lyotard and Thébaud 1985). Politics, the authors argue, is one of the genres of discourse that sets the rules for other discourses. Central to the genre of language that is politics, they argue, are the concepts of justice and injustice. But in their view, injustice is not simply the opposite of justice; rather, it is the condition that arises when the possibility of questioning the distinction between the just and the unjust cannot arise (1985: 67). Justice is the regulatory idea in the political arena (1985: 91), but it is also a (language) game like any other game. What makes it distinctive is, first, the centrality of politics in human life and, second, the fact that the language game of justice includes a distinctive feature: transcendence, finality and Idea (1985: 71). The authors claim that "Transcendence is immanent to the prescriptive game." In the language game of justice one is "taken ahold of by something beyond us," thereby producing an obligation (1985: 72).

If I am interpreting Lyotard and Thébaud correctly here, they are advancing a position similar to the one I advanced in the first section of this chapter: an effort to explain the claim to rightness in moral language games without recourse to a meta-narrative. Their theory is that transcendence within immanence is the distinctive character of the prescriptive game. This sounds contradictory, but the contradiction disappears once we abandon the epistemological assumptions of modernist discourse. This perspective explains an intriguing passage in *The Differend*: "Or is postmodernity the pastime of an old man who scrounges in the garbage heap of finality looking for leftovers, who brandishes unconsciousnesses, lapses, limits, confines, goulags, paratoxes, non-senses, or paradoxes, and who turns this into the glory of his novelty, into his promise of change?" (1988: 136).

In modernist discourse, concepts such as justice must be grounded in finality, in absolute knowledge. If such finality is abandoned, then we are left with nothing, and no meaning or action is possible. This is the conclusion reached by the apolitical postmoderns, the conclusion that drove Derrida to a quasi-metaphysical stance in his effort to explain the phenomenon of justice. Lyotard and, I am arguing, Gadamer and Wittgenstein as well take a different tack. As Lyotard puts it, we can either mourn our lost unanimity or find another means of thinking and acting (1989: 316). Finding another means of thinking means thinking without meta-narratives and examining local, discursive grounds for truth. Finding another means of acting means exploring the possibilities of politics without grounding meta-narratives. That this is not a simple matter is clear from Lyotard's discussion of justice. Finding a way of talking about justice that retains the transcendence of the language game is a challenging task. But, unlike Derrida, Lyotard does not retreat into metaphysics in order to accomplish his goal. Whereas Derrida relegates the concept of justice to a realm beyond analysis, Lyotard analyzes the language game of justice and attempts to explain its unique aspects. He tries to fashion a way of talking about justice and politics that will account for both the immanent and the transcendent elements of the language game. The result is an extensive body of political writings (1993). These writings, particularly those dealing with the Algerian war, illustrate Lyotard's willingness to jettison the sacred cows of Marxist analysis, the dominant meta-narrative of leftist intellectuals, and to formulate concrete political positions tailored to the specificities of the political situation (1993: 165–326).

Lyotard's work offers a model for the construction of *a* (not *the*) postmodern approach to ethics and politics. But it is in the work of Foucault that the advantages of employing postmodern themes in ethical and political analysis become most apparent. Much has been written about the political possibilities, or lack thereof, in Foucault's work. I approach this topic by focusing on Foucault's methodology. My contention is that Foucault's method represents a radical epistemological shift from previous ethical and political theories. Viewed from the perspective of these theories, his work is deficient: it fails to provide universally applicable ethical or political standards. But I see this as precisely the strength of his theory and the aspect that makes it particularly appropriate to feminist theory. A central aspect of my argument is that it is more useful to interpret Foucault as a chronicler of change than as its advocate and that in his role as "historian of the present" he collapses the modernist dichotomy between description and prescription. Like Lyotard, Foucault argues that we *do*, in fact, live in a different world from that theorized by the moderns, not that we *should* live in such a world or that we should do thus and so to achieve that world. Thus, he argues that the Cartesian subject is not adequate to describe the situation of subjects in our society, that knowledge is no longer grounded in a widely accepted meta-narrative, and that power is dispersed rather than concentrated. This situation dictates a very different role for the intellectual, the creator of theories of this world, and also a very different form of resistance. In other words, what Foucault discovers about the world he seeks to understand dictates the role he adopts as an intellectual, as well as the kind of politics he advocates. The line between description and prescription is necessarily and deliberately blurred.

This perspective on Foucault's thought is most clearly illustrated in his work on the subject. His attitude toward the subject in all his work is both descriptive and critical. His analysis is designed to understand the construction of subjectivity in the postmodern world and, thereby, suggest ways of improving the situation of subjects through a politics of resistance. In summing up his genealogy of the subject in his later work, Foucault argues:

> Maybe our problem is now to discover that the self is nothing else than the historical correlation of the technology built in our history. Maybe the problem is to change those technologies. And in this case, one of the main political problems would be nowadays, in the strict sense of the word, the politics of ourselves. (1993: 222–3)

Foucault's attitude to truth also illustrates this methodology in which description and critique are linked. Like Lyotard, Foucault believes that there are multiple truths in our society, not a single truth or founding meta-narrative. His theory of truth and knowledge is descriptive; it looks at how truths are constructed by discourses and how those discourses change over time. But, as with his theory of subjectivity, the impulse behind these descriptions is a critical one. Foucault's interest in what he calls "subjugated knowledges" reveals this impulse. Subjugated knowledges are "blocs of historical knowledge present but disguised within the body of functionalist systematizing criticism and which criticism – which obviously draws upon scholarship – has been able to reveal" (1980: 82). Although much of Foucault's work is concerned with elaborate analyses of the hegemonic discourses that structure knowledge, truth, subjects, and power in the modern world, he never loses sight of the critical possibilities of his analyses. And it is the presence of subjugated knowledges that realizes those possibilities. He argues that "it is through the re-appearance of this knowledge, of these local popular knowledges, these disqualified knowledges, that criticism performs its work" (1980: 82).

This same method – the effort to both describe a new phenomenon and, in describing it, to suggest the possibility of critique – informs Foucault's discussion of another controversial aspect of his theory: power. Critics of Foucault have used his theory of multiple truths to argue that a Foucaultian ethics or politics is impossible. The same argument is invoked with reference to his theory of power. Foucault argues that the modern concept of power as emanating from a single source fails to describe the unique character of power in the modern world. As a counter, he advances a number of theses with regard to power. He claims that a distinctive kind of power was inaugurated by bourgeois society: disciplinary power. This kind of power is unique, in that it is inseparable from the production of truth in bourgeois society. Discourses of truth produced by the "experts" so revered in bourgeois society create institutions of power that govern both bodies and minds. This Foucaultian linking of truth and power flies in the face of the

Enlightenment belief that truth will free us from power, that truth is transcendent, power immanent. Further, Foucault's theory of power is unique because, he claims, power is everywhere, it is not localized in a single source. Foucault uses the metaphor of capillaries to describe the phenomenon: power circulates like blood through capillaries, permeating every aspect of the body politic.

In one of the more famous critiques of Foucault's theory of power, Nancy Hartsock (1990) suggests that the argument that power is everywhere entails that power is nowhere and, consequently, that resistance to power is obviated. Both Marxists and liberals argue that power is concentrated in a single source, that all power is derivative of, respectively, the economic or the political. The problem with this approach is that the economic or political source of power theorized by the Marxists or the liberals is by definition monolithic and overpowering. Combatting such power necessitates violent revolution, not a project to be undertaken lightly. Foucault's theory of power, by contrast, theorizes resistance to power in more accessible terms. He argues:

> [Resistances to power] are the odd term in relations of power; they are inscribed in the latter as an irreducible opposite. Hence they too are distributed in irregular fashion: the points, knots or focuses of resistance are spread over time and space at varying densities, at times mobilizing groups and individuals in a definitive way, inflaming certain types of behavior . . . more often one is dealing with mobile and transitory points of resistance, producing cleavages in a society that shift about, fracturing unities and effecting regroupings, furrowing across individuals themselves, cutting them up and remolding them, marking off irreducible regions in them, in their bodies and minds. (1978: 96)

Foucault's theory of power assumes that resistance to power is an integral aspect of the phenomenon of power. Most importantly, he suggests that power can be effectively combatted on the local level, that local resistance to a specific form of oppression can be productive. This is in sharp contrast to the Marxist tradition that defines the hegemonic power of capitalism as creating an almost helpless proletariat. This centralized theory of power dismisses local resistance as ineffective; only striking at the heart of power would achieve its overthrow. Foucault, by contrast, defines resistance to power as everywhere.

The critical relevance of these speculations about the subject, truth, and power come together in Foucault's theory of the role of the intellectual. Once more, Foucault's explicit goal is descriptive rather than prescriptive, but his description necessarily entails critique. The age of the "universal intellectual," he claims, is passing (1980: 126). The universal intellectual was "universal" in two senses: first, he [sic] relied on universal truths and principles to ground his arguments, and, second, he pronounced on the global order of things, the total picture. In

opposition to this, Foucault describes what he calls the "specific intellectual," the intellectual who is concerned with local and immediate
forms of power and oppression, who utilizes a "local" scientific truth to
formulate arguments (1980: 128–9). The task of the specific intellectual,
Foucault argues, is "to struggle against the forms of power that transform him into its object and instrument in the sphere of 'knowledge,'
'truth,' 'consciousness,' and 'discourse'" (1977a: 208). As Foucault defines her/him, the specific intellectual is both a product of the changing
configuration of the modern world – the diversity of subjects, the
dispersal of power – and a commentator on those changes. The specific
intellectual also embodies the possibility of resistance in such a world.
If the struggle is directed against power, Foucault argues, then all those
on whom power is exercised to their detriment can begin the struggle
on their own terrain (1977a: 216). "The essential political problem for
the intellectual is not to criticize the ideological content supposedly
linked to science, or to ensure that his own scientific practice is accompanied by a correct ideology, but that of ascertaining the possibility of
constituting a new politics of truth" (1980: 133).

Central to the tradition of political theory is the analysis of discrete
aspects of the formulations of the theorists who constitute the canon.
Thus we have analyses of Hobbes's theory of power, Locke's individualist subject, Marx's economics. Foucault's approach defies these neat
divisions; it is impossible to separate his "theory" of power from his
"theory" of the subject or resistance. In abandoning the epistemology
of modernity, Foucault embraces an alternative epistemology that
centers on the analysis of discourses; all his "theories" are a function
of this analysis. Central to that epistemology is the collapsing of the
descriptive/prescriptive distinction so fundamental to political theory.
Foucault's adoption of this radically different epistemology, more than
any other factor, accounts for his rejection by traditional political
theorists.

The similarities between Foucault's discourse analysis and
Wittgenstein's concept of language games are notable. These similarities are particularly relevant to the questions of moral and political
theory that Wittgenstein so studiously avoids. Foucault's method is
not only compatible with Wittgenstein's concept of language games;
it supplies the missing political dimension of that concept. For
Wittgenstein, the analysis of language games is wholly descriptive;
he even asserts that philosophy itself can do nothing *but* describe.
Foucault's discourse analysis is similarly descriptive, but, by challenging the distinction between description and evaluation, Foucault attributes a moral/political dimension to this analysis. He argues that

> when I say "game" I mean an ensemble of rules for the production of the
> truth. It is not a game in the sense of imitating or entertaining . . . it is an

ensemble of procedures which lead to a certain result, which can be considered a function of its principles and its rules of procedures, as valid or
not, as winner or loser. (1988: 16)

Elsewhere he concludes, "Only the simple minded can say that for me
truth does not exist" (1984b: 25). The goal of the intellectual's analysis
of games of truth is, for Foucault, to "reinterrogate the obvious and the
assumed, to unsettle habits, ways of thinking and doing, to dissipate
accepted familiarities, to evaluate rules and institutions and . . . to participate in the formation of a political will" (1984b: 30). The result is
what one critic calls the "logic of dissent" (Bannet 1989). What has been
created by discourse can also be overthrown by discourse. This is
accomplished not by appealing to universal truths or by reference to a
transcendent subject (Foucault 1972: 55) but by exploring the gaps and
silences within discourse itself and by applying a discourse where it
does not "belong" to effect a political disruption.

At various points in his work Foucault attempts to connect his critical
method to that established by the Enlightenment in general and Kant in
particular (1986). He claims that in expressing a critical "ontology of
ourselves" (1988: 95), he is continuing the spirit of the Enlightenment.
In his work on Blanchot (1987b) he even moves toward a kind of
mysticism about language that is reminiscent of Wittgenstein's
Tractatus. Whether these specific arguments are individually successful
is unimportant. What is important is that he is trying to define a critical
role for his methodology, a methodology that eschews the disembodied universalism of the Enlightenment and construes critique on
radically different grounds.

In the context of the ongoing debate over whether Foucault's work
provides the basis for moral or political action, it is ironic that
Foucault's later work is specifically concerned with the question of
ethics. His topic in the volumes of *The History of Sexuality* is the
evolution of the ethical subject in Western thought and practice. Thus
he examines the various dimensions of the ethical life: substance,
mode of subjection, ethical self-formation, and ethical action in context
(1985: 26–8). Foucault's analysis of ethics is unique in several respects.
It is, throughout, a particular and historical analysis. Foucault is examining ethics as a historically grounded social practice, not as the attempt to discover the "truth" of ethics in abstract general principles.
Further, his examination of ethics is an examination of the ethical
subject. Ethics and subjectivity are inseparable for Foucault; to be a
subject is to have an *ethos*, an ethical practice that defines moral obliga-
tions. Foucault's ethics is an examination of "who we are said to be," an
examination of the contingent and local practices that constitute us as
ethical subjects.

There has been much discussion in recent commentaries on Foucault concerning whether he can be said to have an "ethics" at all. For example, in his lengthy and erudite *The Question of Ethics* Charles Scott argues that theorists in the Nietzschean tradition, among whom Foucault is prominent, have "interrupted" the values that govern everyday life, causing them to become optional rather than axiomatic (1990: 4). He notes quite accurately that Foucault is not defining "ethics" in the traditional sense of seeking a morality acceptable to everyone (1990: 57). Scott's conclusion is one that has become increasingly popular in "postmodern" discussions of ethics: "Is it possible that the *question* of ethics holds hope for a life without the ethical subject and without some of the suffering that we ethical subjects bring upon ourselves?" (1990: 93). This same sentiment is evident in another extended commentary on "postmodern ethics." Tobin Siebers argues that, for Derrida, ethics emerges as an attempt to establish order and thus is a form of violence. Therefore, he concludes, the "opening of ethics" is itself nonethical and violent (1988: 95).

These attempts to define a "postmodern ethics" are wrong-headed. First, it is impossible to define a single "postmodern ethic" because of the significant differences among the so-called postmoderns. Second, the question of whether we can define a "Foucaultian ethics" is misleading. Foucault is not offering an "ethics," a "counter-ethics," or even a deconstruction of the whole notion of an ethics. Rather, he is inaugurating a method of analysis that describes the constitution of a particular ethical subject. But, as with all aspects of his methodology, description always involves critique. Another way of characterizing what Foucault is doing here is to say that he is bridging the gap between the sociology or history of ethics and moral philosophy. Sociologists and historians of ethics are descriptive, whereas moral philosophers are prescriptive. Foucault is doing both at once. Uncovering the elements of the dominant Western ethical subject simultaneously reveals the possibility of other constitutions of ethical subjectivity and thus the possibility of resistance.

Many of those who attempt to define a "postmodern ethic" interpret Foucault as arguing that ethics, *qua* ethics, is repressive. One of the common and, I believe, accurate interpretations of what I am calling apolitical postmodernism asserts that any concept of ethics entails subjection and hence violence. This concept inevitably leads to the kind of nihilism that theorists such as Sloterdijk embody. Foucault's position is quite different. The key to his approach to ethics lies in his definition of ethics as moral character. For Foucault, as for Wittgenstein and Gilligan, to be a subject means to be an ethical subject; ethics cannot be discussed apart from subjectivity. Although they are speaking from very different discursive traditions, there is a sense in which Gilligan and Foucault are doing much the same thing in their analyses of ethics. Gilligan is examining the hegemonic moral tradition and suggesting the possibility of another constitution of moral subjectivity. Foucault is describing the historical evolution of that same hegemonic moral tradition and suggesting that other definitions of subjectivity – in particular, ethical subjectivity – are possible. Neither is suggesting that ethics itself is repressive; for both, being a subject means having a moral voice. What both are suggesting, however, is that the dominant moral discourse of the West, a discourse that defines only one moral truth and excludes other moral voices from the realm of the moral, *is* repressive.[21]

Because, as I have been arguing, Foucault's method unites description and critique, he does not articulate a distinct "theory" of resistance. But the possibility of resistance is implicit in his descriptive/critical method. I have discussed various aspects of what he calls "local resistance" in the foregoing. One aspect of that discussion is particularly relevant here: the question of whether a "progressive politics" demands the sovereignty of a "pure subject" (1991: 65). One of the principal objections to the possibility of a Foucaultian politics is that principled political action demands grounding in a sovereign subject, absolutes, and universal truth that can guide it. Foucault's rejection of these concepts, it is argued, precludes the possibility of a Foucaultian politics. But Foucault has a very effective answer to this charge: he turns the question back on his detractors. How, he asks, can a politics rooted in abstract universals effectively deal with the concrete problems of practical politics? He argues that what reformers have defined as a "progressive politics," a politics rooted in a transcendent subject and a *logos*, ignores the analysis of concrete practices, taking refuge instead in "a global history of totalities" (1991: 65). Far from fostering the reform of repressive institutions, "progressive politics" abstracts from the concrete political reality it seeks to reform.

The "local resistance" that Foucault advocates is a counter to this traditional concept of politics. Resistance to power, he claims, does not come from outside power. Rather, resistance "exists all the more by being in the same place as power" (1980: 142). Our task, consequently, should not be to formulate global systemic theory but to "analyze the specificity of mechanisms of power, to locate the connections and extensions, to build, little by little, a strategic knowledge" (1980: 145). It is tempting to interpret Foucault's approach as offering an alternative in the dialectical tradition of Marxism. He makes it clear, however, that he is not seeking to abolish error and replace it with truth. Rather, he characterizes his method as the "freeing of difference:" this requires "thought without contradiction, without dialectics, without negation, thought that accepts divergence; affirmative thought whose instrument is distinction; thought of the multiple – of the nomadic and dispersed multiplicity that is not limited or confined by the constraints of similarity" (1977a: 185).

This Foucaultian view of politics as the freeing of difference is the basis for my claim that a Foucaultian politics is particularly appropriate to contemporary feminist politics. Most of those within the contemporary feminist movement would agree that their goal is not simply to replace the "error" of masculinist theory and politics with the "truth" of feminism. Rather, they recognize that there is not one "truth" for women, but many; that women's situations vary widely, and that to impose a single "woman's truth" would result in marginalizing some women and privileging others. Feminists are also coming to realize that the oppressions that women face are varied and multiple; they require specific (local) resistances designed for the particular situations that different women face.

These dimensions of the contemporary feminist movement suggest the appropriateness of a Foucaultian politics. From a Foucaultian perspective, what the "women's liberation movement" is about is the refusal to accept the discourse on sexuality that has been assigned to women (1980: 219–20). Women in the feminist movement have consciously departed from that discourse, borrowing conceptual elements from other discursive formations and crafting discourses about the feminine and sexuality that are transgressive. "Discourses" is important here. There is no single discourse about woman that will be appropriate to all women. This is where the "freeing of differences" becomes important. In one of his few comments on feminism, Foucault argues that women's defiance of the discourse that scripts their sexuality has led them to reinvent their own type of existence, to use their sexuality as a starting point from which to cross to other affirmations (1977b: 155). This is not only a revealing description of what feminists have indeed accomplished but also a blueprint for future struggles.[22]

A discursive morality

Discussions of the possibility of a postmodern ethics/politics abound in contemporary literature. Much of this literature is concerned with what I see to be the impossible task of defining a specifically "postmodern" ethics/politics. There would be little point in reviewing this literature here. But one question that is raised in this literature is essential to my argument: whether an epistemology that eschews absolute foundations can provide a coherent ethical or political position. My argument in the foregoing was that Foucault does not so much answer this question as displace it. By embracing an epistemology that unites description and critique, he breaks down the fact/value dichotomy that informs modernist discourse. He not only questions the distinction between description and critique, fact and value, but challenges the goal of absolutism in either sphere.

It is instructive to compare Foucault's position on ethics with that of another theorist who challenges the fact/value dichotomy and the possibility of ethical truth: Max Weber. Both Foucault and Weber argue that the contemporary world lacks a meta-narrative that can ground ethical beliefs; both also see this world as devoid of absolute meaning. Weber's solution to this problem is to claim that each individual must accept responsibility for his [sic] own actions and choose a particular ethical stance for himself – in short, *choose* to be a morally responsible individual. Foucault's response rejects the individualism that informs Weber's approach. He claims that the subject is a "work of art," that we fashion our subjectivity from the discursive resources available to us in our particular situation. He would further reject Weber's notion that we should delve into our inner being in order to fashion an ethical self.

What is significant about this comparison is that, despite their different solutions, Weber and Foucault are both trying to articulate an ethical stance in a world that they see as devoid of absolutes. But despite their similarities, the reception of their ethical approaches has been radically different. Weber is rarely criticized for obviating the possibility of an ethical or political position, despite his rejection of absolutes. Yet, although, in a strict sense, both present "relativistic" ethical positions, Foucault's position is frequently rejected out of hand, while Weber's is embraced as an ethical model. I see this difference as revealing a significant presupposition of contemporary thought. Foucault, unlike Weber, abandons the transcendent subject as well as transcendent values; he completes the displacement of modernist discourse that Weber only began. Weber's retention of the transcendent subject lends acceptability to his ethical approach, whereas Foucault's rejection of this subject stigmatizes his effort to define an ethics.

My discussion of what I call "discursive morality"[23] is organized around three theses: first, that rejecting absolute foundations for ethics does not entail either the negation of ethics or a retreat to a strictly individualistic ethics; second, that, far from being a compromise position, a discursive understanding of morality fundamentally deconstructs the tradition of modernist moral theory; and third, that the key to discursive morality is an understanding of the uniqueness of the moral language game and its intimate connection with subjectivity.

In order to elaborate these theses, I examine what I see to be three representative approaches to the question of postmodern ethics/politics. My intent is to distinguish my position from these approaches and, in so doing, to outline the possibilities for a reconceptualization of moral theory. The first of these arguments was mentioned briefly above: the claim that postmodernism necessarily subverts the possibility of ethics, Edith Wyschogrod's work offers a good illustration. In *Spirit in Ashes* (1985) and *Saints and Postmodernism* (1990) Wyschogrod develops what seems to be an odd connection: theology and postmodernism. In her first book she poses her central question: how can we create an ethics that is appropriate to the "postmodern world," particularly since the advent of mass death? Her answer in that book is a new concept of self that is appropriate to that world, a "transactional self" that she defines as a "postmodern selfhood." In her later book, *Saints and Postmodernism*, she takes up the issue of ethics more directly: "A postmodern ethics? Is this not a contradiction in terms? If postmodernism is a critical expression describing the subversion of philosophical language, a mutant of western humanism, then how can one hope for an ethics when the conditions of meaning are themselves under attack?" (1990: xiii). Wyschogrod fashions several answers to this question in the course of the book: that a postmodern ethics constitutes the subversion of ethics and that the "postmodern saintly life" offers us a "new path in ethics" (1990: 257).

Wyschogrod's approach illustrates two commonly held assumptions about the possibility of a "postmodern ethics." First, her narratives of the lives of the saints as ethical rebels entails the definition of a postmodern ethic as radically individualistic and idiosyncratic. This is the opposite of the kind of discursive morality that I am articulating. Discursive morality eschews the individualistic construction of moral principles, assuming, instead, that morality is a pattern of behavior that is socially acquired. Like the acquisition of subjectivity, it is constituted by our common form of life. Second, Wyschogrod's work illustrates an all too common assumption that pervades discussions of postmodern ethics: that any attempt to formulate an "ethics," because it must suppress ethical differences, is an "act of terror" (1990: xix). Her position here is yet another example of a self-proclaimed "postmodern" caught on the horns of a modernist dichotomy that she claims to be deconstructing. Her rejection of ethics presupposes that there are only two alternatives: universal ethical principles or idiosyncratic ethical stances assumed by "rebels," which represent the subversion of all ethics. The discursive morality that I am proposing, by contrast, avoids this polarity. It posits a concrete, discursive ground for ethics that is neither arbitrary nor universalistic.[24]

A very different argument is found in the work of Stephen White. If there is a sense in which Wyschogrod's postmodern ethics goes too far in rejecting ethics, then White's work illustrates the opposite pitfall: not going far enough. In a recent work White considers the implications of postmodernism for the tradition of political theory. He argues that modernity's strong suit is what he calls the "responsibility to act," while postmodernism's strength is the "responsibility to otherness" (1990: 81). But he also sees these strengths as having their attendant weaknesses. Modernity's desire to engage in "conceptual imperialism" causes it to be closed to otherness, a condition that has harmful practical consequences. Postmodernism, on the other hand, has a tendency to fall into "apolitical aestheticism" and the inability to foster collective action (1988: 197–8).

White's solution to this problem is to elaborate a theory in which these two tendencies coexist in "creative tension" with each other (1990: 81). It is significant that he turns to what he calls "difference feminism" as a way of illustrating this creative tension. In *Political Theory and Postmodernism* (1991) he argues that the discourse of care that has been developed in "difference feminism" provides the alternative ethical/political discourse that postmodernism is looking for. In articulating his position, White proposes what he calls a "lighter" version of care, one that avoids "communal suffocation" (1991: 105). But despite the fact that he, unlike most male political theorists, assumes that feminism has something to offer political theory, his solution is inadequate. His version of a "radical pluralist politics" (1991: 138) is not, despite his claim, radical enough. There are similarities between what White is asserting here and what I referred to above as the "dialectical" approach to the subject. Like the advocates of the dialectical subject, White seeks to join the polarities of the debate rather than displace the dichotomy that underlies it. He fails to grasp the radical challenge posed by some aspects of postmodern thought. Bringing modernism and postmodernism into creative tension is not feasible, because the two do not share an epistemological space. The challenge posed by the deconstruction of universalistic ethics is that of imagining a new epistemological space for ethics and politics. This cannot encompass the "good" aspects of modernity but, rather, entails radically rethinking the definition of a ground for ethical and political truths.[25]

The boldest attempt to articulate a postmodern ethics/politics is found in the extensive works of Richard Rorty.[26] Rorty's attack on the institution of Western philosophy began with epistemology and metaphysics (*Philosophy and the Mirror of Nature* (1979)), but he has since ventured into the realm of ethics and politics. In *Contingency, Irony and Solidarity* (1989) Rorty presents his political philosophy, which he labels "liberal ironism." At its heart is a deep and thoroughgoing anti-essentialism. Rorty wants to explore "how things look if we drop the demand for theory" that limits public and private life (1989: xv). He wants to explore the question of how we can assert simultaneously that our beliefs are contingent and that we are willing to defend them to the death.

His answer is that relativism is not a problem for those who do not believe in absolutes, any more than blasphemy is a problem for those who do not believe in God (1989: 50). The hero of Rorty's book is the "liberal ironist": a liberal is a person who thinks cruelty is the worst thing we do, an ironist is a person who faces the contingency of her beliefs (1989: xv).[27] Everyone, even the liberal ironist, has what Rorty calls a "final vocabulary" beyond which she/he cannot go in justifying action. What sets the ironist apart from the rest of us, however, is that she realizes that her final vocabulary is no closer to reality than anyone else's (1989: 73).[28]

There is much to commend in Rorty's formulation. His notion of a "final vocabulary" is much like Wittgenstein's notion of forms of life; for both, this is the point at which justifications necessarily end. Rorty emphasizes that we do not choose our language games, that they are not arbitrary but, quite literally, give us a world to inhabit (1989: 6). But his theory can also accommodate change: someone who uses language as it has never been used before (he gives the example of Freud) will alter our way of speaking and hence acting (1989: 28). In other contexts, Rorty applies this theory of change to feminism. What feminists are doing, he claims, is suggesting a way of saying things that has never been said before; it is as a result of this new way of speaking that feminists can visualize new social practices (1991a, 1993). The upshot of this is that, for Rorty, beliefs can regulate action and even be worth dying for, even if those who hold them are aware that they are caused by nothing deeper than contingent historical circumstances (1989: 189).

Rorty's position avoids the pitfall that Wyschogrod's work falls into: the assumption that without universal ethical principles there can be no ethics at all. But he encounters another difficulty that is equally serious: ignoring what I have argued is the uniqueness of the moral language game – specifically, its claim to certainty. When we look closely at Rorty's liberal ironist, we find that she (or he) is an exceedingly odd individual. The liberal ironist, we are told, is someone who desperately needs to talk to people because her/his socialization has not completely "taken" (1989: 186). Rorty's goal in constructing such a being is to refute the belief that morality involves reference to some common human value that constitutes our humanity (1989: 177). But, in attempting to do this, Rorty turns from a concept of a universal common humanity to a form of elitism. The ironist is one who *understands* that all human value is contingent and that our beliefs are ungrounded. This implies that the rest of us – presumably most of humanity – do not understand this because with us, unlike the ironist, socialization *has* "taken." Hence there is a wonderful irony implicit in Rorty's ironist: Rorty comes out sounding much like Kant in *What Is Enlightenment?* Kant divides people into moral individuals who act out of duty and "domestic cattle" who act out of habit and thus not morally. Rorty's division is likewise elitist: there are the ironists who "understand" the contingency of all belief and the rest who erroneously assume their beliefs to be true.

But there is a more fundamental problem with Rorty's liberal ironist. Such a person is someone who realizes the contingency of, in this case, liberal beliefs but acts according to them anyway – even to the point of death. I think that Rorty's formulation here is an inadequate account of how we play the moral language game. I argued above that the substance of moral language games is historical and contingent but that their form is not. When I make a moral statement, I do not, as Rorty's liberal ironist presumably does, qualify my statement of belief by proclaiming its contingency. I do not say that I believe this and recognize that this belief is relative and contingent but believe it anyway. Most certainly, I do not, while proclaiming the contingency of my belief, leap onto the barricades and proclaim my willingness to die for it. Rather, making a statement of belief entails a claim of certainty; it is a statement about who I am and what my life is about.

I think that Rorty misinterprets two important elements of the language game of morality. First, when I make a moral statement, it is necessarily unqualified – it is a statement of belief, not a *contingent* statement of belief. The language game in which I might proclaim the contingency of that moral belief is *another* language game; it is not part of the language game of moral action and judgment, but the language game of philosophical analysis.[29] Second, Rorty ignores the connection between morality and subjectivity. He implies that liberal ironists can abstract themselves from their moral beliefs and examine them at will. Against this, I have argued that morality is constitutive of subjectivity: my moral beliefs make me who I am. The picture of Rorty's liberal ironist coolly proclaiming the contingency of her moral beliefs and then womaning the barricades does not ring true.

The pitfalls that these theorists fall into in their attempts to define a postmodern approach to ethics/politics are theoretical pitfalls; they make no attempt to deal with anything approaching practical politics. There is, however, a growing literature on the practical side of the question of postmodern politics. This literature is relevant to my attempt to theorize a discursive morality; it suggests ways in which a nonfoundational approach to morality can provide guidelines for political practice. One of the most ambitious and useful contributions to this literature is that of Laclau and Mouffe. Their aim is to define a political program that operates "deconstructively within Marxist categories" (Laclau and Mouffe 1985: 3). What they call their "radical and plural democracy" provides the lens through which they reformulate the socialist project by proposing a new imaginary that speaks to the tradition of great emancipatory struggles. Postmodernism is necessary to this task, they argue, because it allows us to understand the complexity of contemporary social movements and the multiplicity of subjects (Mouffe 1988: 32–4).

Laclau and Mouffe's radical, plural democracy abandons the abstract universalism of Enlightenment politics along with the essentialism of the unitary subject (Mouffe 1988: 44). Departing from Marxism, they eschew the notion of a privileged standpoint for the theorist, arguing that there are only discourses that articulate resistance (Laclau and

Mouffe 1985: 169). They further argue that abandoning the myth of foundations leads not to nihilism, as critics have claimed, but to a proliferation of discursive interventions (Laclau 1988: 79). What Laclau and Mouffe imagine is a resistance politics that has shed the ontological baggage of Enlightenment politics. In a similar argument Michael Ryan maintains that a postmodern politics is a politics that is "up for grabs," a politics in which all categories are contingent and power is movable and therefore removable (1989: 97).[30]

Once more, I would argue that the attempt to define a distinctively "postmodern" politics is a futile one. What is valuable in this literature is the attempt to explore what politics would look like if we were to deconstruct the epistemology of modernism. Two aspects of this effort are particularly relevant to feminist politics. First, this literature has begun to define in a concrete way a politics of resistance that is not grounded in absolutes. It is a politics of resistance that is inspired by the emancipatory aims of Marxism but distinct from the critique of totalities that informs Marxism. It is, instead, a politics of local resistance. What this means for feminism is the possibility of political strategies that focus on the particular oppressions of specifically located women. Such a politics is uniquely relevant to the contemporary feminist movement. Feminists have become acutely aware that different women are subjected to very different forms of oppression. It follows that no single feminist political strategy can encompass these different situations. The politics of local resistance speaks directly to this fact of feminist politics.[31]

Second, this literature has begun to explore what many contemporary authors define as a "politics of difference."[32] Two senses of "difference" implicit in this definition are relevant to feminist politics. This politics is different in the sense of eschewing the ontological and epistemological assumptions that define modernist politics. It would displace the gendered dichotomies that ground modernist politics and define and reinforce the inferiority of women. Such a politics is also a politics of difference in the sense that it would emphasize the differences among political actors. Contemporary feminism needs an understanding of politics that can accommodate the differences among women. Most important, feminist politics must discard the assumption that only our common identity *as women* can serve as the basis for a feminist politics. The politics of difference suggests that we can unite politically without positing a common identity, that we can unite *through* our differences.

A discursive morality for feminism

My aim in this book has not been to define in detail the elements of a nonfoundationalist feminist politics or even to elaborate the full range of a reconstructed feminist morality.[33] Rather, in the spirit of Foucault, it has been at once descriptive and prescriptive. I am, on the one hand, documenting a paradigm shift, an epistemological break, or rupture, that is occurring in contemporary intellectual life. Through an examination of the work of Gilligan and a variety of other writers, I have argued that moral theory, one of the last bastions of modernist thought, has begun to crumble and that the paradigm shift that has occurred across a range of academic disciplines is having a profound effect on moral theory. Further, I have argued that this paradigm shift necessitates a radical reconceptualization of morality, a reformulation of the moral language game. I have attempted to outline, though not detail, a discursively constituted approach to morality.

At the same time, I have been making a prescriptive claim, asserting that such a radical reconceptualization is beneficial for feminism and that feminists should not only embrace this new paradigm but be at the forefront of it. Perhaps the best way of summarizing the argument that I am advancing in this book is to construct answers to a series of questions that a critic might quite reasonably raise against this prescriptive claim. Why, she might ask, does moral theory need to be restructured at all, much less to the radical degree that I am proposing? In particular, why should we abandon the notion of a universal morality, of "getting it right" in moral theory? And, most important, why should feminists follow the discursive morality outlined here?

Throughout this book I have offered three different reasons for the discursive reconstruction of morality. The first is the most obvious: the masculinist construction of moral theory that has dominated the West, particularly since the advent of modernity, is hierarchical and exclusionary. It marginalizes and silences the moral voices not only of women but, as Kohlberg's categories reveal, of any one who cannot attain the ideal of moral knowledge: the disembodied application of abstract universal principles. This includes everyone who does not have access to the advanced philosophical education that produces "true" moral knowledge. Feminists have little to lose and much to gain from the demise of this moral theory. The plurality of moral voices that I am suggesting here counters the hierarchicalization and marginalization that characterizes modernist moral theory. It gives these "different" voices equal standing and imagines a world in which they would be granted the status "moral."

The second set of arguments I have presented are variants of arguments presented by Foucault and Lyotard. Foucault maintains that the disembodied, autonomous Cartesian subject of modernity fails to describe the condition of subjects in the contemporary world. Subjects, he argues, are more subjected than subjecting. They are situated in all respects of the term: embodied, historical, cultural, and discursively constituted. It follows from this that if we are to come to grips with subjectivity in this world, we need a radically different concept of the subject from that offered by modernist epistemology. The discursive concept of the subject that is emerging in a range of contemporary disciplines is suited to this task. In a similar vein, Lyotard argues that the modernist concept of knowledge, which presupposes a meta-narrative that informs all judgments and defines all truth, is an inadequate description of the "condition of knowledge" that we face. We live in a world of multiple truths and multiple discourses of knowledge, a world devoid of absolutes.

In the foregoing I have applied these insights to the moral sphere, arguing that we need a reconstructed concept of the moral subject and moral knowledge that can comprehend moral action in the contemporary world. Central to this argument is the assertion that morality and subjectivity are inseparable: that what we recognize as a subject is a moral subject.[34] I have further argued that just as there are multiple subjectivities, so there are multiple moralities. This does not entail, however, that morality is either arbitrary or individualistic. We acquire a moral voice from the social, cultural, historical setting that also constitutes our subjectivity; moral voices vary with race, class, and gender even within a particular social situation. It is never *my* voice, but always *our* voice. Those who claim a strictly individual, idiosyncratic moral voice are not recognized as moral agents. Finally, I have argued that moral language games are unique in their claim to certainty. Although I may know on some abstract epistemological level that there are many moral language games, when I make a moral judgment, I am necessarily asserting its truth.

The third reason I have offered is that feminism needs a reconstructed moral theory in order to provide the theoretical ground for a "politics of difference." As I understand it, a politics of difference is a politics that is local, contextual, and concrete.[35] It eschews the need for absolute grounding, looking instead to the resistances implicit in localized discursive formations.[36] I have suggested that Foucault's political approach provides a model for a feminist politics of difference. Foucault suggests a politics that is local, contextual, and resistant, a politics that defines the specific nature of particular instances of repression and attacks them as such. Feminists have quite profitably employed this methodology in their analyses, using discourse analysis to unmask instances of social control. A particularly apt example is an article by Sander Gilman (1985) that analyzes the ideological impact of medical models in defining the character of black women's sexuality. Using a Foucaultian methodology, Gilman establishes that black women's sexuality has been constructed as a pathology by medical discourse. He then goes on to detail how this institutionalized discourse of female sexuality constitutes black women as deviant and to explain the social consequences of this deployment of knowledge. It is analyses such as these, analyses that explore and devise resistance to particular in-stances of repression, that a feminist politics of difference requires.

I stated in the previous section that the politics of difference I am advancing defines "difference" in two senses. This argument is central to the thesis I am advancing here. A feminist politics of difference rests on a different metaphysical and epistemological basis than does tradi-tional politics. It does not assume that a moral meta-narrative is neces-sary to ground political action. It assumes, rather, that power produces resistance, that resistance is and must be local, and that the relativism/absolutism dichotomy is not relevant to defining political action. It represents a new paradigm both epistemologically and metaphysically. In this respect my concept stands in contrast to that of many "postmodern" positions. What I am advocating is a paradigm shift, an entry into what Althusser calls "a new continent of thought." Postmoderns who deny that their position represents an alternative to modernist thought, or even constitutes a position at all, are, I think, deluding themselves.

A feminist politics of difference, further, is a politics in which differ-ences among women are confronted and theorized rather than ignored. It involves the assumption that a single identity for "woman" is not, and cannot be, the foundation of a feminist politics. Chantal Mouffe puts this nicely when she argues that a feminist politics that allows us to understand how the subject is constructed through different discourses is more adequate than one that reduces all women to one identity (1992: 382). Jane Flax suggests that the postmodern deconstruction of power opens up spaces in which suppressed hetero-geneity, discontinuity, and differences will reappear (1990: 41). As we begin to explore the variety of power relations that script the lives of women, we are discovering that these scripts differ by class, race, and culture. But the spaces that this opens up need not divide us – unless, that is, we assume that *only* a common identity can found our politics. This assumption is yet one more modernist concept that feminists should displace.

The outlines of such a politics of difference are beginning to emerge in feminist writings. Feminist legal scholars have struggled with the sameness/difference dichotomy that imposes a straitjacket on legal thinking in the United States. Some creative displacements of this di-chotomy are appearing in feminist legal thought. Christine Littleton (1987) has developed a theory of "equality and acceptance" that seeks to eliminate the inequitable consequences that follow from differences. Mary Joe Frug turns to Gilligan's work to displace the sameness/difference dichotomy. Utilizing what she calls a "progressive" reading of Gilligan's work, Frug argues that identifying sex-linked differences in the law is a way of critiquing dominant interpretations (1992: 40). She rejects the idea that differences are universal, arguing instead that they are linguistic and contextual. She sees her method as challenging the gendered character of discourses and thereby providing a strategy for challenging the extensive and complicated network of social and cultural practices that legitimate the subordination of women (1992: 112).

Other feminist writers have moved toward what I am calling the politics of difference by challenging the hegemony of the justice voice in our political/legal system. Patricia Williams (1991) imagines a legal system in which moral, religious, and psychological considerations enter the sphere of law, displacing the dominance of the justice voice. Virginia Held (1984, 1993) argues that we need different moral approaches for different spheres of life, since no single morality can encompass the diversity of our lives. And in one of the most insightful discussions of the possibilities of a feminist politics of difference, Nancy Fraser (1991b) argues for a multi-sectored public sphere that would replace the unitary concept of the public that dominates our political life. In an argument that converges with my advocacy of multiple moral voices, Fraser contends that, at present, all voices in the public arena are filtered through a single, all-encompassing lens. But, she claims, no lens can be culturally neutral. What is required is a plurality of public arenas in which groups with diverse values and rhetorics can be heard.[37]

Instead of engaging in fruitless discussions of whether such theories are "postmodern" or not, feminist theorists should instead continue to explore the parameters of the politics of difference. Foucault's model can serve us well in this endeavor. Foucault encourages us to look at concrete instances of power and how these instances and the discourses that constitute them shape and constrain subjects' lives. There is nothing abstract about this methodology. It is concrete and particular; it comes to grips with the very real instantiations of power in the very real lives of subjects.

It is also a critical methodology. One of the principal aims of this book has been to illustrate how discursive analysis can be used critically, particularly for the construction of a feminist moral theory. The key to this argument is that our language provides us with all the critical tools we require; we do not need to assume a transcendent subject or transcendent moral values in order to effect this critique. There are many ways of characterizing this critical potential within language: Barthes (1986) talks about "acractic" language; Bakhtin (1986) theorizes about "heteroglossia"; Foucault defines subjugated knowledges and counter discourses; Mary Hawkesworth talks about the ambiguities in language, its "interstices" (1988: 456); Nancy Fraser talks about creating rather than discovering feminist moral identities (1991a: 263); and Wittgenstein says simply that "Grammar gives language the necessary degrees of freedom" (1975: 74).

It has been my aim to employ this critical methodology to reconstruct moral theory along feminist lines. That our society possesses a hegemonic moral discourse seems indisputable; that this discourse is the "justice voice" that Gilligan identifies is also clear. What Gilligan argued is that there is another, "different" moral voice that the hegemonic voice has silenced. I have extended this argument to theorize a multiplicity of moral voices constituted by race, class, and culture, as well as gender. Moral voices are connected to moral persons, persons who are concrete rather than disembodied. To have a moral voice is to participate in a common discourse, to embrace a form of life. There is nothing arbitrary, anarchic, or idiosyncratic about this. It is, quite simply, what we do.

Notes

Chapter 1   *The Different Voice*

1 I examine this thesis in Chapter 3.
2 It is interesting to note that Gilligan frequently employs aural metaphors in her work – hearing, listening, voice, resonance – rather than the visual metaphors that dominate masculinist theories.
3 At one point Gilligan refers to the autonomous moral voice as an "adolescent ideal" (1982: 98). But this does not so much privilege the care voice as argue for the interdependence of the two voices.
4 For a compatible argument see Jack (1991).
5 In a compatible study, Tappan and Brown (1989) explore the role of narrative in moral education. I discuss this in Chapter 4.
6 Brown and Gilligan developed a "Listeners' Guide" for their researchers, which involved listening to each narrative four times, for a different theme each time. The result was that a "polyphony of voices were heard" (1992: 26).
7 See Moody-Adams (1991); L. Walker (1984); and Broughton (1983) for similar critiques.
8 See next section of this chapter.
9 Benhabib (1992) also makes an attempt to unite justice and care. But, unlike the other commentators, she identifies Gilligan's work as representing a paradigm shift in moral theory. See also Leffers (1993).
10 In her most recent work Tronto (1993) continues her criticism of Gilligan's work but also argues that it contains a radical potential.
11 Deborah Tannen's (1990) description of women and men's conversational styles has been immensely popular for much the same reason.
12 Rorty (1991b: 185) denies that Rawls assumes a disembodied subject, but I do not think this can be sustained.
13 It is significant that in *Political Liberalism* (1993) Rawls abandons his quasi-universalistic claims and adopts a pluralistic approach.
14 See Hekman (1990: 119–35); Harding (1986, 1991); Fausto-Sterling (1985); Code (1991); Longino (1990).

15 See Haraway (1988, 1991); Longino (1990); and Smith (1990) for feminist accounts of discursive knowledge.

16 This is Derrida's term.

Chapter 2   *Alternative or Displacement?*

1 See Lloyd (1984) for one of the best accounts.

2 See Nussbaum's "Equity and Mercy" (1993) for an insightful analysis of the relationship between justice and mercy. It is also relevant in this context to note that justice and mercy are represented in the Christian tradition in the tension between God the Father (justice) and God the Son (mercy) and that Jesus, the merciful son, is cast in feminine terms.

3 Elizabeth Anscombe (1968) also advances a specifically Aristotelian conception of ethics, which challenges modernist moral theory. Bakhtin (1990) argues for the moral relevance of novels.

4 Murdoch presents a more detailed theory in *Metaphysics as a Guide to Morals* (1992). I discuss this in the next chapter.

5 Owen Flanagan's *Varieties of Moral Personality* (1991) is another attempt to reject Kantian moral theory along these lines. But Flanagan's counter to Kant is even less viable than Blum's. Although Flanagan rejects Kant's exclusion of empirical factors from moral theory, he nevertheless sides with Kant in his search for one, true, universal moral theory. He is not interested, as the title of his book would suggest, in the *varieties* of moral personality but, rather, in a universal psychological theory. See also Flanagan and Rorty 1990.

6 I explore this further in Chapter 4.

7 See Tronto (1993) for another feminist appropriation of Hume.

8 I am referring specifically to the work of Kurt Baier (1965), William Frankena (1963), Jeffrey Stout (1988), Bernard Williams (1985), J. L. Mackie (1977), and Stephen Toulmin (1986).

9 See Downing and Thigpen's (1986) review of Walzer for more on this critique.

10 See Hekman (1992a) for another version of this argument.

11 For a counterpoint to Sandel see Buchanan (1989).

12 See also his *Three Rival Versions of Moral Inquiry* (1990).

13 Unger (1975) presents a concept of community that involves a dialectic between the individual and the social, the public and the private; Michael Taylor (1982) advances a concept of community that he claims is compatible with individual liberty; Barber's (1984) "strong democracy" strikes a balance between participation (autonomy) and community (sociality); Balbus's (1982) concept of community is rooted in reciprocal recognition. See also Buchanan (1989).

14 For another brief, and ultimately dismissive, account of women and communitarianism see Fowler (1991).

15 See M. Friedman (1989a) for a variant of this argument.

16 See also Holland (1990).

17 For other accounts of the ethic of care see Tronto (1993); Fuller (1992); and Pappas (1993).

18 I have certain problems with this concept that will become clear in subsequent discussions. Friedman argues that the complex self includes "female nature and embodiment" that exceeds social regulation, a position that courts essentialism.

19 See Hirschman (1989); Flax (1990); and Benson (1990) for discussions of agency in feminist theory.

20 I explore the politics of difference more extensively in Chapter 4. See Young (1986) for an earlier discussion of this topic.

Chapter 3　*Subject Strategies*

1 For an insightful analysis of this process see Coward and Ellis (1977).

2 See Benjamin (1988) for an extended defense of the intersubjective self. See Westkott (1986) for commentary on Horney.

3 For another discussion of the rejection of individualistic concepts in psychology see Henriques et al. (1984).

4 An interesting parallel to Coward and Ellis's analysis of the evolution of the postmodern subject is Charles Taylor's massive *Sources of the Self* (1989). Although Taylor is by no means a postmodern, his effort to trace the evolution of the modern sense of identity, like that of Foucault, emphasizes historicity and the societal "framework" that defines identity.

5 See Hekman (1991) for a fuller discussion of this point.

6 In her analysis of the connection between Foucault and feminism, Lois McNay (1993) maintains that, for many of the reasons I have cited, Foucault is not a postmodern. Although I agree with her in many respects, I see it as making more sense to argue for different strands of postmodernism than to remove Foucault from this category.

7 McNay (1993) argues that in his later works Foucault's approach to the subject changes significantly, from a concept of the subject as social dupe to a concept of the subject as active agent. I see the change as much more gradual.

8 See Rajchman (1991) for a discussion of Foucault's ethics.

9 McNay's interpretation of Foucault's ethics and its relevance for feminism contradicts this. McNay argues that Foucault's later writing contains Enlightenment normative values and hence that he is not a postmodern. She further argues that feminism needs moral universals and that Foucault, precisely because he is not a postmodern and because he espouses such moral universals, is of relevance to feminism. My interpretation, by contrast, moves both Foucault and feminism into a post-Enlightenment epistemological space.

10 See Cornell (1992) for a similar reason for rejecting the "postmodern" label.

11 See Hekman (1992b); Di Stefano (1991).

12 For a fuller discussion of these issues see Hekman (1994).

13 See Margaret Whitford's (1991) book on Irigaray for a discussion of Irigaray as a philosopher of change.

14 Jane Gallop (1988: 8) refutes this criticism quite effectively.

15 Referring to this problem in a public address, Catherine Stimpson characterized it as the "political coach potato" problem.

16 Ebert classifies Foucault as a "ludic postmodern," which I see as a misreading of his work. But in other respects our arguments are very similar.

17 See Radhakrishnan (1987) and Awkward (1989) for more explicit defenses of the applicability of postmodernism to ethnic literary criticism.

18 See the collection by Benstock (1988) for other arguments that black women write autobiographies about a collective self. Susan Friedman (1988) argues that this is true of women's autobiographies in general.

Chapter 4   *Back to the Rough Ground: Theorizing the Moral Subject*

1 See May (1993) for a discussion of the similarities between Foucault and Wittgenstein on this point.

2 Commentators on Wittgenstein's ethics have interpreted what I have identified as the contradiction in his thought in a variety of ways. I discuss the positions of Murdoch and Johnston in the text. The positions of Pitkin and Lovibond are also noteworthy. Pitkin (1972), who argues against the fact/value dichotomy, asserting that moral discourse has a logic of its own, turns to Oakeshott rather than Wittgenstein in her attempt to formulate a position on ethics. Lovibond (1983) also offers a "Wittgensteinian ethics," which she calls "moral realism." Lovibond uses the contextualism of Wittgenstein's theory of language games to develop an approach to morality, but without acknowledging the contradiction this creates.

3 This is the basis of Staten's (1984) argument regarding the similarity between Wittgenstein and Derrida: both are rejecting the whole tradition of Western philosophy.

4 Several commentators have discussed Wittgenstein's attitude toward subjectivity from this perspective. Lee-Lampshire (1992) and Descombes (1991) identify Wittgenstein's philosophy as necessarily entailing the death of the Cartesian subject. Murdoch (1992), however, shies away from such a radical conclusion. She argues that we must retain a concept of the individual that is conscious, inward, and private (1992: 294).

5 Despite the fact that Wittgenstein rarely discusses either morality or the subject, two recent commentaries on his work have focused on the moral subject. Using Wittgenstein's philosophy as a guideline, Wendy Lee-Lampshire (1992) argues that morality and subjectivity are inescapably connected and that to speak is to commit oneself as a moral agent. Iris Murdoch makes a similar claim with her thesis that consciousness is a form of moral activity (1992: 167).

6 In another context, however, Habermas (1989–90) makes clear that he believes there to be a moral point of view that can claim universal validity.

7 It is interesting that the position that Murdoch takes in *Metaphysics as a Guide to Morals* (1992) is much less compatible with Gilligan's position than the one she adopts in *The Sovereignty of Good* (1970).

8 The position taken by Pitkin in *Wittgenstein and Justice* (1972) appears to be compatible with my position here. Pitkin rejects Wittgenstein's explicit statements about ethics, adopting instead a position similar to that of Oakeshott, which characterizes morality as a habit of affection and conduct (1972: 52).

9 Richard Flathman also notes this in *Willful Liberalism* (1992) but then goes on to use Wittgenstein's theory for political purposes.

10 For an extended discussion of Gadamer see my *Hermeneutics and the Sociology of Knowledge* (1986).

11 Several other feminist authors have argued that hermeneutics provides a useful vehicle for feminist theorizing (Fiorenza 1991; Warnke 1993).

12 Murdoch (1992) makes this point as well.

13 Oakeshott makes similar observations regarding politics, asserting that politics is an activity and that political education is education into a way of life (1962: 123ff.).

14 See Clarke and Simpson (1989) for another version of the argument that "conservative" moral theory opposes the theoretical bias of modern moral philosophy.

15 Tappan and Brown even claim that the narrative approach constitutes a "postmodern" theory of moral development. See Kearney (1987) and Tappan (1991) for other versions of the narrative self and morality.

16 For an extended discussion of Derrida's value for feminism see my *Gender and Knowledge* (1990: 163–73) and Holland (1990).

17 For a similar argument see McCarthy (1989–90).

18 Much the same argument could be made regarding "Declarations of Independence" (1986b), an article in which Derrida examines the text of the Declaration of Independence.

19 See especially *Of Spirit* (1989).

20 It is significant that Baudrillard also turns to metaphysics in his most recent work. See also Kariel (1989), which wants to revive the "playfulness" of politics.

21 For other discussions of a Foucaultian ethics see Merrill (1988); Minson (1985); and Harpham (1988).

22 See Shapiro (1992); Oliver (1991); and Gordon (1991) for discussions of Foucaultian politics.

23 I want to distinguish this concept from Habermas's universalistic "discourse ethics."

24 See Caputo (1993) for another argument against the possibility of ethics from a postmodern position.

25 See Dana Villa's (1993) review of White's book for a related argument. For other discussions of postmodernism and politics see Chambers (1990) and the articles in Arac (1986).

26 Rorty prefers the label "pragmatist" to "postmodern."

27 Throughout the book Rorty uses the female pronoun in presenting the position he favors, the male pronoun for the position he attacks.

28 For another connection between liberalism and postmodernism see McClure (1992).

29 Habermas makes much the same point when he claims that moral norms must take the *form* of unconditional universal "ought" statements (1990: 64).

30 For arguments against the compatibility of Marxism and deconstruction see Aronowitz (1988) and Ross (1988).

31 In this same vein Naomi Scheman argues that feminism is a politically responsible form of postmodernism (1993: 186).

32 See especially Connolly (1991).

33 See Held (1993) for a comprehensive outline of a feminist morality.
34 For a compelling argument linking ethics and subjectivity see Bakhtin (1990: 226).
35 A good example of what I do *not* mean here is found in the work of Drucilla Cornell (1991, 1992). Cornell attempts to apply Derridian deconstruction to legal theory and in so doing, offers a number of formulations that are stunning in their indecipherability. Like Derrida, she ultimately turns to metaphysics to ground her argument. See Kramer (1991) and Dalton for other discussions of deconstruction and legal theory.
36 See James Scott (1990) for an excellent discussion of how such local resistance operates.
37 See also Young (1990).

References

Addelson, Kathryn 1991: *Impure Thoughts: essays on philosophy, feminism and ethics*. Philadelphia: Temple University Press.

Alcoff, Linda 1988: Cultural feminism versus post-structuralism: the identity crisis in feminist theory. *Signs*, 13 (3), 405–36.

Allen, Paula Gunn 1986: *The Sacred Hoop: recovering the feminine in American Indian traditions*. Boston: Beacon Press.

Anscombe, G. E. M. 1968: Modern moral philosophy. In Judith Thomson and Gerald Dworkin (eds), *Ethics*, Cambridge, Mass.: MIT Press, 186–210.

Arac, Jonathan (ed.) 1986: *Postmodernism and Politics*. Minneapolis: University of Minnesota Press.

Aronowitz, Stanley 1988: Postmodernism and politics. In Andrew Ross (ed.), *Universal Abandon*, Minneapolis: University of Minnesota Press, 46–62.

Awkward, Michael 1989: Appropriate gestures. In Linda Kaufman (ed.), *Gender and Theory*, Cambridge, Mass.: Basil Blackwell, 238–46.

Baier, Annette 1985a: *Postures of the Mind: essays on mind and morals*. Minneapolis: University of Minnesota Press.

—— 1985b: What do women want in a moral theory? *Nous*, 19, 53–63.

—— 1987a: Hume, the women's moral theorist? In Eva Kittay and Diana Meyers (eds), *Women and Moral Theory*, Totowa, NJ: Rowman & Littlefield, 37–55.

—— 1987b: The need for more than justice. In Marsha Hanen and Kai Nelson (eds), *Science, Morality and Feminist Theory*, Calgary: University of Calgary Press, 41–56.

Baier, Kurt 1965: *The Moral Point of View*. New York: Random House.

Bakhtin, M. M. 1981: *The Dialogic Imagination*, tr. Caryl Emerson and Michael Holquist. Austin: University of Texas Press.

—— 1986: *Speech Genres and Other Late Essays*, tr. Vern W. McGee. Austin: University of Texas Press.

—— 1990: *Art and Answerability: early philosophical essays by M. M. Bakhtin*, ed. Michael Holquist and Vadim Liapunov. Austin: University of Texas Press.

Balbus, Isaac 1982: *Marxism and Domination*. Princeton: Princeton University Press.

Bannet, Eve 1989: *Structuralism and the Logic of Dissent: Barthes, Derrida, Foucault, Lacan*. Urbana: University of Illinois Press.

Barber, Benjamin 1974: *The Death of Communal Liberty*. Princeton: Princeton University Press.

—— 1984: *Strong Democracy*. Berkeley: University of California Press.

Barthes, Roland 1986: *The Rustle of Language*. New York: Hill and Wang.

Baudrillard, Jean 1988: *Selected Writings*, ed. Mark Poster. Stanford, Calif.: Stanford University Press.

Baumrind, Diana 1986: Set differences in moral reasoning: response to Walker's (1984) conclusion that there are none. *Child Development*, 57, 511–21.

Bellah, Robert N., et al. 1985: *Habits of the Heart: individualism and commitment in American life*. New York: Harper and Row.

Benhabib, Seyla 1987: The generalized and the concrete other: the Kohlberg–Gilligan controversy and feminist theory. In Seyla Benhabib and Drucilla Cornell (eds), *Feminism as Critique*, Minneapolis: University of Minnesota Press, 77–95. Cambridge: Polity Press.

—— 1992: *Situating the Self: gender, community, and postmodernism in contemporary ethics*. New York: Routledge. Cambridge: Polity Press.

Benjamin, Jessica 1988: *The Bonds of Love*. New York: Pantheon.

Benson, Paul 1990: Feminist second thoughts about free agency. *Hypatia*, 5 (3), 47–64.

Benstock, Shari (ed.) 1988: *The Private Self: theory and practice of women's autobiographical writing*. Chapel Hill: University of North Carolina Press.

Bernstein, Elizabeth and Gilligan, Carol 1990: Unfairness and not listening: converging themes in Emma Willard girls' development. In Carol Gilligan, Nona Lyons, and Trudy Hanmer (eds), *Making Connections*, Cambridge, Mass.: Harvard University Press, 147–61.

Bernstein, Richard 1987: Serious play: the ethical-political horizon of Jacques Derrida. *Journal of Speculative Philosophy*, 1, 93–117.

Blum, Lawrence 1980: *Friendship, Altruism, and Morality*. Boston: Routledge and Kegan Paul.

—— 1986: Iris Murdoch and the domain of the moral. *Philosophical Studies*, 50, 343–67.

—— 1988: Gilligan and Kohlberg: implications for moral theory. *Ethics*, 98 (3), 472–91.

Bowlby, John 1988: *A Secure Base: parent–child attachment and healthy human development*. New York: Basic Books.

Braidotti, Rosi 1989: The politics of ontological difference. In Teresa Brennan (ed.), *Between Feminism and Psychoanalysis*, New York: Routledge, 89–105.

Brodribb, Somer 1992: *Nothing Mat(t)ers: a feminist critique of postmodernism*. New York: New York University Press.

Brodzki, Bella and Schenck, Celeste (eds) 1988: *Life/Lines: theorizing women's autobiography*. Ithaca: Cornell University Press.

Broughton, John 1983: Women's rationality and men's virtues: a critique of gender dualism in Gilligan's theory of moral development. *Social Research*, 50 (3), 597–642.

Brown, Lyn 1990: When is a moral problem not a moral problem? In Carol Gilligan, Nona Lyons, and Trudy Hanmer (eds), *Making Connections*, Cambridge, Mass.: Harvard University Press, 88–109.

Brown, Lyn Mikel and Gilligan, Carol 1992: *Meeting at the Crossroads: women's psychology and girls' development*. Cambridge, Mass.: Harvard University Press.

Buchanan, Allen 1989: Assessing the communitarian critique of liberalism. *Ethics*, 99, 852–82.

Butler, Judith 1989: Gendering the body: Beauvoir's philosophical contribution. In Ann Garry and Marilyn Pearsall (eds), *Women, Knowledge, and Reality*, Boston: Unwin Hyman, 253–62.

—— 1990a: *Gender Trouble: feminism and the subversion of identity*. New York: Routledge.

—— 1990b: Gender trouble, feminist theory and psycho-analytic discourse. In Linda Nicholson (ed.), *Feminism/Postmodernism*, New York: Routledge, 324–40.

—— 1991: Contingent foundations: feminism and the question of post-modernism. *Praxis International*, 11 (2), 150–65.

Caputo, John 1993: *Against Ethics: contributions to a poetics of obligation with constant reference to deconstruction*. Bloomington: Indiana University Press.

Card, Claudia 1991: The feistiness of feminism. In Claudia Card (ed.), *Feminist Ethics*, Lawrence: University of Kansas Press, 3–31.

Carothers, Suzanne 1990: Catching sense: learning from our mothers to be black and female. In Faye Ginsburg and Anna Lowenhaupt Tsing (eds), *Uncertain Terms: negotiating gender in American culture*, Boston: Beacon Press, 232–47.

Chambers, Iain 1990: *Border Dialogues: journeys in postmodernism*. London: Routledge.

Chodorow, Nancy 1978: *The Reproduction of Mothering*. Berkeley: University of California Press.

—— 1986: Toward a relational individualism: the mediation of self through psychoanalysis. In Thomas Heller, Morton Sosua, and David Wellberg (eds), *Reconstructing Individualism*, Stanford: Stanford University Press, 197–207.

—— 1987: Feminism and difference: gender, relation, and difference in psychoanalytic perspective. In Mary Walsh (ed.), *The Psychology of Women*, New Haven: Yale University Press, 249–64.

—— 1989: *Feminism and Psychoanalytic Theory*. New Haven: Yale University Press. Cambridge: Polity Press.

Christian, Barbara 1987: The race for theory. *Cultural Critique*, 6, 51–63.

Cixous, Hélène 1988: Extreme fidelity. In Susan Sellars (ed.), *Writing Differences*, New York: St. Martin's Press, 11–36.

Clarke, Stanley and Simpson, Evan (eds) 1989: *Anti-theory in Ethics and Moral Conservatism*. Albany: SUNY Press.

Code, Lorraine 1988: Experience, knowledge, and responsibility. In Margaret Whitford and Morwenna Griffiths (eds), *Feminist Perspectives in Philosophy*, Bloomington: Indiana University Press, 187–204.

—— 1991: *What Can She Know? Feminist theory and the construction of knowledge*. Ithaca: Cornell University Press.

Collins, Patricia Hill 1990: *Black Feminist Thought*. Boston: Unwin Hyman.

Connolly, William 1991: *Identity/Difference: democratic negotiations of political paradox*. Ithaca: Cornell University Press.

Cornell, Drucilla 1991: *Beyond Accommodation: ethical feminism, deconstruction, and the law*. New York: Routledge.

—— 1992: *The Philosophy of the Limit.* New York: Routledge.

Coward, Rosalind and Ellis, John 1977: *Language and Materialism: developments in semiology and the theory of the subject.* London: Routledge and Kegan Paul.

Cudjoe, Selwyn 1984: Maya Angelou and the autobiographical statement. In Mari Evans (ed.), *Black Women Writers*, Garden City, NY: Doubleday, 6–24.

Culler, Jonathan 1982: *On Deconstruction: theory and criticism after structuralism.* Ithaca: Cornell University Press.

Curtin, Deanne 1991: Toward an ecological ethic of care. *Hypatia*, 6 (1), 60–74.

Dalton, C. 1985: An essay in the deconstruction of contract doctrine. *Yale Law Journal* 94 (5), 999–1114.

De Lauretis, Teresa 1984: *Alice Doesn't: feminism, semiotics, cinema.* Bloomington: Indiana University Press.

—— 1986: Feminist studies/critical studies: issues, terms, and contexts. In Teresa de Lauretis (ed.), *Feminist Studies/Critical Studies*, Bloomington: Indiana University Press, 1–19.

—— 1987: *The Technologies of Gender.* Bloomington: Indiana University Press.

—— 1990: Eccentric subjects: feminist theory and historical consciousness. *Feminist Studies*, 16 (1), 115–50.

Derrida, Jacques 1973: *Speech and Phenomena*, tr. David Allison. Evanston, Ill.: Northwestern University Press.

—— 1984: No apocalypse, not now. *Diacritics*, 14 (2), 20–31.

—— 1986a: But beyond . . . (open letter to Anne McClintoele and Rob Nixon). *Critical Inquiry*, 13 (1), 155–70.

—— 1986b: Declarations of independence. *New Political Science*, 15, 7–15.

—— 1989: *Of Spirit: Heidegger and the question.* Chicago: University of Chicago Press.

—— 1990: Force of law: the mystical foundation of authority. *Cardozo Law Review*, 11 (5–6), 921–1045.

—— 1992: *The Other Heading: reflections on today's Europe.* Bloomington: Indiana University Press.

Descombes, Vincent 1991: A propos of the "critique of the subject" and the critique of this critique. In Eduardo Cadava et al. (eds), *Who Comes After the Subject?*, New York: Routledge, 120–34.

Diamond, Irene and Quinby, Lee (eds) 1988: *Feminism and Foucault.* Boston: Northeastern University Press.

Di Stefano, Christine 1991: *Configurations of Masculinity: a feminist perspective on modern political theory.* Ithaca: Cornell University Press.

Donzelot, Jacques 1991: Pleasure in work. In Graham Burchel, Colin Gordon, and Peter Miller (eds), *The Foucault Effect*, Chicago: University of Chicago Press, 251–80.

Downing, Lyle and Thigpen, Robert 1986: Beyond shared understandings. *Political Theory*, 14, 451–72.

Dreyfus, Hubert and Rabinow, Paul 1982: *Michel Foucault: beyond structuralism and hermeneutics.* Chicago: University of Chicago Press.

DuBois, Page 1988: *Sowing the Body: psychoanalysis and ancient representations of women.* Chicago: University of Chicago Press.

Ebert, Teresa 1991: The "difference" of postmodern feminism. *College English*, 53 (8), 886–904.

Eisenberg, Nancy and Lennon, Rondy 1983: Sex differences in empathy and related capacities. *Psychological Bulletin*, 94 (1), 100–31.

Eisenstein, Zillah 1988: *The Female Body and the Law*. Berkeley: University of California Press.

Elshtain, Jean Bethke 1981: *Public Man, Private Woman*. Princeton: Princeton University Press.

Engelmann, Paul 1968: *Letters from Ludwig Wittgenstein with a memoir*. New York: Horizon Press.

Fausto-Sterling, Ann 1985: *Myths of Gender*. New York: Basic Books.

Ferguson, Kathy 1989: The man question in metatheory: interpretation and genealogy in feminism. Paper presented at Western Political Science Association Convention.

—— 1993: *The Man Question: visions of subjectivity in feminist theory*. Berkeley: University of California Press.

Findlay, John 1978: *Values and Intentions*. Atlantic Highlands, NJ: Humanities Press.

Fiorenza, Elizabeth 1991: Bread not stone: the challenge of feminist biblical interpretation. In Sneja Gunew (ed.), *A Reader in Feminist Knowledge*, New York: Routledge, 263–76.

Flanagan, Owen 1991: *Varieties of Moral Personality: ethics and psychological realism*. Cambridge, Mass.: Harvard University Press.

—— and Jackson, Kathryn 1987: Justice, care, and gender: the Kohlberg–Gilligan debate revisited. *Ethics*, 97, 622–37.

—— and Rorty, Amélie (eds) 1990: *Identity, Character, and Morality: essays in moral psychology*. Cambridge, Mass.: MIT Press.

Flathman, Richard 1992: *Willful Liberalism: voluntarism and individuality in political theory and practice*. Ithaca: Cornell University Press.

Flax, Jane 1990: *Thinking Fragments: psychoanalysis, feminism, and postmodernism in the contemporary west*. Berkeley: University of California Press.

Foucault, Michel 1971: *The Order of Things*. New York: Random House.

—— 1972: *The Archaeology of Knowledge*, tr. A. M. Sheridan Smith. New York: Random House.

—— 1977a: *Language, Counter-Memory, Practice*, tr. Donald Bouchard and Sherry Simon. Ithaca: Cornell University Press.

—— 1977b: Power and sex: an interview with Michel Foucault. *Telos*, 32, 152–61.

—— 1978: *The History of Sexuality*, tr. Robert Hurley. New York: Random House.

—— 1980: *Power/Knowledge*. New York: Pantheon Books.

—— 1982: The subject and power. In Hubert Dreyfus and Paul Rabinow (eds), *Michel Foucault: beyond structuralism and hermeneutics*, Chicago: University of Chicago Press, 208–26.

—— 1984a: *The Foucault Reader*, ed. Paul Rabinow. New York: Pantheon Books.

—— 1984b: The regard for truth. *Art and Text*, summer, 20–31.

—— 1985: *The Use of Pleasure*. New York: Pantheon Books.

—— 1986: *The Care of the Self*. New York: Pantheon Books.

—— 1987a: The ethic of the care of the self as a practice of freedom. *Philosophy and Social Criticism*, 12–13, 112–31.

—— 1987b: Maurice Blanchot: the thought from outside. In *Foucault/Blanchot*, New York: Zone Books, 7–58.

—— 1988: *The Final Foucault*, ed. James Bernauer and David Rasmussen. Cambridge, Mass.: MIT Press.

Foucault, Michel 1991: Politics and the study of discourse. In Graham Burchell, Colin Gordon, and Peter Miller (eds), *The Foucault Effect*, Chicago: University of Chicago Press, 53–72.

—— 1993: About the beginnings of the hermeneutics of the self. *Political Theory*, 21 (2), 198–227.

Fowler, Robert 1991: *The Dance with Community: the contemporary debate in American political thought*. Lawrence: University of Kansas Press.

Frankena, William K. 1963: *Ethics*. Englewood Cliffs, NJ: Prentice-Hall.

Fraser, Nancy 1991a: From irony to prophecy to politics: a response to Richard Rorty. *Michigan Quarterly Review*, 30 (2), 259–66.

—— 1991b: Rethinking the public sphere: a contribution to the critique of actually existing democracies. *Social Text*, 25–6, 56–80.

—— 1991c: The uses and abuses of French discourse theory. In Nancy Fraser and Sandra Bartky (eds), *Revaluing French Feminism*, Bloomington: Indiana University Press, 177–94.

Freud, Sigmund 1961: Some psychical consequences of the anatomical distinction between the sexes. In James Strachey (ed.), *The Standard Edition of the Complete Psychological Works of Sigmund Freud*, 19, 248–58.

Friedman, Marilyn 1987a: Beyond caring: the de-moralization of gender. In Marsha Hanen and Kai Nelson (eds), *Science, Morality and Feminist Theory*, Calgary: University of Calgary Press, 87–110.

—— 1987b: Care and context in moral reasoning. In Eva Kittay and Diana Meyers (eds), *Women and Moral Theory*, Totowa, NJ: Rowman and Littlefield, 190–204.

—— 1989a: Feminism and modern friendship: dislocating the community. *Ethics*, 99 (2), 275–90.

—— 1989b: Self-rule in social context. In James Sterba and Creighton Peden (eds), *Freedom, Equality, and Social Change*, Lewiston, Me.: Edwin Mellen Press, 158–69.

—— 1991: The social self and the partiality debates. In Claudia Card (ed.), *Feminist Ethics*, Lawrence: University of Kansas Press, 161–79.

Friedman, Susan S. 1988: Women's autobiographical selves: theory and practice. In Shari Benstock (ed.), *The Private Self*, Chapel Hill: University of North Carolina Press, 34–62.

Frug, Mary Joe 1992: *Postmodern Legal Feminism*. New York: Routledge.

Frye, Marilyn 1990: A response to *Lesbian ethics*. *Hypatia*, 5 (3), 132–7.

—— 1991: A response to *Lesbian ethics*: why ethics? In Claudia Card (ed.), *Feminist Ethics*, Lawrence: University of Kansas Press, 52–9.

Fuller, Robert 1992: *Ecology of Care*. Louisville, Ky.: Westminster/John Knox Press.

Fuss, Diana 1989: *Essentially Speaking*. New York: Routledge.

Gadamer, Hans-Georg 1975: *Truth and Method*. New York: Continuum.

—— 1976: *Philosophical Hermeneutics*, tr. David E. Linge. Berkeley: University of California Press.

—— 1981: *Reason in the Age of Science*. Cambridge, Mass.: MIT Press.

Gallop, Jane 1988: *Thinking Through the Body*. New York: Columbia University Press.

Gatens, Moira 1991: *Feminism and Philosophy*. Bloomington: Indiana University Press.

Gates, Henry Louis 1985: Writing "race" and the difference it makes. *Critical Inquiry*, 12 (1), 1–21.

—— 1987a: *Figures in Black*. New York: Oxford University Press.

—— 1987b: "What's love got to do with it?" Critical theory, integrity, and the black idiom. *New Literary History*, 18 (2), 345–62.

Gilligan, Carol 1982: *In a Different Voice*. Cambridge, Mass.: Harvard University Press.

—— 1983a: Do changes in women's rights change women's moral judgment? In Martina Horner, Carol Nadelson, and Malka Notman (eds), *The Challenge of Change: perspectives on family, work, and education*, New York: Plenum Press, 39–60.

—— 1983b: Do the social sciences have an adequate theory of moral development? In Norma Haan (ed.), *Social Science as Moral Inquiry*, New York: Columbia University Press, 33–51.

—— 1986a: Exit-voice dilemmas in adolescent development. In Alejandro Foxley, Michael McPherson, and Guillermo O'Donnell (eds), *Development, Democracy, and the Art of Trespassing: essays in honor of Albert O. Hirschman*, Notre Dame, Ind.: University of Notre Dame Press, 283–300.

—— 1986b: Reply by Carol Gilligan. *Signs*, 11 (2), 324–33.

—— 1987a: Moral orientation and moral development. In Eva Kittay and Diana Meyers (eds), *Women and Moral Theory*, Totowa, NJ: Rowman and Littlefield, 19–33.

—— 1987b: Remapping development: the power of divergent data. In Christine Farnham (ed.), *The Impact of Feminist Research in the Academy*, Bloomington: University of Indiana Press, 77–94.

—— 1988a: Adolescent development reconsidered. In Carol Gilligan et al. (eds), *Mapping the Moral Domain*, Cambridge, Mass.: Harvard University Press, vii–xxxix.

—— 1988b: Remapping development: creating a new framework for psychological theory and research. In Carol Gilligan et al. (eds), *Mapping the Moral Domain*, Cambridge, Mass.: Harvard University Press, 3–19.

—— 1990a: Joining the resistance: psychology, politics, girls, and women. *Michigan Quarterly Review*, 24 (9), 501–36.

—— 1990b: Preface to Carol Gilligan, Nona Lyons, and Trudy Hanmer (eds), *Making Connections*, Cambridge, Mass.: Harvard University Press, 6–29.

—— 1991: Women's psychological development: implications for psychotheory. In Carol Gilligan, Annie Rogers, and Deborah Tolman (eds), *Women, Girls, and Psychotherapy: reframing resistance*, New York: Harrington Park Press, 5–31.

—— and Wiggins, Grant 1988: The origins of morality in early childhood relationships. In Carol Gilligan et al. (eds), *Mapping the Moral Domain*, Cambridge, Mass.: Harvard University Press, 111–38.

——, Brown, Lyn and Rogers, Annie 1990: Psyche embedded: a place for body, relationship, and culture in personality theory. In A. I. Rabin et al. (eds), *Studying Persons and Lives*, New York: Springer, 86–147.

——, Johnston, D. Kay and Miller, Barbara 1988: *Moral Voice, Adolescent Development, and Secondary Education: a study at the Green River School*. Cambridge

MA Project on the Psychology of Women and the Development of Girls, Harvard Graduate School of Education, monograph no. 3.

Gilligan, Carol, Rogers, Annie and Brown, Lyn 1990: Epilogue to Carol Gilligan, Nona Lyons, and Trudy Hanmer (eds), *Making Connections*, Cambridge, Mass.: Harvard University Press, 314–34.

————— and Tolman, Deborah (eds) 1991: *Women, Girls, and Psychotherapy: reframing resistance.* New York: Harrington Park Press.

Gilman, Sander 1985: Black bodies, white bodies: toward an iconography of female sexuality in late nineteenth-century art, medicine, and literature. *Critical Inquiry*, 12 (1), 204–42.

Gordon, Colin 1991: Government rationality: an introduction. In Graham Burchell, Colin Gordon, and Peter Miller (eds), *The Foucault Effect*, Chicago: University of Chicago Press, 1–51.

Greeno, Catherine and Maccoby, Eleanor 1986: How different is the "Different Voice"? *Signs*, 11 (2), 310–16.

Gutmann, Amy 1985: Communitarian critiques of liberalism. *Philosophy and Public Affairs*, 14, 308–22.

Habermas, Jürgen 1989–90: Justice and solidarity: on the discussion concerning "stage 6." *Philosophical Forum*, 21 (1–2), 32–52.

———— 1990: *Moral Consciousness and Communicative Action.* Cambridge, Mass.: MIT Press. Cambridge: Polity Press.

Hampshire, Stuart 1989: Morality and conflict. In Stanley Clarke and Evan Simpson (eds), *Anti-Theory in Ethics and Moral Conservatism*, Albany: SUNY Press, 135–64.

Haraway, Donna 1985: A manifesto for cyborgs: science, technology, and socialist feminism in the 1980s. *Socialist Review*, 80, 65–107.

———— 1988: Situated knowledges: the science question in feminism and the privilege of partial perspective. *Feminist Studies*, 14 (Fall), 575–99.

———— 1989: *Primate Visions: gender, race, and nature in the world of modern science.* New York: Routledge.

———— 1991: *Simians, Cyborgs, and Women: the reinvention of nature.* New York: Routledge.

Harding, Sandra 1986: *The Science Question in Feminism.* Ithaca: Cornell University Press.

———— 1987: The curious coincidence of feminine and African moralities. In Eva Kittay and Diana Meyers (eds), *Women and Moral Theory*, Totowa, NJ: Rowman and Littlefield, 296–315.

———— 1991: *Whose Science? Whose Knowledge? thinking from women's lives.* Ithaca: Cornell University Press.

Harpham, Geoffrey 1988: Foucault and the "ethics" of power. In Robert Merrill (ed.), *Ethics/Aesthetics: postmodern positions*, Washington, DC: Maissonneuve Press, 71–81.

Hartsock, Nancy 1990: Foucault on power: a theory for women? In Linda Nicholson (ed.), *Feminism/Postmodernism*, New York: Routledge, 157–75.

Hawkesworth, Mary 1988: Feminist rhetoric: discourses on the male monopoly of thought. *Political Theory*, 6 (3), 444–67.

Hekman, Susan 1986: *Hermeneutics and the Sociology of Knowledge.* Cambridge: Polity Press.

—— 1990: *Gender and Knowledge: elements of a postmodern feminism*. Cambridge: Polity Press. Boston: Northeastern University Press.

Hekman, Susan 1991: Reconstituting the subject: feminism, modernism and postmodernism. *Hypatia*, 6 (2), 44–63.

—— 1992a: The embodiment of the subject: feminism and the communitarian critique of liberalism. *Journal of Politics*, 54 (4), 1098–119.

—— 1992b: John Stuart Mill's *The Subjection of Women*: the foundations of liberal feminism. *History of European Ideas*, 15 (4–6), 681–6.

—— 1994: Subjects and agents: the question for feminism. In Judith Kegan Gardiner (ed.), *Provoking Agents*, Urbana/Champagne: University of Illinois Press, 370–95.

Held, Virginia 1984: *Rights and Goods: justifying social action*. New York: Free Press.

—— 1993: *Feminist Morality: transforming culture, society and politics*. Chicago: University of Chicago Press.

Henderson, Mae 1992: Speaking in tongues: dialogics, dialectics, and the black woman writer's literary tradition. In Judith Butler and Joan Scott (eds), *Feminists Theorize the Political*, New York: Routledge, 144–66.

Henriques, Julian et al. 1984: *Changing the Subject: psychology, social regulation and subjectivity*. London: Methuen.

Hilmy, Stephen 1987: *The Later Wittgenstein*. Oxford: Basil Blackwell.

Hirschman, Nancy 1989: Freedom, recognition and obligation: a feminist approach to political theory. *American Political Science Review*, 83 (4), 1227–44.

Hoagland, Sarah 1988: *Lesbian Ethics: toward a new value*. Palo Alto, Calif.: Institute of Lesbian Studies.

—— 1991: Some thoughts about "caring." In Claudia Card (ed.), *Feminist Ethics*, Lawrence: University of Kansas Press, 246–63.

Holland, Nancy 1990: *Is Women's Philosophy Possible?* Savage, Md.: Rowman and Littlefield.

Holmes, Stephen 1988: The community trap. *The New Republic*, 28 Nov., 24–8.

Hooks, bell 1989: *Talking Back: thinking feminist, thinking black*. Boston: South End Press.

—— 1990: *Yearning: race, gender, and cultural politics*. Boston: South End Press.

Horney, Karen 1967: *Feminine Psychology*. New York: Norton.

Irigaray, Luce 1985a: *Speculum of the Other Women*, tr. Gillian C. Gill. Ithaca: Cornell University Press.

—— 1985b: *This Sex Which is Not One*, tr. Catherine Porter. Ithaca: Cornell University Press.

Jack, Dana 1991: *Silencing the Self: depression and women*. Cambridge, Mass.: Harvard University Press.

Jaggar, Alison 1989: Feminist ethics: some issues for the nineties. *Journal of Social Philosophy*, 20 (1–2), 91–107.

—— 1991: Feminist ethics: projects, problems, prospects. In Claudia Card (ed.), *Feminist Ethics*, Lawrence: University of Kansas Press, 78–104.

Jarratt, Susan 1990: The first sophists and feminism: discourses of the "other." *Hypatia*, 5 (1), 27–41.

Johnston, Paul 1989: *Wittgenstein and Moral Philosophy*. New York: Routledge.

Jordon, Judith 1991: The meaning of mutuality. In Judith Jordon et al. (eds), *Women's Growth in Connection*, New York: Guilford Press, 81–96.

Joyce, Joyce 1987: The black canon: reconstructing black American literary criticism. *New Literary History*, 18 (2): 335–44.

Kariel, Henry 1989: *The Desperate Politics of Postmodernism*. Amherst: University of Massachusetts Press.

Kearney, Richard 1987: Ethics and the postmodern imagination. *Thought*, 62, 39–58.

Keller, Catherine 1986: *From a Broken Web: separation, sexism and self*. Boston: Beacon Press.

Kerber, Linda et al. 1986: On *In a Different Voice*: an interdisciplinary forum. *Signs*, 11 (2), 304–33.

Kohlberg, Lawrence 1981: *The Philosophy of Moral Development*. San Francisco: Harper and Row.

—— 1982: A reply to Owen Flanagan and some comments on the Puka–Goodpaster exchange. *Ethics*, 92 (3), 513–28.

—— 1984: *The Psychology of Moral Development: essays on moral development, 2*. San Francisco: Harper and Row.

Kohlberg, Lawrence, Levine, C. and Hewar, A. 1983: *Moral Stages: a current formulation and response to critics*. New York: Karger.

Kramer, Matthew 1991: *Legal Theory, Political Theory and Deconstruction: against Rhadamanthus*. Bloomington: Indiana University Press.

Kristeva, Julia 1984: *Revolution in Poetic Language*, tr. Margaret Waller. New York: Columbia University Press.

—— 1988: On melancholic imagination. In Hugh Silverman and Donn Welton (eds), *Postmodernism and Continental Philosophy*, Albany: SUNY Press, 12–23.

Laclau, Ernesto 1988: Politics and the limits of modernity. In Andrew Ross (ed.), *Universal Abandon?*, Minneapolis: University of Minnesota Press, 63–82.

—— and Mouffe, Chantal 1985: *Hegemony and Socialist Strategy: towards a radical democratic politics*. London: Verso.

Lee-Lampshire, Wendy 1992: Moral "I": the feminist subject and the grammar of self-reference. *Hypatia*, 7 (1), 34–51.

Leffers, M. Regina 1993: Pragmatists Jane Addams and John Dewey inform the ethic of care. *Hypatia*, 8 (2), 64–77.

Littleton, Christine 1987: Reconstructing sex equality. *California Law Review*, 75, 1279–1337.

Lloyd, Genevieve 1984: *The Man of Reason: "male" and "female" in western philosophy*. Minneapolis: University of Minnesota Press.

Longino, Helen 1990: *Science as Social Knowledge*. Princeton: Princeton University Press.

Lorde, Audre 1981: The master's tools will never dismantle the master's house. In Cherrie Moraga and Gloria Anzuldua (eds), *This Bridge Called My Back*, Watertown, Mass.: Persephone Press, 98–101.

Lorraine, Tamsin 1990: *Gender, Identity and the Production of Meaning*. Boulder, Colo.: Westview Press.

Lovibond, Sabina 1983: *Realism and Imagination in Ethics*. Minneapolis: University of Minnesota Press.

Lugones, Maria and Spelman, Elizabeth 1983: Have we got a theory for you! feminist theory, cultural imperialism and the demand for "the woman's voice." *Women's Studies International Forum*, 6 (6), 573–81.

Lyotard, Jean François 1984: *The Postmodern Condition: a report on Knowledge*, tr. Geoff Bennington and Brian Massumi. Minneapolis: University of Minnesota Press.

Lyotard, Jean François 1988: *The Differend*, tr. George van den Abbeele. Minneapolis: University of Minnesota Press.

—— 1989: *The Lyotard Reader*, ed. Andres Benjamin. Oxford: Basil Blackwell.

—— 1993: *Political Writings*, tr. Bill Readings. Minneapolis: University of Minnesota Press.

—— and Thébaud, Loup 1985: *Just Gaming*, tr. Wlad Godzich. Minneapolis: University of Minnesota Press.

MacIntyre, Alasdair 1983: Moral philosophy: what next? In Stanley Nauerwas and Alasdair MacIntyre (eds), *Revisions: changing perspectives in moral philosophy*, Notre Dame, Ind.: University of Notre Dame Press, 1–15.

—— 1984: *After Virtue*, 2nd edn. Notre Dame, Ind.: University of Notre Dame Press.

—— 1988: *Whose Justice? Which Rationality?* Notre Dame, Ind.: University of Notre Dame Press.

—— 1990: *Three Rival Versions of Moral Inquiry: encyclopedia, genealogy and tradition*. Notre Dame, Ind.: University of Notre Dame Press.

Mackie, J. L. 1977: *Ethics: inventing right and wrong*. Harmondsworth: Penguin.

Manning, Rita 1992: *Speaking from the Heart: a feminist perspective on ethics*. Lanham, Md.: Rowman and Littlefield.

Marcus, Isabel and Spiegelman, Paul 1985: Feminist discourse, moral values and the law – a conversation: the 1984 James MacCormick Mitchell lecture. *Buffalo Law Review*, 34, 11–87.

May, Todd 1993: *Between Genealogy and Epistemology: psychology, politics and knowledge in the thought of Michel Foucault*. University Park, Pa.: Penn State Press.

McCarthy, Thomas 1989–90: The politics of the ineffable: Derrida's deconstructionism. *Philosophical Forum*, 21 (1–2), 146–68.

McClure, Kirstie 1992: On the subject of rights: pluralism, plurality and political identity. In Chantal Mouffe (ed.), *Dimensions of Radical Democracy*, New York: Verso, 108–27.

McNay, Lois 1993: *Foucault and Feminism: power, gender and the self*. Boston: Northeastern University Press.

Meese, Elizabeth 1990: *(Ex)tensions: re-figuring feminist criticism*. Urbana: University of Illinois Press.

Merrill, Robert 1988: Forward to Robert Merrill (ed.), *Ethics/Aesthetics: postmodern positions*. Washington, DC: Maissonneuve Press, vii–xiii.

Meyers, Diana 1989: *Self, Society and Personal Choice*. New York: Columbia University Press.

Mill, John Stuart 1971: *On Liberty, Representative Government, the Subjection of Women*. London: Oxford University Press.

Minh-ha, Trinh T. 1989: *Woman, Native, Other: writing post-coloniality and feminism*. Bloomington: Indiana University Press.

Minow, Martha 1990: *Making All the Difference: inclusion, exclusion, and American law*. Ithaca: Cornell University Press.

Minson, Jeffrey 1985: *Genealogies of Morals*. New York: St Martin's Press.

Mitchell, Steven 1988: *Relational Concepts in Psychoanalysis: an integration*. Cambridge, Mass.: Harvard University Press.

Moody-Adams, Michelle 1991: Gender and the complexity of moral voices. In Claudia Card (ed.), *Feminist Ethics*, Lawrence: University of Kansas Press, 196–212.

Moraga, Cherrie 1981: La Güera. In Cherrie Moraga and Gloria Anzuldua (eds), *This Bridge Called My Back*, Watertown, Mass.: Persephone Press, 27–34.

—— 1983: *Loving in the War Years: Lo gue hunea paso por sus labios*. Boston: South End Press.

Mouffe, Chantal 1988: Radical democracy: modern or postmodern? In Andrew Ross (ed.), *Universal Abandon?* Minneapolis: University of Minnesota Press, 31–45.

—— 1992: Feminism, citizenship and radical democratic politics. In Judith Butler and Joan Scott (eds), *Feminists Theorize the Political*, New York: Routledge, 369–84.

Murdoch, Iris 1970: *The Sovereignty of Good*. London: Routledge and Kegan Paul.

—— 1983: Against dryness: a polemical sketch. In Stanley Hauerwas and Alasdair MacIntyre (eds), *Revisions: changing perspectives in moral philosophy*, Notre Dame, Ind.: University of Notre Dame Press, 43–50.

—— 1992: *Metaphysics as a Guide to Morals*. New York: Penguin.

Murphy, John and Gilligan, Carol 1980: Moral development in late adolescence and adulthood. *Human Development*, 23, 77–104.

Nagel, Thomas 1986: *The View from Nowhere*. New York: Oxford University Press.

—— 1991: *Equality and Partiality*. New York: Oxford University Press.

Nails, Debra 1983: Social-scientific sexism: Gilligan's mismeasure of man. *Social Research*, 50 (3), 643–64.

Nelson, John 1990: Political foundations for the rhetoric of inquiry. In Herbert Simons (ed.), *The Rhetorical Turn: invention and persuasion in the conduct of inquiry*, Chicago: University of Chicago Press, 258–89.

Nelson, Lynn Hankinson 1990: *Who Knows: from Quine to a feminist empiricism*. Philadelphia: Temple University Press.

Noddings, Nel 1984: *Caring*. Berkeley: University of California Press.

—— 1989: *Women and Evil*. Berkeley: University of California Press.

Nunner-Winkler, Gertrude 1984: Two moralities? a critical discussion of an ethic of care and responsibility vs. an ethic of rights and justice. In W. Kurtines and J. Gewirtz (eds), *Morality, Moral Behavior and Moral Development*, New York: Wiley Interscience, 348–61.

Nussbaum, Martha 1986: *The Fragility of Goodness*. New York: Cambridge University Press.

—— 1990: *Love's Knowledge: essays on philosophy and literature*. New York: Oxford University Press.

—— 1992a: Human functioning and social justice: in defense of Aristotelian essentialism. *Political Theory*, 20 (2), 202–46.

—— 1992b: Virtue revived. *Times Literary Supplement*, 3 July, 9–11.

—— 1993: Equity and mercy. *Philosophy and Public Affairs*, 22 (2), 83–125.

Oakeshott, Michael 1962: *Rationalism in Politics*. New York: Basic Books.

—— 1975: *On Human Conduct*. Oxford: Oxford University Press.

Okin, Susan Moller 1979: *Women in Western Political Thought*. Princeton: Princeton University Press.

Oliver, Kelly 1991: Fractal politics: how to use "the subject." *Praxis International*, 11 (2), 178–94.

Pappas, Gregory 1993: Dewey and feminism: the affective and relationship in Dewey's ethics. *Hypatia*, 8 (2), 78–95.

Pateman, Carole 1988: *The Sexual Contract*. Stanford, Calif.: Stanford University Press. Cambridge: Polity Press.

—— 1989: *The Disorder of Women*. Stanford, Calif.: Stanford University Press. Cambridge: Polity Press.

Piaget, Jean 1965 (1932): *The Moral Judgment of the Child*. New York: Free Press.

Pitkin, Hanna 1972: *Wittgenstein and Justice*. Berkeley: University of California Press.

Radhakrishnan, R. 1987: Ethnic identity and post-structuralist différance. *Cultural Critique*, 6, 199–220.

Rajchman, John 1991: *Truth and Eros: Foucault, Lacan and the question of ethics*. New York: Routledge.

Rawls, John 1971: *A Theory of Justice*. Cambridge, Mass.: Harvard University Press.

—— 1980: Kantian constructivism in moral theory. *Journal of Philosophy*, 78 (9), 515–72.

—— 1993: *Political Liberalism*. New York: Columbia University Press.

Riley, Denise 1988: *"Am I That Name?" feminism and the category of "women" in history*. London: Macmillan.

Robinson, Tracy and Ward, Janie W. 1991: A belief in self far greater than anyone's disbelief: cultivating resistance among African-American female adolescents. In Carol Gilligan, Annie Rogers, and Deborah Tolman (eds), *Women, Girls and Psychotherapy: reframing resistance*, New York: Harrington Press, 87–103.

Rorty, Richard 1979: *Philosophy and the Mirror of Nature*. Princeton: Princeton University Press.

—— 1989: *Contingency, Irony and Solidarity*. New York: Cambridge University Press.

—— 1991a: Feminism and pragmatism. *Michigan Quarterly Review*, 31 (2), 231–58.

—— 1991b: The priority of democracy to philosophy. In *Objectivity, Relativism and Truth: philosophical papers*, vol. 1, 175–96.

—— 1993: Feminism, ideology and deconstruction: a pragmatist view. *Hypatia*, 8 (2), 96–103.

Ross, Andrew 1988: Introduction to Andrew Ross (ed.), *Universal Abandon?*, Minneapolis: University of Minnesota Press, vii–xviii.

Ruddick, Sarah 1989: *Maternal Thinking*. Boston: Beacon Press.

Ryan, Michael 1989: *Politics and Culture: working hypotheses for a post-revolutionary society*. Baltimore: Johns Hopkins University Press.

Said, Edward 1978: *Orientalism*. New York: Vintage Press.

Sandel, Michael 1982: *Liberalism and the Limits of Justice*. New York: Cambridge University Press.

Sandoval, Chela 1991: U.S. third world feminism: the theory and method of oppositional consciousness in the postmodern world. *Genders*, 10, 1–24.

Sawicki, Jana 1986: Foucault and feminism: toward a politics of difference. *Hypatia*, 1 (2), 23–36.

——— 1991: *Disciplining Foucault: feminism, power and the body*. New York: Routledge.

Scheman, Naomi 1993: Though this be method, yet there is madness in it: paranoia and liberal epistemology. In Louise Antony and Charlotte Witt (eds), *A Mind of One's Own*, Boulder, Colo.: Westview Press, 145–70.

Scott, Charles 1990: *The Question of Ethics: Nietzsche, Foucault, Heidegger*. Bloomington: Indiana University Press.

Scott, James 1990: *Domination and the Arts of Resistance: hidden transcripts*. New Haven: Yale University Press.

Shapiro, Michael 1992: *Reading the Postmodern Polity: political theory as textual practice*. Minneapolis: University of Minnesota Press.

Siebers, Tobin 1988: *The Ethics of Criticism*. Ithaca: Cornell University Press.

Silverman, Kaja 1988: *The Acoustic Mirror*. Bloomington: Indiana University Press.

Sloterdijk, Peter 1987: *The Critique of Cynical Reason*. Minneapolis: University of Minnesota Press.

Smith, Dorothy 1990: *The Conceptual Practices of Power: a feminist sociology of knowledge*. Boston: Northeastern University Press.

Spelman, Elizabeth 1988: *Inessential Woman*. Boston: Beacon Press.

Spivak, Gayatri 1976: Translator's preface to Jacques Derrida, *Of Grammatology*, Baltimore: Johns Hopkins University Press, ix–xxxvii.

——— 1987: *In Other Worlds: essays in cultural politics*. New York: Methuen.

Stack, Carol 1990: Different voices, different visions: gender, culture and moral reasoning. In Faye Ginsburg and Anna Lowenhaupt Tsing (eds), *Uncertain Terms: negotiating gender in American culture*, Boston: Beacon Press, 19–27.

Staten, Henry 1984: *Wittgenstein and Derrida*. Lincoln: University of Nebraska Press.

Stern, Lori 1990: Conceptions of separation and connection in female adolescents. In Carol Gilligan, Nona Lyons, and Trudy Hanmer (eds), *Making Connections*, Cambridge, Mass.: Harvard University Press, 73–87.

Stocker, Michael 1987: Duty and friendship: toward a synthesis of Gilligan's contrastive moral concepts. In Eva Kittay and Diana Meyers (eds), *Women and Moral Theory*, Totowa, NJ: Rowman and Littlefield, 56–68.

Stout, Jeffrey 1988: *Ethics After Babel*. Boston: Beacon Press.

Tannen, Deborah 1990: *You Just Don't Understand: women and men in conversation*. New York: William Morrow.

Tappan, Mark 1991: Narrative, language and moral experience. *Journal of Moral Education*, 20 (3), 243–56.

——— and Brown, Lyn 1989: Stories told and lessons learned: toward a narrative approach to moral development and moral education. *Harvard Educational Review*, 59 (2), 182–205.

Taylor, Charles 1989: *Sources of the Self: the making of the modern identity*. Cambridge, Mass.: Harvard University Press.

Taylor, Michael 1982: *Community, Anarchy and Liberty*. Cambridge: Cambridge University Press.

Toulmin, Stephen 1986: *The Place of Reason in Ethics*. Chicago: University of Chicago Press.

Tronto, Joan 1987: Women's morality: beyond gender differences to a theory of care. *Signs*, 12 (4), 644–63.

—— 1993: *Moral Boundaries: a political argument for an ethic of care*. New York: Routledge.

Unger, Roberto M. 1975: *Knowledge and Politics*. New York: Free Press.

Villa, Dana 1993: Review of *Political Theory and Postmodernism*. *Political Theory*, 21 (1), 142–6.

Walker, Lawrence 1984: Sex differences in the development of moral reasoning: a critical review. *Child Development*, 55, 677–91.

Walker, Margaret 1989: Moral understandings: alternative "epistemology" for a feminist ethics. *Hypatia*, 4 (2), 15–28.

—— 1992: Feminism, ethics and the question of theory. *Hypatia*, 7 (3), 23–38.

Walzer, Michael 1983: *Spheres of Justice*. New York: Basic Books.

—— 1990: The communitarian critique of liberalism. *Political Theory*, 18 (1), 6–23.

Warnke, Georgia 1993: Feminism and hermeneutics. *Hypatia*, 8 (1), 81–98.

Weil, Simone 1977: *The Simone Weil Reader*, ed. G. Panichas. New York: David McKay.

Westkott, Marcia 1986: *The Feminist Legacy of Karen Horney*. New Haven: Yale University Press.

White, Stephen 1988: Post-structuralism and political reflection. *Political Theory*, 16, 186–208.

—— 1990: Heidegger and the difficulties of a postmodern ethics and politics. *Political Theory*, 18 (1), 80–103.

—— 1991: *Political Theory and Postmodernism*. Cambridge: Cambridge University Press.

Whitford, Margaret 1991: *Luce Irigaray: philosophy in the feminine*. New York: Routledge.

Williams, Bernard 1985: *Ethics and the Limits of Philosophy*. Cambridge, Mass.: Harvard University Press.

Williams, Patricia 1991: *The Alchemy of Race and Rights*. Cambridge, Mass.: Harvard University Press.

Wilson, James Q. 1993a: The moral sense. *American Political Science Review*, 87 (1), 1–11.

—— 1993b. *The Moral Sense*. New York: Free Press.

Wittgenstein, Ludwig 1958: *Philosophical Investigations*. New York: Macmillan.

—— 1960: *The Blue and Brown Books*. New York: Harper and Row.

—— 1961: *Tractatus Logico-Philosophicus*. London: Routledge and Kegan Paul.

—— 1965: A lecture on ethics. *Philosophical Review*, 74, 3–12.

—— 1969: *On Certainty*. New York: Harper and Row.

—— 1970: *Zettel*. Berkeley: University of California Press.

—— 1974: *Philosophical Grammar*. Berkeley: University of California Press.

—— 1975: *Philosophical Remarks*. Chicago: University of Chicago Press.

—— 1980: *Culture and Value*. Chicago: University of Chicago Press.

Wong, David 1984: *Moral Relativity*. Berkeley: University of California Press.

Wyschogrod, Edith 1985: *Spirit in Ashes*. New Haven: Yale University Press.

—— 1990: *Saints and Postmodernism: revisioning moral philosophy*. Chicago: University of Chicago Press.

Young, Iris 1986: The ideal of community and the politics of difference. *Social Theory and Practice*, 12 (1), 1–26.

—— 1990: *Justice and the Politics of Difference*. Princeton: Princeton University Press.

Index